30 Key
Moments
in the
History
of
Christianity

30 Key Moments in the History of Christianity

Inspiring True Stories from the Early Church Around the World

—

Mark W. Graham

BakerBooks
a division of Baker Publishing Group
Grand Rapids, Michigan

© 2026 by Mark W. Graham

Published by Baker Books
a division of Baker Publishing Group
Grand Rapids, Michigan
BakerBooks.com

Printed in the United States of America

Library of Congress Cataloging-in-Publication Control Number: 2025020243
ISBN 9781540905017 (paper)
ISBN 9781540905352 (casebound)
ISBN 9781493452866 (ebook)

Cover design by Studio Gearbox

The author is represented by the literary agency of Wolgemuth & Wilson.

Baker Publishing Group publications use paper produced from sustainable forestry practices and postconsumer waste whenever possible.

26   27   28   29   30   31   32   7   6   5   4   3   2   1

Contents

Contents

Foreword

When I arrived at Grove City College, I asked Mark Graham what student rebellion looked like at the institution. Perhaps the question seems a little loaded, but Mark's answer was fascinating. He told me that it looked like students coming to GCC from broad evangelical churches but then attending Grace Anglican, the Anglican Church in North America's local congregation. In the years since then, I have asked students who have followed this pattern to explain why. The answer usually has three parts: They love the priest's preaching, they love the liturgy, and they love the sense of history that shapes both.

That answer indicates that a small but encouraging development is taking place among some young Christian people: a growing desire to understand and to practice the Christian faith with a consciousness of its rich historical background and development. And these students are not only interested in the typical and somewhat fantastical history so often used to buttress modern evangelical identity—the one that usually starts with a mythical Luther single-handedly dealing a deathblow to the papacy after a thousand years when nobody apparently understood anything of the gospel. Instead, these young people increasingly want to know what happened in the early church and the Middle Ages and how

9

this provides a positive background for understanding their own Christian faith today.

This welcome historical interest nonetheless raises a challenge. There are many books on church history out there, but they tend to fall into one of two categories: the scholarly and the popular. In this, church history is perhaps no different from other types of history. Many of us love reading history but do not have time to wade through the heavily footnoted specialist tomes that are the stock-in-trade of the scholar. That is what makes popular history books so useful. One does not need to be an expert in the field to read, enjoy, and learn from Andrew Roberts on Napoleon or Simon Sebag-Montefiore on Stalin. So should it be with popular church history books too.

But there is a difference with church history, a difference that has shaped the scholarly–popular divide in a distinct way. For Christians, the history of the church is also the history of their personal faith, at least as expressed in the life, contribution, and conflicts of its fundamental institution. That means the stakes are very high indeed. Professional scholars of church history are often concerned with important questions that yet hold little interest to the Christian amateur historian. The former want to know about broader cultural context and themes. They want to engage with a variety of interdisciplinary approaches that shed light on how the church developed. And even when touching on doctrine, they typically avoid the issue of whether a particular dogma or creed is true. In contrast, the Christian who wants to learn something about church history often wants to be informed mainly to be inspired and finds the question of truth to be of paramount importance. The result is that popular church history often tilts toward the sensational and the hagiographic, avoiding all those pesky contextual questions for the sake of a good, straightforward story. When one recalls the intuitive Protestant antipathy to the Middle Ages and even to many elements of the early church, the picture is made more discouraging: Books written for the nonspecialist Protestant on these periods tend to reinforce precisely that prejudice.

This is where Mark Graham's book is so useful. Not only does it introduce the reader to an era of history that is often neglected in evangelical circles—the first millennium—but it does so in a way that connects the careful and sober approach of a professional historian to the kinds of questions that interest Christian believers. Here is judicious use of broader context helping the reader understand, for example, what the second-century Roman governor Pliny meant when he described Christianity as a *superstitio*. And here is also care to help us understand the qualitative difference between a heresy like Arianism and what one might characterize as an egregious but not soul-damning error like Nestorianism.

Graham takes the reader not merely outside the usual chronological boundaries of the Protestant world but also beyond the geographical boundaries of the Western world. There are discussions of Ethiopia, China, and the Umayyad Islamic Empire. There's a cast of characters that includes John of Damascus, the great defender of icons, and Cyril of Thessaloniki, whose linguistic prowess and missionary adventures would be remarkable even today in our era of computers and easy travel. That he was a ninth-century churchman verges on incredible. In short, in an era when the question of the global status of Christianity is uppermost in many minds, Graham helps us see how the faith has always been worldwide in its scope.

Yet Graham does more. Each chapter ends with recommendations for further reading, forging that difficult connection between popular presentation and further scholarly depth. The interested reader's appetite will be whetted by each chapter and then pointed to further intellectual and theological feasts.

This is a remarkable book. The only parallel I can think of is Robert Louis Wilken's *The First Thousand Years: A Global History of Christianity*. Graham, like me, is an admirer of Wilken's work—another true scholar who can also speak movingly of church history to a broader audience. I can think of no higher praise than to draw such a comparison. For this is that rarest of books—a popular presentation of church history that could only have been written by a scholar. Take up and read. You will be informed, entertained, and edified.

Carl R. Trueman, professor of biblical and religious studies, Grove City College; author, *The Rise and Triumph of the Modern Self*

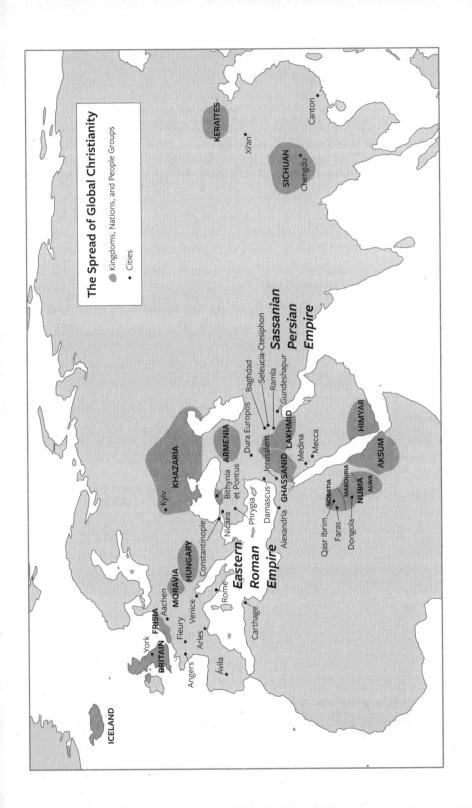

The Spread of Global Christianity

- Kingdoms, Nations, and People Groups
- Cities

ICELAND

York
BRITAIN
FRISIA
MORAVIA
HUNGARY
Aachen
Fleury
Venice
Arles
Angers
Ávila
Rome
Carthage
Constantinople
Nicaea
Bithynia et Pontus
Phrygia
Damascus
Alexandria

KHAZARIA
Kyiv

ARMENIA

KERAITES
Xi'an
SICHUAN
Chengdu
Canton

Eastern Roman Empire

Sassanian Persian Empire

Dura Europos
Baghdad
Seleucia-Ctesiphon
Ramla
Gundeshapur
Jerusalem
GHASSANID
LAKHMID
Medina
Mecca
HIMYAR
AKSUM

NOBATIA
Qasr Ibrim
Faras
MAKOURIA
Dongola
NUBIA
ALWA

Timeline of the Early Church

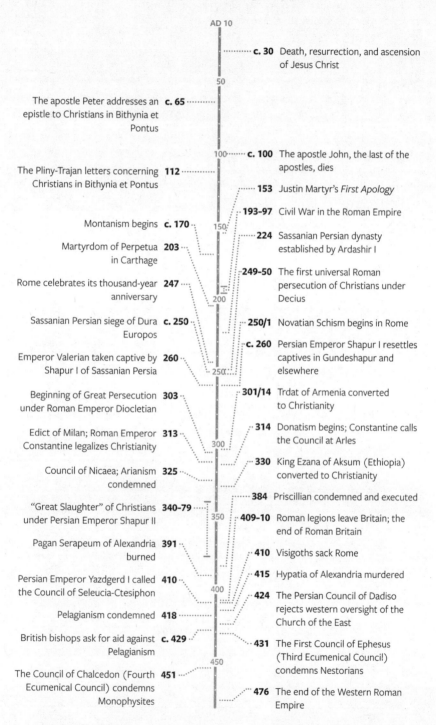

AD 10

c. 30 Death, resurrection, and ascension of Jesus Christ

50

The apostle Peter addresses an **c. 65** epistle to Christians in Bithynia et Pontus

100 **c. 100** The apostle John, the last of the apostles, dies

The Pliny-Trajan letters concerning **112** Christians in Bithynia et Pontus

153 Justin Martyr's *First Apology*

193-97 Civil War in the Roman Empire

Montanism begins **c. 170**

150

224 Sassanian Persian dynasty established by Ardashir I

Martyrdom of Perpetua **203** in Carthage

249-50 The first universal Roman persecution of Christians under Decius

Rome celebrates its thousand-year **247** anniversary

200

Sassanian Persian siege of Dura **c. 250** Europos

250/1 Novatian Schism begins in Rome

c. 260 Persian Emperor Shapur I resettles captives in Gundeshapur and elsewhere

Emperor Valerian taken captive by **260** Shapur I of Sassanian Persia

250

Beginning of Great Persecution **303** under Roman Emperor Diocletian

301/14 Trdat of Armenia converted to Christianity

Edict of Milan; Roman Emperor **313** Constantine legalizes Christianity

314 Donatism begins; Constantine calls the Council at Arles

300

Council of Nicaea; Arianism **325** condemned

330 King Ezana of Aksum (Ethiopia) converted to Christianity

384 Priscillian condemned and executed

"Great Slaughter" of Christians **340-79** under Persian Emperor Shapur II

350 **409-10** Roman legions leave Britain; the end of Roman Britain

Pagan Serapeum of Alexandria **391** burned

410 Visigoths sack Rome

415 Hypatia of Alexandria murdered

Persian Emperor Yazdgerd I called **410** the Council of Seleucia-Ctesiphon

424 The Persian Council of Dadiso rejects western oversight of the Church of the East

400

Pelagianism condemned **418**

British bishops ask for aid against **c. 429** Pelagianism

431 The First Council of Ephesus (Third Ecumenical Council) condemns Nestorians

450

The Council of Chalcedon (Fourth **451** Ecumenical Council) condemns Monophysites

476 The end of the Western Roman Empire

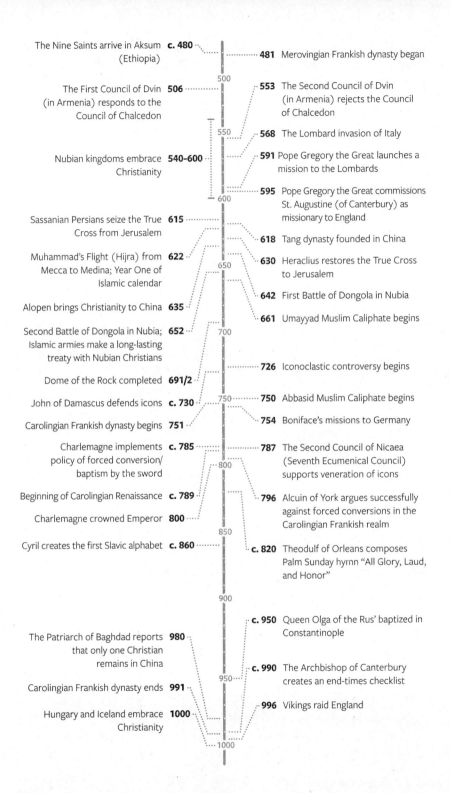

The Nine Saints arrive in Aksum **c. 480**
(Ethiopia)

481 Merovingian Frankish dynasty began

500

The First Council of Dvin **506**
(in Armenia) responds to the
Council of Chalcedon

553 The Second Council of Dvin
(in Armenia) rejects the Council
of Chalcedon

550

568 The Lombard invasion of Italy

Nubian kingdoms embrace **540–600**
Christianity

591 Pope Gregory the Great launches a
mission to the Lombards

600

595 Pope Gregory the Great commissions
St. Augustine (of Canterbury) as
missionary to England

Sassanian Persians seize the True **615**
Cross from Jerusalem

618 Tang dynasty founded in China

Muhammad's Flight (Hijra) from **622**
Mecca to Medina; Year One of
Islamic calendar

650

630 Heraclius restores the True Cross
to Jerusalem

642 First Battle of Dongola in Nubia

Alopen brings Christianity to China **635**

661 Umayyad Muslim Caliphate begins

Second Battle of Dongola in Nubia; **652**
Islamic armies make a long-lasting
treaty with Nubian Christians

700

726 Iconoclastic controversy begins

Dome of the Rock completed **691/2**

John of Damascus defends icons **c. 730**

750

750 Abbasid Muslim Caliphate begins

Carolingian Frankish dynasty begins **751**

754 Boniface's missions to Germany

Charlemagne implements **c. 785**
policy of forced conversion/
baptism by the sword

787 The Second Council of Nicaea
(Seventh Ecumenical Council)
supports veneration of icons

800

Beginning of Carolingian Renaissance **c. 789**

796 Alcuin of York argues successfully
against forced conversions in the
Carolingian Frankish realm

Charlemagne crowned Emperor **800**

850

Cyril creates the first Slavic alphabet **c. 860**

c. 820 Theodulf of Orleans composes
Palm Sunday hymn "All Glory, Laud,
and Honor"

900

c. 950 Queen Olga of the Rus' baptized in
Constantinople

The Patriarch of Baghdad reports **980**
that only one Christian
remains in China

c. 990 The Archbishop of Canterbury
creates an end-times checklist

950

Carolingian Frankish dynasty ends **991**

996 Vikings raid England

Hungary and Iceland embrace **1000**
Christianity

1000

Introduction

Our People

In the 1930s, archaeologists digging in Syria discovered the earliest known Christian building to date. Inside they found a baptistery and frescoes of New Testament scenes, precious glimpses of the vibrant worship and liturgical life of a community of what I refer to as "Our People" from a little over two centuries after the resurrection and ascension of Jesus Christ. The building was in use for barely two decades before this early Christian community disappeared entirely and their church was completely buried and forgotten for almost seventeen hundred years, a sort of "Christian Pompeii."

This site, the Roman frontier city of Dura Europos, was caught in a clash between two superpower rivals during the mid-250s. The Sassanian Persian Empire had declared war on the Roman Empire and was sacking Roman cities along their mutual frontier. The inhabitants of Dura Europos took desperate measures to defend against a Persian siege. In an attempt to thwart the Persian enemy's famous tunneling attacks, defenders piled rubble and dirt deep over the structures built along the inside of the city walls, completely burying several of them, including this Christian building. Their efforts to save the city failed. The Persians

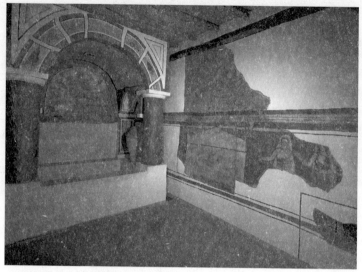

Dura Europos baptistery and frescoes
Public domain

tunneled in anyway, seized the city, and deported its inhabitants, leaving Dura Europos abandoned and desolate. Its buried buildings were forgotten and thus remained remarkably intact over the centuries.

We have a good idea of what happened to the captured people of Dura Europos, including its vibrant Christian community. The victorious Sassanian Persians resettled them deep in Persian territory where many of the Christians would flourish and spread the gospel in that land, as we will see in chapter 6. This story might well call to mind lines from Scripture such as "God meant it for good" (Gen. 50:20) or perhaps address the age-old question "How shall we sing the LORD's song in a foreign land?" (Ps. 137:4). In the pages that follow, you will encounter many such stories from the first millennium of the church along with the messages they still hold for us today.

In the first millennium, Our People could be found among empires and kingdoms from Britain to Sudan to China. You will meet some of these Christian brothers and sisters—including martyrs and tyrants, saints and schismatics, exiles and avengers, poets and administrators. Recalling and recounting their stories can inspire, challenge, encourage, convict, and at times even rebuke God's people today.

Some of these stories will be familiar to many readers, such as some accounts of early Roman martyrs, the emperor Constantine's conversion, and the reforms of medieval Frankish emperor Charlemagne. I hope, though, that all readers will learn something new even within familiar stories. Most of the stories will likely not be so familiar—for example, a Sassanian Persian "king of kings" calling and hosting a church council, the massacre of Christians by an Arabic-speaking convert to Judaism in a southern Arabian kingdom, and skilled archers saving the Nubian church from takeover by Muslim invaders. It is no secret that the historical memory of many modern Western Christians, especially Protestants, is rather hazy for most of this first millennium (and usually the next half millennium too).

We also do not know many of these stories because we tend to tether historic Christianity to a narrative of Western civilization. When we do remember that first millennium of the church, we tend to focus exclusively on a narrative that moves directly from the ancient Roman Mediterranean world into medieval western Europe. The way we sometimes speak of the church "becoming global" in the nineteenth and twentieth centuries results in part from this tendency to equate church history with the Christian history of Western civilization. If we have not encountered stories of vibrant Christianity from many other areas across time, then it certainly would appear as if a global church emerged only recently. But Christianity was, in fact, global from its earliest years, even if its roots were deepest in the Mediterranean region.

This emphasis on Our People across space and time might prompt us to question the extent to which our own national, political, and cultural identities compete with or even overshadow our most foundational (and eternal) identity as Christians. In some important ways, modern American Christians have more in common with Christians from seventh-century Nubia, Persia, and southern Arabia than with agnostic neighbors who share our national flag.

Moments

Contrary to popular belief, real history can never simply be about names, dates, and facts. It can, however, recapture moments. Each chapter of this book pursues a particular moment (or several related moments) in the history of Christianity. The moments generally do not flow from one to another or build upon each other, so the chapters need not be read in order. Where topics and themes overlap with other chapters (e.g., the Aksumite/ Ethiopian kingdom or the apocalypse), the text will refer readers to those places (e.g., "see chap. 5"). This allows for the book to be read one chapter per day (or perhaps one per week) for a book group.

Each moment begins with an introduction titled "The Background" that aims to set it within its historical context.[1] This section explains and explores the bigger picture surrounding the chosen moment, giving some necessary or helpful background details and narrative information. Some moments happen to be turning points in Christian history (if not history in general), but as you will see, that is not why I selected them. The second section of each chapter, simply titled "The Moment" (or in a few instances "The Moments"), explores crucial persons and events.

The final section of each chapter suggests what it is that Christians today can learn from Our People then. I have titled these sections "The Mathēma," employing an ancient Greek word meaning "that which is learned; a lesson." Here I aim to integrate my professional background as a historian of ancient and early medieval empires with my many years serving as a Sunday school teacher and elder in my church. The idea of history "lessons" was fundamental to all ancient storytelling. Balancing historical analysis with history lessons from and for Our People does not come particularly easily or naturally to this modern historian, though. At the same time, emphasizing lessons at the expense of solid historical understanding comes almost instinctively to some popular versions of Christian history. In some circles, Christian history can be full of simple moralisms, hagiography (i.e., embellished or idealized biographies and self-affirming narratives), and romanticism. While this may be simply comforting or chiding, it is inadequate as history and is sometimes even dishonest or naive. This third section seeks to strike a balance between historical analysis and drawing out the message(s) that each moment can still hold for us today within the family of God.

A Global House Subdivided

Two particular groups, Nestorians and Monophysites, have a vital place in global Christianity's first thousand years. Due to their roles in so many of the thirty key moments included here, they need special introduction and description up front. Expect to see cross-references to this introduction when either term appears in a chapter.

At the famous Council of Nicaea in 325 (see chap. 10), also known as the First Ecumenical Council, the church definitively affirmed that Jesus Christ is "very God of very God . . . of one substance with the Father." The council condemned the teachings of Arius and his followers, known as Arians, who denied the full divinity of Christ. Recognizing Jesus Christ as fully God is a foundational and nonnegotiable marker of orthodox Christian belief. Though it was essential, the subsequent question of exactly how Christ's divinity is related to his humanity proved to be an extremely difficult one for the church. How did Christ's person (or was it persons) interact with his nature (or was it natures)? In the fifth century, two councils—the Council of Ephesus in 431 and the Council of Chalcedon in 451—were called to address these and other related questions. Many Christians, both inside and outside the Byzantine Empire (where the councils were hosted), did not affirm the decisions they reached. The theological issues are extremely complex, and even today theologians continue to debate the specifics.

One group, whom scholars usually call Nestorians (or, less commonly, Dyophysites), proposed that the incarnate Christ has essentially two persons to go along with his two natures. The Council of Ephesus condemned this view. Twenty years later, the Council of Chalcedon condemned another group, the Monophysites (also called Miaphysites), for holding that the incarnate Christ had essentially one unified nature, combining human and divine. Variations of these two groups have made up a significant number of the world's Christians over time, as we will see. The opponents of both groups are sometimes collectively known as Chalcedonians (i.e., affirming the decisions of both the Chalcedon and Ephesus Councils), and they maintained that the divine Jesus Christ is one person with two natures. To use the technical term, they affirmed the hypostatic union. Roman Catholics, Eastern Orthodox, and most Protestants to this day would be considered Chalcedonians.

Both Nestorians and Monophysites affirmed the Council of Nicaea, and for this and other reasons this study unambiguously numbers them among Our People. Outside the Roman and Byzantine Empires, Nestorians and Monophysites represent a majority report. Within the Roman and Byzantine Empires, treatment of the two groups could range from grudging coexistence to harassment to outright persecution, driving many of these Christians to seek refuge and opportunities elsewhere. They were arguably the greatest of premodern missionaries.

This study, then, rejects the often unacknowledged assumption that all heresies are created equal. There is a fundamental divide between Arians, for example, and Nestorians. The former are not included among Our People any more than Jehovah's Witnesses should be today. This is not to assert that the doctrinal differences between Nestorians and Chalcedonians are unimportant. (I refer readers to the excellent study *The Cruelty of Heresy* by Anglican bishop C. FitzSimons Allison for an explanation of the very real pastoral consequences to getting the hypostatic union wrong.[2]) Rather, it is a simple claim that one should be extremely hesitant to dismiss groups that affirmed the Council of Nicaea in those early Christian centuries, especially rank-and-file Christians. One might instead wonder what those early Nestorians and Monophysites would think of the significant percentage of regularly surveyed American evangelicals who respond "true" to the statement "Jesus Christ is the first and greatest being created by God."[3]

The Big Picture

Focusing only on specific moments in global church history has clear limitations and downsides. Readers might well find themselves wishing for the larger historical picture and searching to fill in the gaps between and among the moments covered here. I am indebted to several great works on global Christianity. I have compiled a brief list of such works in an appendix for you to explore further and connect the dots between the flashes and moments here.

You are about to embark on a journey where, in any given chapter, you may find yourself on the shores of the Black Sea, the Red Sea, or the Mediterranean Sea, or deep in the Middle East, Britain, or China. The selections here give glimpses into much larger worlds. Amidst world empires and kingdoms, you will meet brothers and sisters whose lives—victories, tragedies, and sorrows—still hold meaning for us today.

Notes

1. For an excellent study of the historical significance of key moments in the history of the church, see Mark Noll, *Turning Points: Decisive Moments in the History of Christianity*, 2nd ed. (Baker Academic, 2001).

2. C. FitzSimons Allison, *The Cruelty of Heresy: An Affirmation of Christian Orthodoxy* (Morehouse, 1994).

3. Stephen Nichols, "The State of Theology: The Questions That Matter Most," Ligonier, October 16, 2018, https://www.ligonier.org/posts/state-theology -questions-matter-most.

1

A Christian "Contagion" and a "Good Sense" Governor

(Black Sea, 112)

The Background

The Roman province of Bithynia et Pontus was in trouble. Nestled on the south shores of the Black Sea in Asia Minor (present-day Turkey), it was a very wealthy province. Though it had been a site of much political and military drama during the second and first centuries BC, things had been quiet now for more than a hundred years. But as the second century AD dawned, financial mismanagement and political turmoil threatened the stability of the cities and towns throughout the province. The emperor Trajan took control of the province away from the Roman Senate in order to deal with the problems more directly himself. Such crises were particularly rare during the Pax Romana, the period of Roman peace that had been launched by the emperor Augustus over a century earlier. Trajan, one of the empire's legendary five "good emperors," needed a top-notch and trustworthy administrator to get things back into shape. By all Roman measures, he made a perfect choice in his longtime friend Pliny the Younger.

There were few who could match the intellectual and administrative background and pedigree of Pliny the Younger, who had been adopted, raised, and educated by his famous uncle and namesake, Pliny the Elder.[1] The elder Pliny was renowned for his *Natural History*, one of the most extensive encyclopedias of human knowledge from the premodern world. The younger Pliny continued his studies in Rome under Quintilian, author of one of history's most influential works on rhetoric. A noted orator in his own right, Pliny began his career in the law courts, where he distinguished himself with some high-profile cases against corrupt officials. He climbed the ranks of the Roman political scene, from one increasingly important office to another, before getting the call from the emperor to take on the delicate assignment in Bithynia et Pontus. It would be the final achievement of an illustrious career. Trajan's confidence in him was clear: "I chose you for your good sense, so that you could guide that province in changing their ways and establish institutions that would lead to permanent peace there."[2]

We can follow Pliny's efforts throughout the province in unusual and almost unique detail, thanks to about sixty letters that he wrote to the emperor. Each letter zeroes in on a particular matter of administration—for example, inquiring about funding for and reporting on maintenance of public works such as baths, aqueducts, theaters, temples, a firefighting force, and much more. Many of Trajan's succinct replies also survive, revealing the mind of the good emperor at work. One specific emergency seems to have taken Pliny by surprise: A very dangerous religious movement was overrunning the province.

The Moment

The Christian movement had arrived in the province at least two generations before Pliny. The apostle Peter had addressed his first epistle to Christians of Bithynia et Pontus (among others), and the movement apparently had been growing rapidly. Pliny's letters are the earliest account of Christian life and worship written by an outsider. Dating to the year 112, they reveal the lives of Our People in the generation just following the close of the apostolic age. Some of those examined by Pliny had become Christians while the apostle John was still alive.

Pliny's careful Roman administrative eye helped him compile a profile of the movement. Christians came from "every age, social class, and men and women alike."[3] Some of them were even Roman citizens and so had to be dealt with specially. The movement had spread not just to cities and towns but even to villages and rural districts. Their witness had threatened attendance and sacrifices at the local temples, though dutiful Pliny assured Trajan that the numbers at those Roman religious ceremonies were rebounding under his watch. The major practices of the movement consisted of meeting on a given day before dawn and "singing responsively a hymn to Christ as to a god."[4] They swore a sacred oath to abstain from all wrongdoing: They vowed not to steal, rob, commit adultery, break promises, or fail to return money entrusted to them. Later in the day, they would eat a meal together.[5]

This all might seem innocuous enough. Yet throughout his letter, Pliny's obvious mistrust of and disgust for Christians are on full display. Alarmed that their movement has "spread like a contagion," he categorizes the Christians as obstinate and unyielding in ways he describes as "lunacy."[6] When he tortured two "slave women who were called deaconesses" to extract a confession, he concluded that he was dealing with "an extreme and misguided *superstitio*."[7] A trained and seasoned criminal lawyer and public official, Pliny was following standard Roman practice here, and we can be sure that he knew danger when he saw it. The qualifier "extreme" in particular signals a very serious threat.

Defining *superstitio* is not simple.[8] Often it is helpful that Latin words look a lot like English ones—cognates, as linguists call them. But sometimes cognates complicate or confuse matters, as is the case with the word *superstitio*. The English translation "superstition" is not quite right. To a sound, reasonable, and highly educated Roman like Pliny, the term *superstitio* had specific legal connotations. *Superstitio* was recognized as a crime not simply because it was considered a silly or untenable set of beliefs (think black cats, umbrellas opened indoors, crossed fingers, and the like) but because it was seen as illegitimate and dangerous. It had its counterpart in *religio*, legitimate religious rites and practices. Religious rites and rituals not sanctioned by antiquity or supporting the public order could be classified as *superstitio* by tradition-minded Romans. Practices intended to coerce deities or humans through magic or spells were *superstitio*. It was a serious charge, and because it was widely seen as a threat to public order, it was punishable by death. The issue was not that the rites or incantations were mere "superstitions" and unreasonable but rather that they could get divine favor in an illicit way. The charge was one that Christians would frequently face in years to come.

It is clear enough from the exchange between Pliny and Trajan that the Romans did not have a specific policy at that time for dealing with the Christians. The methods that Pliny and Trajan worked out would shape treatment of Christians in the Roman Empire for roughly the next century and a half. After considering Pliny's analysis and questions, Trajan specifically cautioned Pliny not to rely on anonymous accusations or seeking Christians out. He also noted a straightforward way for an accused Christian to avoid punishment: If the accused would simply pray to the gods— that is, images of the emperor and other major Roman deities—in the presence of an official, they were to be released. Failure to do so would result in punishment, most often execution. Persecution of Christians was neither constant nor empire-wide in the first two centuries of the church age (see chap. 5), but this moment shows it was an ever-present possibility.

The Mathēma

This earliest glimpse into Christian communities from the outside reveals a variety of commitment levels. Some Christians remained faithful, even firm under torture and until death. Others drifted away over time. Still others denied the faith under pressure. The study of history often affirms that some things never change. Would modern Christians be any different? This moment should challenge any notion that the early church was some sort of golden age we should aspire to return to, as some Christians today believe.

Our People in Bithynia et Pontus had a broad cultural impact for a time. Faithfully gathering together was a crucial part of their lives. They sang together. They dined together. They came from all social classes. Their ranks included both citizens and slaves, men and women. Women were even given titles like deaconess. Their communities were multigenerational, both urban and rural. Faithful Christians could not bow the knee to other gods and maintain their identity. Pliny himself recognized as much.

Pliny (and Trajan) were neither unhinged nor hysterical in their evaluation and treatment of Christians. They were veritable paragons of Roman education, reason, law, and order. Pliny was, by the standards of the day, the epitome of a competent, excellent, and rational administrator. Trajan let it be known that the "enlightened" spirit of the age was incompatible with people bringing anonymous accusations against others.[9] Such seems a universal good and sound principle. Yet note that the very name "Christian" was seen as a defensible reason to persecute and execute the accused if they were unwilling to deny Christ. In the next chapter, we will explore how one early Christian strove to mount a reasonable defense of Christianity using the very standards of the Greco-Roman world.

The episode at Bithynia et Pontus raises a vital question for Christians of all times: What could these faithful Christians have done to be more acceptable, maybe even winsome, to their superiors and contemporaries? While we can speculate about other factors at play in this moment of persecution, the initial evidence suggests there was little or nothing they could have done. The words of the apostle Peter to a previous generation of Christians in Bithynia et Pontus ring true to their experience, as to the experiences of many others throughout time: They will "suffer for righteousness' sake" (see 1 Pet. 3:14–17). Peter encouraged the saints there to be ready to respond to anyone who asked about the hope that was in them. And he urged them to do so with gentleness and reverence, a good reminder to Christians of all eras. These early Christians who sang hymns to Christ in their early morning gatherings could rest upon the words of Christ himself: "Blessed are you when others revile you and persecute you and utter all kinds of evil against you falsely on my account. Rejoice and be glad, for your reward is great in heaven" (Matt. 5:11–12). We too can rest upon those words.

Further Reading

Freeman, Charles. *A New History of Early Christianity*. Yale University Press, 2011.

González, Justo L. and Catherine Gunsalus González. *Worship in the Early Church*. Westminster John Knox, 2022.

Kruger, Michael. *Christianity at the Crossroads: How the Second Century Shaped the Future of the Church*. IVP Academic, 2018.

Wilken, Robert Louis. *The Christians as the Romans Saw Them*. 2nd ed. Yale University Press, 2003.

Notes

1. For a thorough description of Pliny himself, see chap. 1 of Robert Louis Wilken, *The Christians as the Romans Saw Them*, 2nd ed. (Yale University Press, 2003), and the references in his notes.

2. Pliny the Younger, *Letters to Trajan* 10.117, as quoted in R. Scott Smith and Christopher Francese, *Ancient Rome: An Anthology of Sources* (Hacket Publishing, 2014), 299–331.

3. Pliny, *Letters to Trajan* 10.96.
4. Pliny, *Letters to Trajan* 10.96.
5. Pliny, *Letters to Trajan* 10.96.
6. Pliny, *Letters to Trajan* 10.96.
7. Pliny, *Letters to Trajan* 10.96.
8. See John Scheid, *An Introduction to Roman Religion* (Edinburgh University Press, 2003), 23, 173; and James B. Rives, *Religion in the Roman Empire* (Wiley-Blackwell, 2006).
9. Pliny, *Letters to Trajan* 10.97.

2

---•---

Justin Martyr Invents Christian Apologetics

(Rome, 153)

The Background

In 153, a Christian convert named Justin made his way to the office of the imperial secretary in Rome and hand delivered a petition addressed to the emperor Antoninus Pius, his sons, the "Sacred Senate," and the whole Roman people. Consisting of sixty-eight sections, it was unusually long, "fifteen times the length of a normal petition to the emperor."[1] In it, Justin energetically rebutted a series of accusations that had been circulating about Christians. Using traditional Roman petition language and format, Justin also boldly presented the gospel throughout the work. We know this piece today as Justin Martyr's *First Apology*; it was the first ever work of Christian apology, and this moment marks the birth of Christian apologetics.

By the middle of the second century, the Romans were not simply criticizing those who identified as Christians but were beginning to level serious accusations against them. Among these were atheism (for rejecting known gods) and various types of sexual debauchery (for imagined goings-on at their secret gatherings and "love feasts"). Most of what we know about these charges comes from the Christian reactions and responses they provoked rather than from pagan Roman sources.

However, one unlikely but very telling source gives us a glimpse of the popular perceptions and caricatures of Christians. In his book *The Metamorphosis* (or *The Golden Ass*), which is one of the world's oldest surviving novels, the pagan philosopher Apuleius, who was a contemporary of Justin, at one point introduces a woman from whom "not a single vice was wanting." Many scholars believe that Apuleius created this fictitious woman with Roman stereotypes of a Christian in mind. She was "hard-hearted, perverse, man-mad, drunken, and stubborn to the last degree"; and "worse still, she had rejected and spurned the heavenly gods . . . and blasphemously set up a deity of her own whom she proclaimed as the One and Only God." She threw her life away pursuing "meaningless rituals of her own invention" and engaging in drunkenness and sexual debauchery.[2] Unlike most people in today's culture, Romans distrusted and even explicitly despised innovation and novelty, so the author's denunciations of this woman's invented rituals would land effectively on Roman ears. Christians were seen as evil because, along with this raft of obviously despicable allegations, their rituals were outright newfangled. Apuleius himself was likely aware of Justin's *First Apology*, or certainly of the types of arguments made in it,[3] and thus this imaginary character gives us a rather concrete sense of accusations Justin and other Christians of that day were up against as well as some ways a pagan might refute Christian attempts at self-defense.

Justin Martyr, as his famous epithet declares, ultimately died a martyr's death at the hands of Roman officials around the year 165. He had sought to defend not only himself but all Christians from the circulating accusations. Paradoxically, he did so by a real innovative achievement of his own: the Christian apology.[4] In writing it, he has been hailed as "one of the most original thinkers Christianity ever produced."[5] He would have been surprised at such an accolade, as he was simply exercising a Roman citizen's standard recourse when responding to perceived injustice.

The Moment

Justin was born into a pagan family in Samaria sometime between the late 90s and 110. He once described his personal journey through the various strands of Greek philosophy before he came to Christ—from Stoic to Aristotelian to devotee of Pythagoras to Platonist. Sometime in his early adulthood, a wise old man he encountered by the sea opened up the Scriptures to him, and "a fire was suddenly kindled in my soul. I fell in love with the prophets and those who had loved Christ. I reflected on their words and found that this philosophy alone was true and profitable."[6]

Around two decades after his conversion, Justin composed his *First Apology*. There was likely a very personal dimension to this defense. Right around the time he delivered his petition to the imperial office, Justin knew a certain well-off woman who became a Christian. Before her conversion, she and her husband had (actually) lived lives of wanton drunkenness, sexual debauchery, and other named and unnamed vices involving themselves and their servants. Once she became a Christian, the woman could no longer abide her husband's expectations and actions, so she divorced him in accordance with Roman law. Her angry husband then reported her to the authorities as a Christian.[7] She, in turn, petitioned the emperor to delay her trial so she could put some matters in order, and the emperor granted her a delay. Not getting his way, her husband then denounced her Christian teacher, who was ultimately executed along with several of the teacher's vocal supporters. This sad moment prompted Justin to compose his famous petition to the emperor; in fact, he even followed the same petition format as did the woman who had successfully managed to postpone her trial.[8]

In his petition Justin appealed to the reason and justice for which Romans prided themselves. He also responded directly to all the popular accusations against Christians. He began by dismissing the charge of atheism at some length. He also argued that true Christians were not sexually deviant but counterculturally chaste, citing Christ's teaching about lust and adultery in explicit detail.[9] In direct response to caricatures like those in the work of Apuleius, he added that "promiscuous intercourse is not one of our mysteries," a word that referred to their secret acts of worship.[10]

But Justin added a new dimension to a regular procedure of legal and administrative appeals: a powerful presentation of the gospel in terms that Romans would recognize and, he hoped, appreciate. He "turned a petition into an apology," as one leading scholar put it, thus starting the whole tradition of Christian apologetics.[11] Justin wanted Romans to see the very deep history of the Christian faith as it was laid out through all of Scripture—no innovation or novelty here! Jesus and Christianity clearly fulfilled the old Hebrew prophecies. Christianity was not newfangled, and thus Romans should not dismiss it as such.

Justin concluded his piece by explaining Christian worship practices, one of the earliest such descriptions available. He argued that rituals in worship were anything but contrived or "meaningless"; what's more, they helped produce truly virtuous citizens. Christians gathered on Sundays for extensive reading of the Scriptures—both ancient prophets and more recent apostles. They heard expositions on how to apply the Scriptures to their lives. They celebrated the Eucharist. They took up mercy offerings. A "president" led their gatherings. Contra the lurid accusations circulating about them, Christians gathered in decency, something the Romans should have appreciated. To refute Apuleius's charge, their rituals and gatherings were neither scandalous nor meaningless.

The Mathēma

No doubt Justin faced the same fundamental frustration as many other Christian apologists throughout the years: In spite of solid efforts to reach and persuade outsiders, it is primarily those already inside the fold who read their work for encouragement and comfort. Any non-Christian who might have read Justin's *First Apology* would simply have responded with contempt.[12] But Christians who read it, especially new converts, would have appreciated him defending their lives as ones of reasonable and patient virtue.[13]

Woven throughout Justin's petition is a presentation of the gospel using normal means of the day to persuade the emperor and defend Christians. Justin assumed here a "common universe of discourse accessible to all human beings," a world in which "it was possible for all men and women to meet on the common ground of truth."[14] He wrote as a normal person using normal methods addressing normal people in a normal petition. However, when explaining what had brought some Romans into the faith, Justin did not actually highlight the role of argumentation and persuasion. Instead, he noted above all else that it was simply the lives of integrity that Christians had lived out before their neighbors and everyday business contacts. Their patience, gentleness, and honesty, he reported, were the actual reason that many who were once "of your way of thinking" had embraced Christ.[15]

Modern Christian apologists and philosophers (and their promoters) sometimes have missed Justin's crucial point: Defending the faith is not really about careful rhetorical training and practice to win arguments. Nor is it a call to any species of heady elitism or rarefied intellectualism. We can learn, Justin claims, "from those who do not even know the shapes of the letters, uneducated folk and barbarians in speech, but wise and trustworthy in their understanding."[16] The point of his apology was not the classical education, the polished defense, the clever turn of phrase, or the triumphant argument but rather true and godly wisdom lived out in front of the world. Justin was merely using the accepted means of his day to state his case directly; he was simply trying to talk to the authorities and citizens around him who had imbibed all those slanderously inaccurate portrayals of his fellow Christians.[17]

Justin's argument was fairly straightforward: Christians are not crazy or criminally deviant or creatively innovative. Rather, following true Reason, "We imitate the excellences which reside in [God], temperance, and justice, and philanthropy," and all the other virtues associated with him.[18] That particular calling—to live reasonable, just, and self-effacing lives in front of our neighbors and associates—is the most powerful defense of all for the Christian faith, at least according to the Father of Apologetics.

Further Reading

Parvis, Paul. "Justin Martyr." In *Early Christian Thinkers: The Lives and Legacies of Twelve Key Figures*. Edited by Paul Foster. IVP Academic, 2010.

Parvis, Sara, and Paul Foster, eds. *Justin Martyr and His Worlds*. Fortress, 2007.

Smith, Warren S. *Religion and Apuleius' Golden Ass: The Sacred Ass*. Routledge, 2022.

Stead, Christopher. *Philosophy in Christian Antiquity*. Cambridge University Press, 1994.

Wilken, Robert Louis. *The Christians as the Romans Saw Them*. 2nd ed. Yale University Press, 2003.

Notes

1. Paul Parvis, "Justin Martyr," in *Early Christian Thinkers: The Lives and Legacies of Twelve Key Figures*, ed. Paul Foster (IVP Academic, 2010), 7.

2. Apuleius, *The Golden Ass: A New Translation*, trans. E. J. Kenney (Penguin 1998), 9.14.

3. See Warren S. Smith, "Apuleius' *Metamorphoses* and Jewish/Christian Literature," *Ancient Narrative* 10 (2012): 47–87, and his *Religion and Apuleius' Golden Ass: The Sacred Ass* (Routledge, 2022).

4. Sara Parvis, "Justin Martyr and the Apologetic Tradition," in *Justin Martyr and His World* (Fortress, 2007), 115–27.

5. Theodore Stylianopoulos, "Justin Martyr," in *Encyclopedia of Early Christianity* (Routledge, 1990).

6. Justin Martyr, *Dialogue with Trypho* 8.1.

7. Justin Martyr, *Second Apology* 2; Paul Parvis, "Justin Martyr," 4–5.

8. Paul Parvis, "Justin Martyr," 6.

9. Justin Martyr, *First Apology* 15.

10. Justin Martyr, *First Apology* 29.

11. Paul Parvis, "Justin Martyr," 7.

12. Paul Parvis, "Justin Martyr," 10.

13. See Alan Kreider, *The Patient Ferment of the Early Church: The Improbable Rise of Christianity in the Roman Empire* (Baker Academic, 2016), 16–17.

14. Paul Parvis, "Justin Martyr," 12.

15. Justin Martyr, *First Apology* 16.

16. Justin Martyr, *First Apology* 60.

17. Paul Parvis, "Justin Martyr," 9.

18. Justin Martyr, *First Apology* 10.

3

---•---

A "City in the Sky"
and a New Prophecy

(Phrygia, Late Second Century)

The Background

In the year 198, a walled city hovered in the sky over Judea for
forty days . . .

It was yet another sign of extremely unsettled times. The years
prior to this alleged sighting had been strangely tumultuous, almost unprecedented. The first major civil war within the Roman
Empire in over two hundred years had raged from 193 to 197; the
emperor himself was away at war with the Parthian Empire to the
east. Cracks and fissures were beginning to appear in the facade
of the Pax Romana, the period of peace that had begun under
the emperor Augustus just prior to the birth of Christ. Septimius
Severus, the emperor at the time of the strange sighting, would
be the last to have a successful rule for a good long while. For the
next hundred years, nearly every one of his successors would have

their reigns cut short by an assassin or by death in battle—more often than not amidst civil war. Septimius Severus would be the last emperor to die a natural death for quite some time. As he lay dying, he reportedly advised his sons to "take care of the army; never mind everyone else."[1]

Many hints of a coming age of crisis stood out in high relief against the backdrop of two centuries of relative peace and stability. For Christians, local persecutions were beginning to erupt throughout the empire. Until this point, most of them had been able to live in relative peace. Empire-wide persecution was still fifty years or so in the future (see chap. 5). No Roman—Christian or otherwise—could yet imagine the full extent of the coming crisis. But for one group of Christians, the signs of the times were clear enough—the end of the world was nigh! The divine Bridegroom was preparing to come meet his bride. Would she be ready?

The Moment

Just a few decades prior to that strange portent in Judea, a new Christian movement had begun in the region of Phrygia (modern-day central western Turkey). It soon spread among local rural settlements and villages, then throughout the Roman Empire. The exact date is uncertain, but sometime around the year 170, a certain man named Montanus and his two closest followers, Priscilla (or Prisca) and Maximilla, began receiving prophetic visions and delivering ecstatic utterances. According to the early church historian Eusebius, Montanus himself was a recent convert and newly baptized even as a movement coalesced around him.[2]

Some have asserted that Montanus's pagan past as a priest for the Phrygian mystery cult of the goddess Cybele was a formative part of his background that he carried into his newfound faith in Christ.[3] Others have instead emphasized the fact that Christians in this region apparently had long fixated on eschatological and apocalyptic passages in the writings of the apostle John, particularly those in Revelation 2–3 that described congregations nearby. The Montanist movement, however, pushed beyond traditional interpretations of Scripture, calling itself "the New Prophecy." Its opponents simply labeled it "the Phrygian Prophecy" wherever they happened to encounter it.

The beliefs and practices of the new movement appear in a few of the Montanists' surviving writings and in the more plentiful accounts of their detractors. All agree that Montanists looked for ongoing revelations from living prophets who had visions and could speak with ecstasies (i.e., trancelike declarations). These prophecies often breathed imminent apocalypse. Montanist leaders were called *illuminati* ("enlightened ones"), and those who followed them were known as *spirituales* ("truly spiritual") or *pneumati* ("Spirit-led" or "Spirit-filled ones"). Professing Christians who did not recognize or follow the guidance of these leaders were labeled *psychici* or "animal men," a lower tier led by the flesh and not by the Spirit. Only the *spirituales* were truly prepared to meet the impending Final Day, and to recognize an antichrist who would soon appear, the "man of sin [or lawlessness]" of 2 Thessalonians 2:3–10.

There was an urgency to their message, as there usually is with such apocalyptic movements. They claimed they had recovered an apocalyptic eschatology that the church at large had woefully neglected in the century and a half since the age of the apostles. Now, truly spiritual Christians were called to renounce the world and live lives of constant expectation, rigor, and even asceticism.

Leaders in the Phrygian town of Pepuza, where the movement was particularly strong, declared their city the "New Jerusalem." Some followers went even further, urging true believers to sell their possessions and retreat to the hills in preparation for the end times. The bride, so their thinking went, must be ready for the Bridegroom.[4] They were accused of encouraging voluntary martyrdom by actively seeking out execution for the faith. In their passion to get the church back to the pristine origins they imagined, they were one of the first Christian revivalist movements. Some saw them as schismatics, others as outright heretics, and still others as a sort of "holiness club" within the church.

The Montanist movement spread fairly quickly throughout Asia Minor and beyond to Egypt, North Africa, Alexandria, Rome, and Gaul. In countrysides where the authority of traditional bishops was weaker, the movement could gain a foothold. In North Africa, the movement scored a major victory by attracting the well-known church leader Tertullian, bishop of Carthage, who joined in 208. It was he who recorded the reports of a walled city hovering over Judea.[5] To illustrate Tertullian's importance in Christian history, he is the one credited with inventing the word Trinity (Latin: *Trinitas*), so he was no small fish. In Carthage, the Montanist movement had already helped inspire a vigorous and public Christian witness, as we will see with Saints Perpetua and Felicity in chapter 4. So despite its problems, it had praiseworthy parts as well.

Most church leaders, though, had little sympathy for the Montanist movement. The Phrygian bishop Apollinarius of Hierapolis denounced the movement just as it was starting. A number of nearby Phrygian bishops came together to cast out what they saw as a false spirit within their church region. Their synods represent the first local councils in Christian history. Church leaders at a distance were not always sure exactly what to do when they encountered the Phrygian Prophecy. Irenaeus, the famous bishop of Lyon in Gaul, at first hesitated to condemn the movement outright, while Eleutherus, bishop of Rome, was more decisive and condemned Montanists in 177.

By the late second century, the movement was facing firm opposition. The tombstone of a certain Avircius (or Abercius) Marcellus from Phrygia, which was discovered by famed biblical archaeologist Sir William Ramsay in 1883 and is perhaps the earliest known Christian tombstone, appears to be one bishop's protest of the movement through its explicit praise of the church universal. Church historian Eusebius would later denounce the movement because, as he put it, its adherents opposed the "custom which belongs to the tradition and succession of the Church from the beginning."[6] His and others' denunciations invoked Jude 3, affirming "the faith that was once for all delivered to the saints."

The Montanist movement would continue well after its major moment; tiny pockets survived here and there even into the sixth century (and perhaps beyond). Montanists appointed their own separate bishops and leaders, both men and women, separate from those of the universal church. Within a century the movement would be dealt a serious blow with the emperor Constantine's conversion to Christianity (see chap. 8). Sustaining a vision of the imminent end of the world turned out to be a real challenge once Rome's very earthly leaders embraced the faith and showed it favor.

The Mathēma

Unsettled political conditions provoked and nurtured this early moment of apocalyptic fervor. The civil war of 193–197 and subsequent crises did not give birth to the Montanist movement itself, but they certainly helped sustain it. More frequent and widespread persecution of Christians further fanned the apocalyptic fervor. During times of crisis, the fertile soil for apocalypticism often nurtures both hope and despair simultaneously.

Centuries later, the Montanists had dwindled and then disappeared but not without leaving their mark on the church, for better or for worse. While Montanism was a sort of prod to purity, church leaders generally saw it as a threat; subsequent historical circumstances did not play well to the Montanists' motivating fascinations and fears. At the very moment when apologists like Justin Martyr were striving to establish Christianity as rational and thus in tune with the best of ancient philosophy (see chap. 2), many saw ecstatic utterances as irrational.

This was not the first moment, nor indeed the last, when Christians have interpreted the unsettling events of their immediate day as signs of the end. More historically noteworthy, perhaps, might be moments when Christians did *not* jump to unwarranted conclusions amidst tumultuous times. No less rational an observer than the famed American pastor Jonathan Edwards once believed that the French and Indian War signaled the end times. Many American evangelicals during the Cold War had their own conflicting varieties of apocalypticism. Learning about moments like this in the history of Our People can help keep us grounded. Those we often recognize in retrospect as being advocates of extreme and bizarre claims can serve as cautionary tales for us today. At the same time, the witness of Our People who rejected unwarranted claims can likewise guide against the excesses and paranoia to which Our People are too often susceptible.

Maintaining a proper balance regarding preparedness for the promised coming of Christ has often been a challenge for the church. Like Abraham, we too look for "the city that has foundations, whose designer and builder is God" (Heb. 11:10). On the one hand, a stance of indifference to the promised coming of the Lord is clearly in error. But on the other hand, so is an excessive indulgence of apocalyptic fears.

Further Reading

Butler, Rex D. *The New Prophecy and the New Visions: Evidence of Montanism in The Passion of Perpetua and Felicitas.* Catholic University of America Press, 2011.

Tabbernee, William. *Fake Prophecy and Polluted Sacraments: Ecclesiastical and Imperial Reactions to Montanism.* Brill, 2007.

Trevett, Christine. *Montanism: Gender, Authority, and the New Prophecy.* Cambridge University Press, 1996.

Notes

1. Cassius Dio, *Roman History* 77.115.
2. Eusebius, *Ecclesiastical History* 5.16–19.
3. Eusebius, *Ecclesiastical History* 5.16.9.
4. Eusebius, *Ecclesiastical History* 18.
5. Tertullian, *Against Marcion* 3.24.
6. Eusebius, *Ecclesiastical History* 5.16.

4

"No Other Name": The Trials and Death of Vibia Perpetua

(Carthage, 203)

The Background

It is an odd family portrait. Three faces—two adults and a boy—are clearly visible. But the face of a fourth figure, another boy, has been deliberately removed. The color and odor of the erasure suggest it may have been defaced with feces. The portrait depicts the royal family: Emperor Septimius Severus, his wife Julia Domna, and their two sons. The boy whose face remains intact is Caracalla, the older brother. The erased figure is Geta, the younger of the two. After their father's death, the brothers briefly ruled as co-emperors until 211 when Caracalla murdered his younger brother and erased his memory through the Roman decree of *damnatio memoriae*.

On March 7, 203, eight years before Geta's demise, the Roman Empire celebrated his fourteenth birthday with games and festivities. Carthage, the provincial capital of North Africa, put on spectacular entertainments in its large amphitheater. There were gladiators with swords and whips; wild beasts such as bears, leopards, wild boars, and mad heifers; and the highlight—condemned criminals meeting brutal deaths before eager Roman eyes. Those in the stands already knew they were in for a rare opportunity, for among the condemned were two young women, and one of them, Vibia Perpetua, was particularly distinguished: "well born, liberally educated, and honorably married."[1] What's more, she was a Roman citizen, and citizens were almost never thrown to the beasts.

The year before this, in 202, the emperor had forbidden any conversion to Christianity "under heavy penalties."[2] The enforcement of such a prohibition would have been short-lived and local, as the Roman Empire declared no general law against Christianity until

Portrait of Emperor Septimius Severus and the royal family
Public domain

about a half century later (see chap. 5). Enforcement ultimately depended on the zeal of local officials. Carthage was in the province of Africa Proconsularis, which apparently had a particularly pious procurator (governor) at this time. His name was Hilarianus, and he took his task of honoring the imperial family and the state gods with drop-dead seriousness.[3]

What the cheering crowd could not have known was that among those whose deaths they cheered that day was one who was (1) one of the very earliest Christians ever to write in Latin, (2) the first author of a Christian autobiography, and (3) the writer of the earliest surviving ancient diary by a woman. We know much about this moment from that diary, *The Passion of Saints Perpetua and Felicity*.

The Moment

Governor Hilarianus was poised to make the most of this occasion, as the emperor himself had lately been in North Africa.[4] The emperor was North African and was much beloved in this region. In the days leading up to the celebration, a small but fervent group of Christians was rounded up, interrogated, imprisoned, and brought to trial before Hilarianus. It soon became clear that they were to play a central role in the birthday festivities.

The group that stood trial were all catechumens, new and eager converts to the faith, and all would be baptized in their final days. Two were slaves—Revocatus and Felicity, who was eight months pregnant—and the others were Perpetua, Saturninus, and Secundulus. Vibia Perpetua was a twenty-two-year-old married woman who had a nursing infant son. We know nothing about her husband. The group's Christian teacher, Saturus, would later hand himself over to the authorities to die in solidarity with his catechumens.

Perpetua's own account is introduced by an unknown editor, who also picks up the story where Perpetua leaves off as she goes to face martyrdom. Throughout the portion written by Perpetua herself, her father appears as a major figure. He begged and pleaded for Perpetua to simply perform the sacrifices to the emperor and the gods. She stubbornly refused. In one particularly poignant part of the exchange, she writes:

> When we were still with our arresting officers [or prosecutors], my father wished to make me change my mind with words of persuasion. He persevered in his attempts to defeat me, all because of his love for me.
>
> "Father," I said, "for the sake of argument, do you see this vase, or whatever you want to call it, lying here?"
>
> And he said, "Yes, I see it."
>
> And I said to him, "Can you call it by any other name than what it is?"
>
> And he said, "No, you can't."
>
> "So," I said, "I cannot call myself anything other than what I am—a Christian."
>
> Merely hearing this word upset my father greatly. He threw himself at me with such violence that it seemed he wanted to tear my eyes out.[5]

Deep mutual affection between father and daughter is implicit throughout Perpetua's account. But here she defied the fundamental Roman tradition of *patria potestas*, the ultimate power a Roman father had over his daughters all their lives, even into married adulthood. Perpetua was bothered by the grief she brought her father, but she remained resolute in her faith and refused to deny Christ.

A few days after the initial inquest, the group was arrested and thrown into a dark, overcrowded dungeon. Two deacons, Tertius and Pomponius, managed to bribe the guards to get Perpetua and company temporarily moved to better conditions where she could care for her child. After a few days in prison, the group was brought out for a public hearing. Perpetua's father appeared again to plead with her: "My daughter, have pity on my gray hair, have pity on your father. . . . If with these hands I have raised you to this flower of youth, if I have preferred you to all your brothers, do not shame me among men. Think about your brothers, think about your mother and your mother's sister, think about your son who will not be able to live without you."[6]

Roman due process was at work even with the pending birthday celebration, and the first hearing was followed by a second in which Perpetua's companions confessed to being Christians. At Perpetua's subsequent hearing, her father appeared once again, this time physically dragging her from the inquiry platform as he pleaded with her. The governor Hilarianus intervened and demanded of Perpetua: "Spare the gray hair of your father, spare your infant son. Offer the sacrifice for the health of the emperors." Perpetua refused, and he got right to the point: "Are you a Christian?" "I am a Christian," she replied.[7] And by claiming the name of Christian, her fate was sealed. Her father would not stop his pleas until the governor ordered him thrown to the ground and beaten; Perpetua's actions had further disgraced her father. After the group was sent to a military prison in final preparation for the arena, her father appeared one last time, even tearing out his beard and flinging himself on the ground.

Some have seen Perpetua and her group as Montanists or at least as being strongly influenced by that movement (see chap. 3). This is certainly possible.[8] They appeared eager for martyrdom, which lines up with the accusations of volunteer martyrdom often leveled at Montanists. Perpetua and Saturus both experienced vivid guiding visions, which comforted Perpetua with assurance of ultimate victory. At one point, the whole group prayed earnestly for Felicity to deliver her baby a month early, for Roman law forbade execution of pregnant women and she desired above all else to face the arena along with her friends, not alone at a later time. Immediately after their prayers, Felicity went into labor and delivered a baby girl. More explicitly, in the introduction to the diary is praise for "new prophecies" and "new visions," clearly suggestive of Montanism. Although such praise came from the ancient editor, it might well represent Perpetua and company.

The day before the birthday bash for Geta, the group was given a last meal. A mob jostled to get a glimpse of these prisoners ahead of the big games. Saturus, the teacher of all the catechumens, directly rebuked the pressing mob, and many of them became believers.[9] Earlier in the account we read that their assigned guard even embraced the faith.

When the "day of their victory dawned,"[10] the group was marched to the amphitheater. They were commanded to put on costumes, a common practice, as the amphitheater was almost always performative theater, with condemned criminals playing roles for the further entertainment of the hungry audience. The men were to be dressed as priests of the god Saturn and the women as priestesses of the goddess Ceres. They stubbornly refused to do so and persisted until the authorities finally relented. As expected, they each underwent brutal torment and death involving gladiators, soldiers, and wild beasts. Perpetua ultimately died by a sword to her throat after being attacked and thrown by a mad heifer.

The Mathēma

The anonymous editor concludes the diary by noting that the recounting of recent events—as much as, if not more than, older ones—serves to build up the church. And indeed, Perpetua and Felicity began almost immediately to be memorialized in art, stories, and sermons. Two centuries later, Augustine of Hippo, their fellow North African, would preach a series of powerful sermons in their memory.[11]

Christians throughout the centuries have found themselves at odds with basic manners of their age in one way or another. Along with the obvious ways in which she stood firm in her faith, Perpetua boldly refused to conform to the fundamental mores of her culture. It would have been impossible for her to be a good

Roman daughter and submit to *patria potestas* while also remaining a faithful follower of Christ. Note also that she gladly shared the arena with slaves and even embraced the opportunity to do so. A citizen of high social standing together with outcasts and slaves in an unbreakable bond? Traditional Romans could never understand.

This key moment may cause readers to recall the words of Martin Luther's famous hymn "A Mighty Fortress Is Our God":

> Let goods and kindred go,
> This mortal life also;
> The body they may kill:
> God's truth abideth still,
> His Kingdom is forever.[12]

Sometimes, though certainly not always, we can see victory in the here and now. Eight years after his highly celebrated birthday, Geta was killed at age twenty-two, the same age Perpetua had been when she died in the arena. His images were defaced and even his name was chiseled out of inscriptions. Septimius Severus himself died in fear for the future of his earthly empire. Perpetua's story has inspired multitudes through the ages, and continues to do so. Such a juxtaposition should not drive us to boastful triumphalism—though such a response is awfully tempting when we consider how Geta's portrait was defaced. Rather, it should serve as a sobering reminder that, for every age, the powers that seem so present, so meaningful, and so all-encompassing will soon be cast aside. We know precious little about her life, but we can be sure that our sister Perpetua faced death confident in eternal victory.

Further Reading

Birley, Anthony R. *Septimius Severus: The African Emperor.* Yale University Press, 1988.

Butler, Rex D. *The New Prophecy and the New Visions: Evidence of Montanism in The Passion of Perpetua and Felicitas.* Catholic University of America, 2011.

Heffernan, Thomas J., trans. *The Passion of Perpetua and Felicity.* Oxford University Press, 2012.

Salisbury, Joyce E. *Perpetua's Passion: The Death and Memory of a Young Roman Woman.* Routledge, 1997.

Shaw, Brent, "The Passion of Perpetua." *Past and Present* 139 (1993): 3–45.

Notes

1. *The Passion of Perpetua and Felicity* 1.1, trans. Thomas J. Heffernan (Oxford University Press, 2012).

2. *Historia Augusta, Septimius Severus* 17.1.

3. See James Rives, "The Piety of a Persecutor," *Journal of Early Christian Studies* 4.1 (1996): 1–26.

4. See Thomas J. Heffernen, *The Passion of Perpetua and Felicity* (Oxford University Press, 2012), 225.

5. *Passion of Perpetua and Felicity* 3.1–4, as quoted in Brent Shaw, "The Passion of Perpetua," *Past and Present* 139 (1993): 3–45.

6. *Passion of Perpetua and Felicity* 2.1.

7. *Passion of Perpetua and Felicity* 2.2.

8. See William Tabbernee, "Perpetua, Montanism, and Christian Ministry in Carthage c. 203 C.E.," *Perspectives in Religious Studies* 32, no. 4 (2005): 430. See also Rex D. Butler, *The New Prophecy and the New Visions: Evidence of Montanism in The Passion of Perpetua and Felicitas* (Catholic University of America Press, 2011).

9. *Passion of Perpetua and Felicity* 5.4.

10. *Passion of Perpetua and Felicity* 6.1.

11. Augustine, *Sermons* 280, 281, 282.

12. Martin Luther, "A Mighty Fortress Is Our God" (1529), trans. Frederick H. Hedge.

5

---•---

Persecution, Schism, and a Doctrine of the Church

(North Africa, c. 250)

The Background

In AD 247 the city of Rome flamboyantly celebrated its thousand-year anniversary. The problem was, there was precious little to celebrate. Military threats disrupted frontier and interior alike. A dozen emperors in succession had been assassinated, killed in battle, or died by suicide, most after very short reigns. Rampant inflation and debasement of currency wracked the empire, and a plague was just beginning that would kill a significant portion of its inhabitants. Emperor Decius, who usurped the throne just two years after Rome's millennial celebrations, had his work cut out for him. Had the Romans finally lost the Pax Deorum ("peace of/with the gods") that had guaranteed their health and strength? The recent celebrations had many Romans wistfully imagining a glorious past from a vantage point of chaos and disaster.

Decius desperately needed something definitive to stem the tide of emergency and discontent. Just a few months into his reign, he decreed that all Romans must publicly offer homage to their immortal gods, who would ensure the empire's security and prosperity. He demanded that all participate and, for the first time ever, required a document or certificate called a *libellus* (plural *libelli*) to verify that sacrifices had been offered before an overseeing official. For an otherwise unnoteworthy leader, it was "one of the most remarkable edicts hitherto issued by any Roman emperor."[1]

Even if the whole matter was prompted by obvious and overwhelming Roman insecurity (as the harshest of Roman persecutions always were), the fallout for Christians was real, immediate, and drastic. For the first time in the history of the church, an imperial edict demanded something impossible for Christians everywhere within the empire. Persecution was no longer a local matter as it had been since the beginning of the church. Fabian, the bishop of Rome, was executed in 250 for refusing to sacrifice. Many Christians throughout the empire were killed. Some Christian leaders, however, relented and sacrificed to the gods. Others went into hiding, and some even forged *libelli* or found other legal means of escape. The persecution lasted only a year and a half, until Decius, following the pattern for third-century emperors, was killed in June of 251.

The effect of this short-lived persecution on the church was enduring, however. Those who had capitulated to this edict and publicly sacrificed to the gods were labeled as *lapsi*, meaning "the ones who had lapsed" or "the fallen." Once persecution subsided, there was the glaring question of what should be done about *lapsi* who desired to return to the church. And what if they tried to return to leadership positions within the church? The ensuing debates were no small matter and struck at the very meaning of salvation and the nature of the church.

The Moment

The conflict began right at the center of the empire, in the city of Rome. As soon as it was safe, church leaders gathered to elect and appoint a bishop of Rome to replace the martyred Fabian. They selected Cornelius, a Roman priest, in 251. However, one leading presbyter named Novatian, who was a brilliant theologian, rejected the council's choice. Novatian had a solid reputation and broad support well beyond the city due to his impressive work *On the Trinity*, one of the most important works on the topic written before the mid-fourth century. Novatian rejected Cornelius for being too soft and even conciliatory toward *lapsi*, whom Novatian essentially saw as unredeemable apostates. Novatian's position was fairly straightforward: "No reconciliation was available to those who had sinned gravely; God might forgive, the Church had no such power."[2] Novatian then allowed himself to be ordained the "true" bishop of Rome by three Italian bishops, effectively as a counterbishop to Cornelius. Within the year, Cornelius called a council of bishops that condemned Novatian for schismatic actions.

The controversy soon spread to North Africa, where Cyprian, bishop of Carthage and the leader of the North African church, had already been crying foul at Novatian's actions. At first, Cyprian was sympathetic to Novatian's harsher stance toward *lapsi*, but he drew a hard line at what he saw as Novatian's usurpation. Cyprian quickly found himself in the middle of a very serious controversy.

To begin with, Cyprian's own position as bishop was not entirely secure. Prior to his conversion, he had been a wealthy lawyer, and his ascension to the office of bishop was controversial because he had been a Christian for only two years when he was acclaimed to the office. Christians of long standing had been passed over, and bitterness persisted in some quarters. Additionally, Cyprian butted heads with a group of Christians in North Africa who exercised considerable authority outside of traditional and recognized structures. Known as "confessors," these individuals had suffered bodily during the persecution but had managed to survive and were revered by many lay Christians. Because Cyprian himself had gone into hiding during the persecution (the wealthy could do that, after all), he lost influence with some believers. When some of the confessors declared a general amnesty for all the *lapsi*, Cyprian rebuked them, claiming that only the church and its recognized officers had that right. So Cyprian could not win. He found himself at the same time at odds with both those holding a rigorous line like Novatian and his followers (known as Novatians or Novatianists) *and* those who were less stringent and forgiving in their treatment of *lapsi*.

Novatian sent representatives to North Africa who essentially set up a new church right under Cyprian's nose in Carthage. The rival church set themselves as *katharoi* ("the pure ones") as opposed to the *lapsi* and their defenders, whom they saw as compromisers. Cyprian had gone on record with two short but powerful treatises, *On the Lapsed* and *On the Unity of the Church*, in which he called the *lapsi* to public repentance and (perhaps) restoration while denouncing the schismatic movement begun by Novatian in the strongest of terms.

Within Cyprian's treatises as well as a host of his letters, a powerful idea was taking shape: The church is one and separation from it is damnable. In other words, there is no salvation outside of the unity of the universal communion of the church. The church itself might not be a pure body and would always consist of both those who have failed and those who have confessed, but schism was unjustifiable apostasy. This idea came to dominate the North African church in particular, but it would also exert broader influence in the Latin Western church.

This all played out quite practically through the administration of the sacraments. Cyprian held that neither the *lapsi* nor schismatics like the Novatians could validly administer the sacraments, nor could they legitimately ordain other leaders to do so. Cyprian's thought, as developed in this tense moment, was at times inconclusive and left open questions that would resurface in the next century in debates between Donatists and Catholics (see chap. 9) and that the church has often struggled with ever since. Theologian Alister McGrath helpfully summarizes the two rather different ways Cyprian has been interpreted through the centuries:

1. By lapsing, a church leader committed the sin of apostasy. He therefore placed himself outside the bounds of the church and could no longer be regarded as validly administering the sacraments.
2. By his repentance, the bishop could be restored to grace and thus able to continue validly administering the sacraments.[3]

A later group known as Donatists went with the former interpretation, and their opponents adopted the latter. In Cyprian's own lifetime, he would be attacked from multiple sides, so it would have been no consolation for him to see the conflicting sides later appealing to his work and each claiming him as an authority.

The Mathēma

This was a moment of great importance for clarifying the meaning of the church and its role in salvation. North African Christians living at this time certainly saw and felt the immediate weight of the controversy but probably had no clear idea what a watershed moment they were living through. The Novatian church would continue for centuries, the "pure ones" refusing reconciliation with the compromising rank and file. What was the church supposed to be—a pure and undefiled body or a gathering of sinners dependent upon God's grace?

Despite the adversity Cyprian faced, his tenure as bishop was remarkably fruitful. He held that position for less than a decade before a renewed persecution under the emperor Valerian led to his own martyrdom. Yet in his few trying years, Cyprian began to articulate some of the most important positions of ecclesiology in the history of the church. Crisis prompted profound depth.

Christians who live in times of peace and prosperity and who fancy themselves models of doctrine, life, and practice, sometimes hold to very naive views about persecution. We sometimes hear evangelical Christians saying things like "What the church needs is a good persecution for the sake of purification!" and "All those hangers-on and nominal Christians around us need to be challenged or purged!" I have even heard evangelical organizations on college campuses praying for persecution. The records of the past, however, offer cautionary tales against such self-righteous fantasies. Moments of persecution have produced martyrs and inspiring examples of faithful service at all costs, to be sure, and we should celebrate those. But often they have also produced division, schism, rancor, and unapologetic gracelessness.

It would be far better to always pray and long for peace for the church. We should rejoice in peace, as Luke describes in Acts 9:31: "So the church throughout all Judea and Galilee and Samaria had peace and was being built up. And walking in the fear of the Lord and in the comfort of the Holy Spirit, it multiplied."

Cyprian was aware of the potential pitfalls after persecution. He saw Christian gracelessness and schism as no less the work of Satan than Roman harassment of God's people: "For it is not persecution alone that is to be feared. . . . Caution is more easy where danger is manifest, and the mind is prepared beforehand for the contest when the adversary avows himself. The enemy is more to be feared and to be guarded against, when he creeps on us secretly . . . deceiving by the appearance of peace."[4] Cyprian's example and writings continue to warn us that schism itself can tear the church apart in ways that no persecution by the Roman Empire ever could.

Further Reading

Burns, J. Patout. "Cyprian of Carthage." In *Early Christian Thinkers: The Lives and Legacies of Twelve Key Figures*. Edited by Paul Foster. IVP Academic, 2010.

Evans, G. R., ed. *The First Christian Theologians: An Introduction to Theology in the Early Church*. Blackwell, 2004.

Potter, David S. *The Roman Empire at Bay, AD 180–395*. Routledge, 2004.

Notes

1. David S. Potter, *The Roman Empire at Bay, AD 180–395* (Routledge, 2004), 241.

2. Quoted in Stuart G. Hall, "The Early Idea of the Church," in *The First Christian Theologians*, ed. G. R. Evans (Blackwell, 2004), 52.

3. Alister McGrath, *Christian Theology: An Introduction* (Blackwell, 1994), 408.

4. Cyprian, *On the Unity of the Church* 1.

6

The Christian Captives of Gundeshapur

(Sassanian Persian Empire, c. 260)

The Background

Šābuhr, Šāhān Šāh Ērān ud Anērān. "Shapur, King of Kings of Iran and Not-Iran." It was an innovatively bold title and claim, but warranted, and within it hides a remarkable story of Christianity in Persia. Shapur I (r. 241–272) was the second *shahinshah* (i.e., "king of kings") of a renewed Persian Empire under the Sassanian dynasty and would be one of the greatest Persian leaders of all time. He helped lay the groundwork for a massive empire that included all of modern-day Iran and Iraq, parts of Arabia to the south, and extended east well into central and southern Asia. He was the largest single threat the Romans had faced in centuries. From his day until the eventual defeat of the Sassanians by the Muslims in the seventh century, Romans and Persians would be almost perpetually in conflict, if not outright war.

As we saw in chapter 5, Rome at this time was hardly in a position to handle an expanding and threatening superpower. About a decade into his rule, Shapur I began seizing Roman cities along the frontier. He defeated three Roman emperors over the course of several campaigns from 250 to 260. One of them, Valerian, was the first Roman emperor to ever be captured by a foreign enemy. Shapur advanced deep into Roman territory, seizing land and peoples, most of whom he resettled elsewhere. He even took Antioch, one the most important cities of the eastern half of the Roman Empire.

With these successes, Shapur added the word *Anēran* ("Not-Iran") to his title as a way to describe the territories and peoples he had acquired in his campaigns against Rome. Among the Roman captives he brought back to resettle in the heart of Persia were many Christians, including Demetrius, the bishop of Antioch. During one of his campaigns, Shapur conquered and removed the inhabitants of Dura Europos, a Roman frontier city in Syria. Within the last century, archaeological excavations there have uncovered the earliest known Christian building, which had been covered in earth to strengthen the city walls during this Persian siege (see introduction).

Christianity had a deep history in Persia going back well before the rise of Shapur I and before the Sassanian dynasty. Exactly how far back is hard to say, but it appears that by the time of Shapur's campaign, there was already a well-established church with its own episcopal structure.[1] Some Christian traditions claim Thaddeus of Edessa, one of the seventy-two disciples or apostles (see Luke 10:1), as the founder of the Church of Persia. In Acts 2:9, Luke teases us with the distinct possibility that those "Parthians and Medes and Elamites" returned home to their Persian regions after Pentecost to share the Good News. Jewish communities were spread throughout Persia and likely produced some of the first converts to Christianity, if patterns documented elsewhere hold true here.

Solid historical evidence for Christianity in Persia dates to around the year 170; by 235, Persian Christians "had more than 20 bishops and some 18 dioceses."[2] *The Book of the Law of Countries* (from 196) and the late second- to early third-century heterodox Christian writer Bardesanes both mention Christians in several Persian areas, including Parthia, Kushan, Media, Edessa, Hatra, and Fars.[3] Merchants traveling through Mesopotamia introduced Christianity into Persia "a full generation or more before the rise of the Sassanian dynasty."[4] At moments of intense persecution in the Roman Empire, some Christians moved into Persian territory and found safety there.

If the church in Persia had been growing slowly and often imperceptibly to this point, Shapur's reign marked a clear and decisive moment in its history that has carried forward to the present day.

The Moment

The earlier Assyrian Empire mentioned in the Old Testament had begun the practice of resettling entire communities from the regions they conquered into other areas of their realm. Later empires would follow suit, and Shapur continued (or perhaps revived) this very old Near Eastern practice. His inscription tells the basic story: "And the men, who from the land of the Romans, from Not-Iran, were led back as spoils, into Iran, into Persis, Parthia, Xuzestan [Khuzestan], Asurestand and other lands . . . where settlements were established by me and my father and forebears and ancestors, there they were settled."[5]

Most obviously, this practice helped discourage revolt among resettled peoples, who were no longer living in or seeking to defend their ancestral lands. It was also a way to bolster population in areas that needed construction or agricultural workers. Shapur resettled many of the people he conquered to cultivate sugar and rice in Khuzestan, one of the most fertile regions of his empire.[6] Through civic and agricultural projects, these war captives improved the land and transformed southwest Iran.[7] They also built dams and bridges, the remains of which can still be seen today. In effect, "Shapur I had wrested non-Iranian traditions, skills, and manpower from Aneran [Not-Iran] . . . and had placed them in the heart of Eran."[8]

A major place for such resettlement was Gundeshapur, otherwise known as Beth Lapat (Syriac), which Shapur himself had founded in the region of Khuzestan. The city was also known as Vēh Antiōk Šāpūr ("better than Antioch of Shapur"), which testifies to the Roman–Sassanian rivalry.[9] Many of the transplanted people were Christians, which is unsurprising given the tremendous growth Christianity experienced over the course of the third century. The *Chronicle of Seert*, written centuries later by an Arabic-speaking Christian, names one of the captives as Demetrius the patriarch of Antioch. The role that Christians played among these resettled Roman communities was pivotal. According to the *Chronicle*,

> He [Shapur] settled prisoners . . . and gave them land to cultivate and houses to live in. Christians too became numerous in Persia and they built monasteries and churches. Among them were priests, prisoners from Antioch. They settled in Gundishapur. . . . Christians spread throughout the entire country and became very numerous in the East. . . . They prospered in Persia and their situation became better than in their own country. God did not abandon them. . . . It was through a divine gift that the Romans enjoyed the favour of the Persians; they received land from the Persians and were able to spread Christianity in the East.[10]

Although Shapur himself was a fervent Zoroastrian and helped launch something of a Zoroastrian state church in the Sassanian Empire, he was notably tolerant of other faiths and did not suppress other religious beliefs or practices. Christians at this time were safer among the Sassanians than within the Roman Empire, and they were able to proselytize and grow in numbers.

The resettlement of Christians in the region of Khuzestan in general and Gundeshapur in particular left a clear mark. Three of the five bishops from Khuzestan who attended a synod in the Persian city of Ctesiphon in 410 (see chap. 13) "represented cities where Roman captives had been resettled."[11] Bishop Gadihab of Gundeshapur ordained a man named Miles as bishop of Susa in the early fourth century, prior to the famous ecumenical Council of Nicaea, which itself had a Persian bishop in attendance.[12] In the fourth century, Shapur I's namesake Shapur II would carry out a brutal persecution of Christians (see chap. 11). A number of the martyrs from that brief but intense persecution came from Gundeshapur,[13] which demonstrates that a vibrant and bold Christian community and witness persisted there.

Gundeshapur had a storied future ahead. It became an important city in its own right as an intellectual center, and its bishop would be "one of the most senior in the East."[14] Shapur himself ordered Greek and Sanskrit manuscripts on medicine, astronomy, and philosophy to be translated into Persian.[15] A famous observatory was built there that drew scholars from far and wide as well as a medical school that would last beyond the Sassanian rule and into the Islamic period. Centuries later, when the Christian Roman (Byzantine) emperor Justinian closed down Plato's Academy at Athens, some of those who were exiled resettled in Gundeshapur.[16]

The Mathēma

The Christians of Persia came from diverse cultural backgrounds. Among the captives were both Syriac speakers and Greek speakers, each bringing distinct worship traditions shaped by their cultural heritage. Evidence suggests that these two communities persisted for some time. This contributed to the diverse and multifaceted picture of Christianity in Persia, as seen in other regions as well.[17]

The *Chronicle of Seert* reflects on two biblical texts while rejoicing in what God has done with these Roman Christians who resettled in Persia:

> God did not abandon them [Romans captured and resettled in Persia], in accordance with the word of the prophet to the sons of Israel, consoling them at the moment when the army of Sennacherib invaded and the ten tribes were captured and their hopes were dashed: If a woman forgets the child who is still in her womb, if she has no pity on the fruit of her insides, if it is possible that she forgets it, I will not forget you. Here, I have written your name on my hand and your walls are always before me [Isa. 49:15]. David too said: I have made merciful the heart of those who have taken them into captivity [Ps. 106:46].[18]

Shapur aided Christians in many ways, completely unbeknownst to him. Ironically, the Roman emperor Valerian, who was himself an avid persecutor of Christians, likely died in captivity in Gundeshapur. His successor, Gallienus, rescinded Valerian's edict of persecution, and Roman Christians were able to live in relative peace for a half century before the emperor Diocletian revived the persecutions in the opening years of the fourth century. Through his conquests, Shapur brought decades of peace to Christians in the Roman Empire—again, God is in the details. And the church here would thrive and grow, even amidst some setbacks that were yet to come (see chap. 11). By the end of the sixth century, Christians would make up the largest confessional community in the entire region of Iraq.[19]

This was not the first time God had used a Persian leader to accomplish his plans for his people—recall Cyrus the Great from the Old Testament. God indeed "moves in a mysterious way, his wonders to perform."[20] Yet, the means often are less than mysterious, even if no less remarkable. A Near Eastern monarch employed age-old patterns of resettling conquered people just when Christianity was growing exponentially in the Roman Empire. No earthly ruler intended to spread Christianity into these new areas, where it persists even to the present day. Yet through a combination of Near Eastern practices and benevolent rulership, Shapur was instrumental in building a kingdom that was not his own, an eternal kingdom that would reach far beyond *Anēran*.

Further Reading

Baum, Wilhelm, and Dietmer W. Winkler. *The Church of the East: A Concise History*. Routledge, 2003.

Gilman, Ian, and Hans-Joachim Klimkeit. *Christians in Asia Before 1500*. University of Michigan Press, 1999.

Raheb, Mitri, and Mark Lamport, eds. *The Rowman & Littlefield Handbook of Christianity in the Middle East*. Rowman & Littlefield, 2020.

Walker, Joel. *The Legend of Mar Qardagh: Narrative and Christian Heroism in Late Antique Iraq*. University of California Press, 2006.

Wood, Philip. *The Chronicle of Seert: Christian Historical Imagination*. Oxford University Press, 2013.

Notes

1. Wilhelm Baum and Dietmer W. Winkler, *The Church of the East: A Concise History* (Routledge, 2003), 9.

2. Ian Gilman and Hans-Joachim Klimkeit, *Christians in Asia Before 1500* (University of Michigan Press, 1999), 109.

3. Todd M. Johnson, "Church Growth and Decline in the Middle East Across the Centuries," in Mitri Raheb and Mark Lamport, eds., *The Rowman & Littlefield Handbook of Christianity in the Middle East* (Rowman & Littlefield, 2020), xxiii.

4. Joel Walker, *The Legend of Mar Qardagh: Narrative and Christian Heroism in Late Antique Iraq* (University of California Press, 2006), 95.

5. *Deeds of Shapur* 1.30.

6. Walker, *Legend*, 95.

7. Philip Wood, *The Chronicle of Seert: Christian Historical Imagination* (Oxford University Press, 2013), 25; D. T. Potts, *The Archaeology of Elam*, 2nd ed. (Cambridge University Press, 2015), 415–19.

8. Peter Brown, "The Diffusion of Manichaeism in the Roman Empire," *Journal of Roman Studies* 59, nos. 1–2 (1969): 95.

9. Whether it was given this name by Shapur I or later by Shapur II is a point of disagreement among leading scholars. Walker claims it was Shapur II, but all other scholars cited here claim Shapur I.

10. *Chronicle of Seert* 2.

11. Walker, *Legend*, 96.

12. Roderick Mullen, *The Expansion of Christianity: A Gazeteer of Its First Three Centuries* (Brill, 2004), 68.

13. Sozomen, *Ecclesiastical History*, book 2, chap. 13.

14. Warwick Ball, *Rome in the East: The Transformation of an Empire* (Routledge, 1999), 134.

15. Shahin Nezhad, *Iranshahr and the Downfall of the Sassanid Dynasty* (Logos Verlag, 2023), 23.

16. Ball, *Rome in the East*, 134.

17. James C. Skedros, "Christianity Within the Ancient Empires," in Raheb and Lamport, *Rowman & Littlefield Handbook of Christianity in the Middle East*, xxiii; see also Baum and Winkler, *Church of the East*, 9.

18. *Chronicle of Seert 2.*

19. Jonathan Berkey, *The Formation of Islam: Religion and Society in the Near East, 600–1800* (Cambridge University Press, 2002), 24.

20. William Cowper, "God Moves in a Mysterious Way" (1774), public domain.

7

The Birth of the First "Christian Nation"

(Armenia, 301 or 314)

The Background

The story is told of how the Armenian king Trdat (also known as Tiridates III) was physically transformed into a wild boar as a form of divine punishment for persecuting Christians. He reportedly developed claws, a snout, fangs, and bristly hair, symbolizing his descent into a beastlike state. Ancient church historian Agathangelos tells how Trdat suffered from this strange affliction until divine aid provided a cure. The king's sister had a vision of a man who could heal him—the same man Trdat had years earlier thrown into the aptly named Pit of Oblivion for refusing to sacrifice to an Armenian ancestral goddess. The man's name was Grigor (we know him as Gregory the Illuminator), and he should have died there. But when the Pit of Oblivion was opened, Grigor was found alive thanks to the generosity of a woman who had furtively tossed bread into the pit each day for years. Grigor was brought forth to heal King Trdat, who immediately repented and converted, dedicating the rest of his long reign to tirelessly building up the Armenian Church with Grigor's help.

How should we approach inspiring (and often entertaining) stories like this one, which many cautious historians of Christianity introduce with phrases such as "According to tradition . . ." or "Legend has it that . . ."? The history of the Armenian Church is full of such accounts, yet historians remain divided on whether or how to incorporate them into serious historical narratives. Even the date of Trdat's conversion is deeply controversial, with scholars arguing for either 301 or 314, or somewhere in between. Such challenges are intricately enmeshed with the Armenian national story.

Well before Trdat's conversion, Christianity had been growing steadily in Armenia, as it was elsewhere. Early church traditions declare that Bartholemew and Thaddeus, two of the seventy-two disciples mentioned in Luke 10:1, were the original apostles to the Armenians. Perhaps. Several important trade routes cut through Armenia, and merchants and missionaries shared their faith in the major cities.[1] Over the course of the second and third centuries, Christianity came to Armenia primarily from Edessa in Mesopotamia, which was home to a vibrant Syriac Christianity, and from Cappadocia, which was predominantly Greek. The first recorded Armenian bishop was Meruzanes, who we know corresponded with Dionysius, bishop of Alexandria, around the year 250. By the late third century, some powerful Armenian nobles embraced Christianity as well.

The political situation of Armenia was vital to Christianity's rise there. Armenia was located between two warring superpowers—the Romans to the west and the Sassanian Persians to the east. More often than not, Armenia was at "the whims of imperial powers"[2] owing to a general lack of internal unity among its powerful and assertive nobility. As a buffer zone, Armenia long had to "play a delicate game of balancing major powers in order to maintain independence."[3] Even at moments of relative independence, Armenia was almost never centrally unified and was usually only superficially autonomous. At one such moment, in 298, the Roman and Sassanian Empires signed a peace treaty that recognized Armenian autonomy and acknowledged the Arsacid royal house, which had a strong connection to the Roman Empire.

The Moment

Trdat came to power as part of that treaty but soon faced strong religious and political pressures from all sides. From the east, "the Sassanian Persians were increasing pressure on the Armenians to accept the official Zoroastrian religion of [their] empire" in something akin to forced conversion.[4] From the west, Roman leaders called on Trdat to suppress Christianity and to punish any Christians fleeing to Armenia to escape Roman persecution. Trdat bowed to Roman wishes, reversed a history of religious toleration in Armenia, and began persecuting Christians, declaring his intentions in a letter to Diocletian, the Roman emperor who orchestrated the Great Persecution (see chaps. 8 and 9). But when the Roman emperor Constantine converted to Christianity in 312, Trdat dutifully reversed course, embraced Christianity (if we follow the date of 314), and was taught by Grigor. All along, Trdat also felt pressures from inside his own country, as a number of Armenia's assertive and strong aristocrats had become Christians themselves.[5]

The two central figures in the early Armenian Christian story, Trdat and Grigor, shared strikingly similar backgrounds. Both were born into noble families with roots tracing back to Parthian or Persian heritage. As young children, they narrowly escaped death during periods of intense political upheaval thanks to courageous nurses who smuggled them out of Armenia and into Roman territory after their families were murdered. Interestingly, some accounts suggest a dramatic connection between their families:

Trdat's father was assassinated in a plot in which Grigor's father is said to have played a role. Agathangelos tells us that, while sheltering in the Roman region of Cappadocia as a child or teenager, Grigor "was raised as a devout Christian."[6] Later, in the city of Rome, Trdat befriended influential Romans, laying the groundwork for bonds of friendship.

When Grigor reached adulthood, he returned to Armenia, where he and thirty-three Christian women, led by Hripsime and Gaiane, shared the gospel at the Armenian court. Trdat, however, demanded that Grigor and the others publicly sacrifice to the royal Armenian goddess Anahit. When they refused, they were subjected to torture, though it remains unclear if the infamous Pit of Oblivion was actually involved.

Sometime later, Trdat embraced Christianity. Scholars have proposed various reasons for his conversion, none of which, notably, involve the tale of bristly boar hair. Some point to the influence of powerful Christian nobles within his court, others to the courageous witness of Grigor, Hripsime, Gaiane, and their companions. Another factor may have been Constantine's Edict of Milan in 313, which granted religious toleration throughout the Roman Empire. It is likely that a combination of these factors played a role. What is clear, however, is that once Trdat converted, he immediately began reshaping Armenia in accordance with his new faith. In 313 or 314, a state assembly in Vagharshapat, Armenia, affirmed his choice of a new religion.[7]

The first official act of the Armenian Christian state was to send Grigor back to Cappadocia for ordination as bishop of the Armenians. He received an official political mandate to the entire Armenian people.[8] Grigor returned to continue teaching, and in 314 or 315, he baptized the Armenian king, the army, and, sources say, the Armenian people in the Euphrates River. The areas Trdat controlled most strongly in his fragmented realm and areas controlled by Christian nobility saw immediate conversions. Pockets of paganism remained, as we see Mesrop Mashtots still sharing the gospel with pagan Armenians well into the fifth century.[9] But the royal family and nobility ensured that Christianity would be the religion of the state from the time of Trdat onward. Toward the end of his long reign, he would even send an Armenian representative—Grigor's son Aristaces—to the Council of Nicaea in 325.

The Mathēma

The Roman emperor Constantine, as we will see, embraced the faith himself and extended toleration to others. Trdat went a serious step beyond this when he "established Christianity as a state religion,"[10] the first ruler ever to do so. Whether one accepts the traditional Armenian account and dates Trdat's conversion to 301, making him the first political leader to embrace Christianity, or the current consensus of 314, or somewhere in between, Armenia was the first state to embrace Christianity. The Roman Empire would not declare Christianity the state religion until almost a century later.

The Armenians would come to view themselves as God's chosen people.[11] The ancient writer Agathangelos described his home country as a place "where God's grace has been manifested," with assumptions of exclusivity that have been connected with national pride there ever since. Even the debates over the date of Trdat's conversion are enmeshed. The early date of 301 is the only date officially recognized by the state since it affirms his conversion as an act of Armenian identity that is unrelated to Constantine's conversion.

Not surprisingly, this first "Christian nationalism" bore some unpleasant fruit. Once Christianity became the state religion, "an intense—and at times violent—proselytizing campaign began to enforce the new religion on the entire population."[12] Non-Christians were persecuted, and pagan and Zoroastrian sites and temples were destroyed, with Christian projects often built directly on top of the ruins. Christianity had not functioned this way before, but it would do so in subsequent centuries with great regularity across many different settings. Throughout history, we find similar examples of Christianity being consolidated with political power. Such dangers lurk whenever a people—whether Romans, Franks, Brits, or Americans—claim to be chosen by God and adopt, in effect, a Christian nationalism.

Still, it is impossible to ignore the power Christian nationalism has to sustain a people. Christianity left a unique mark on the Armenian people that has remained strong through the centuries. Despite an often politically fragmented realm, "it was Christianity that cemented the distinctiveness of Armenian identity" in this period.[13] That identity has long sustained our Armenian brothers and sisters through setbacks, conquests, and occupations by Persians, Byzantines, Arabs, Ottoman Turks, and Soviet Russians. They remained a people, sometimes even without any official state to speak of. Within a century of Trdat's conversion, the first Armenian alphabet and script were developed by Mesrop Mashtots, and Armenians now had texts—first the Scriptures, then original literature—written in their own language. Up to that point, Christian writings had only been available in Greek and Syriac. These were powerful markers, statements, and enforcers of Armenian national faith and identity that remain so to this day.

Further Reading

Panossian, Razmik. *The Armenians: From Kings and Priests to Merchants and Commissars*. Columbia University Press, 2006.

Payaslian, Simon. *The History of Armenia from the Origins to the Present*. Palgrave MacMillan, 2007.

Stopka, Krzysztof. *Armenia Christiana: Armenian Religious Identity and the Churches of Constantinople and Rome (4th–15th Century)*. Jagiellonian University Press, 2016.

Notes

1. Krzysztof Stopka, *Armenia Christiana: Armenian Religious Identity and the Churches of Constantinople and Rome (4th–15th Century)* (Jagiellonian University Press, 2016), 18–19.

2. Razmik Panossian, *The Armenians: From Kings and Priests to Merchants and Commissars* (Columbia University Press, 2006), 40.

3. Panossian, *Armenians*, 40.

4. Panossian, *Armenians*, 42.

5. Stopka, *Armenia Christiana*, 31.

6. Agathanangelos, *History of the Armenians* 1.10.

7. Stopka, *Armenia Christiana*, 31.

8. Stopka, *Armenia Christiana*, 31.

9. C. S. Lightfoot, "Armenia and the Eastern Marches," in *Cambridge Ancient History*, vol. 12, ed. Alan Bowman, Averil Cameron, and Peter Garnsey (Cambridge University Press, 2008), 486.

10. Stopka, *Armenia Christiana*, 30.

11. Panossian, *Armenians*, 43–44.

12. Panossian, *Armenians*, 43.

13. Panossian, *Armenians*, 42.

8

"In This Sign Conquer": Constantine Embraces Christianity

(Rome, 312–313)

The Background

Over four decades had passed since Christians in the Roman Empire faced official persecution under Emperor Decius around 250. By the dawn of the fourth century, Christians were living peacefully and openly. They constructed churches, some of which were prominent and impressive. For example, a church in Nicomedia stood on a hill overlooking the palace, while churches in Carthage, Antioch, and Alexandria were large enough to accommodate massive crowds.[1]

Christians also served in the military and held influential government positions. Their numbers continued to grow; although precise figures are uncertain, some estimate that Christians made up as much as 20 percent of the Roman population. More cautious and generally more reliable estimates are closer to 10 percent—between five and seven million people within the empire, with many more outside its borders. With their unwavering commitment to one God and their strong sense of community, Christians had become a significant and influential presence.

The Great Persecution, though, would briefly but decisively upend the church's period of peace and respite in the Roman Empire. Ever since he claimed the throne in 284, Emperor Diocletian had been working tirelessly to stem the tide of the "Crisis of the Third Century," thus named for the ideological, economic, military, and political upheaval that took place (see chap. 5). His reforms, which included the establishment of a tetrarchy—that is, four rulers, two as co-emperors and two as assistant emperors—had brought a general stability to the Roman world the likes of which had not been seen in over a century. He certainly did not need anyone threatening all his hard work to reestablish Pax Deorum, Rome's peace with the gods.

> There is no doubt that the immortal gods, as always friendly towards Rome, will be reconciled to us only if we have ensured that everyone within our empire pursues a pious, religious, peaceful life, and one thoroughly pure in all regards. . . . It is in this way that the majesty of Rome, by the favor of all the divine powers, has attained its greatness.[2]

In 303, well into Diocletian's reign, he and a co-emperor suddenly declared a renewal of persecution. This was likely in response to a group of Christians who disrupted a state religious ceremony, although it was perhaps also fueled by the presence of a church building in his capital at Nicomedia that was actually taller than his imperial palace. An edict was issued directly at Christians, and its terms were crystal clear. It began by striking right at the heart of Christian worship: All church buildings were to be destroyed,[3] and Scriptures were to be burned. Christians were to be removed from public office and were deprived of the legal right to fight back or file charges against anyone who might assault them—a sort of reverse hate crimes law.[4] Authorities were to force submission through imprisonment, torture, and execution, and the ranks of the martyrs grew quickly and memorably.

The Great Persecution did not achieve its desired effect, however, as the church kept on growing. The government's enthusiasm for the persecution faded in many quarters, and it did not even have firm support among all the tetrarchs who now ruled the empire. One of these, Constantius, who was a devotee of the "abstractly monotheist" cult of Sol Invictus, the Unconquered Sun, barely even enforced the edict.[5] Although fierce, the persecution continued uninterrupted for less than two years. A few brief periods of renewed persecution would follow, though these were usually localized, until in 311 the tetrarch Galerius issued the tepid Edict of Toleration as he lay dying. This edict waxed eloquent on the importance of Roman ancestral ways, *mos maiorum*, and accused Christians of abandoning the "practice of their ancestors" because they were possessed by "self-indulgence" and "idiocy."[6] No matter; they could be tolerated—grudgingly. Such could hardly inspire confidence in safety for Christians going forward. Persecution could break out at any time. What the Christians needed above all, to put it in Roman terms, was a protector, a benefactor, a patron.

The Moment

Constantine, the son of the tetrarch Constantius, was a young soldier when he witnessed the launch of the Great Persecution.[7] "Nothing indicates that Constantine opposed" the persecution of Christians "especially strenuously."[8] Acclaimed a tetrarch after the death of his father, Constantine showed more interest in securing a powerful divine protector than anything else. His need for a protector became even more acute after Diocletian retired. (It's worth noting that Diocletian was neither assassinated nor killed in battle—an incredible feat among Roman emperors who came to power in the third century.) Fierce civil war broke out yet again among co-emperors and ambitious rivals, and Constantine's fellow tetrarchs and many others viewed him as a usurper to be eradicated.[9]

Though historians have observed a longer trend toward monotheism both within and beyond the Roman Empire at that time,[10] Constantine's embrace of Christianity was not historically inevitable. Constantine himself had a history of seeing visions associated with a single protective deity, particularly Apollo, whose imagery and attributes often blended with those of Sol Invictus, his father's favored deity. Two years before he embraced Christianity, Constantine visited a shrine of Apollo where he reportedly received a vision assuring him of divine protection and universal rule.

In September 312, Constantine marched forth against his final serious rival amidst the civil struggles engulfing the empire. Not long before the battle, he received new visions. Seeking some all-powerful deity, even if vaguely conceived, Constantine "called on Him with earnest prayer and supplications that He would reveal to him who He was, and stretch forth His right hand to help him in his present difficulties."[11]

Constantine received an answer, as he later reported to church historian Eusebius and even confirmed with oaths:

> About the time of the midday sun, when day was just turning, he said he saw with his own eyes, up in the sky and resting over the sun, a cross-shaped trophy formed from light, and a text attached to it which said, "By this conquer." Amazement at the spectacle seized both him and the whole company of soldiers which was then accompanying him on a campaign.[12]

Eusebius continues,

> He was, he said, wondering to himself what the manifestation might mean; then, while he meditated, and thought long and hard, night overtook him. Thereupon, as he slept, the Christ of God

appeared to him with the sign which had appeared to him in the sky and urged him to make himself a copy of the sign which had appeared in the sky, and to use this as protection against the attack of the enemy.[13]

At the ensuing Battle of Milvian Bridge, Constantine routed his rival and paraded his head on a pike. He was now the undisputed master of the western half of the empire. Within months of his victory, Constantine was busy promoting his newfound faith throughout the empire. In 313 he, along with his co-emperor and erstwhile ally Licinius, issued what is usually called the Edict of Milan. It was the most extensive offer of protection and robust restoration of lost property the church had ever experienced.

The Mathēma

Christians throughout the empire were filled with awe and amazement. Constantine provided acceptance and support at the highest level of government. Just a bit over forty years after the Edict of Milan, it is reasonably estimated that Christians made up 50 percent of the empire's inhabitants.[14] By the end of the fourth century, Christianity would become the Roman state religion, as earlier it had become the Armenian state religion (see chap. 7). But two big questions refuse to go away.

First, did Constantine genuinely convert to Christianity? Some doubt whether he converted at all. Some claim he did eventually convert, but not until much later in 337, the year of his death. No answer will be satisfactory for everyone, but it is clear that Constantine at least saw himself as having gained a new protector who had revealed himself to him. As one major historian has put it, "There is little doubt but that Constantine converted to Christianity because he felt that he was in direct contact with the Christian divinity."[15]

We cannot know what went on in the heart of someone from the distant past, so the question of whether Constantine was really converted will always raise its head and the answers will remain inconclusive. It is worth emphasizing that church leaders of that time unanimously affirmed and rejoiced in his embrace of Christianity. His Christian contemporaries did not doubt it, and that should bear a certain weight. He promoted Christianity within the Roman world and beyond in remarkable ways.

What is clear is that Constantine did switch his highest loyalty to the Christian God. From the outset in 312, he also had at least one Christian bishop as a confidant, Ossius of Cordoba, who advised him and helped him interpret events.[16] What is equally clear is that Constantine's subsequent actions could deviate quite far from Christian ethics and mores. For example, he murdered his wife, Fausta, and his son, Crispus. Also, Sol Invictus and Apollo remained on his new coin issues for over a decade after the Battle of Milvian Bridge. All humans are indeed irreducibly complex, but some are more challenging to understand than others.

Second, was Constantine's profession of Christianity good for the church or bad for the church? To be sure, it was both. If we could invent a time machine and go back to that moment, we would be unlikely to convince any Christian to reject this happy new development. Christian writers rejoiced, envisioning God's kind providence. Christian buildings were being planned and erected everywhere. The symbols of the cross and the Chi Rho (the monogram of Christ) were becoming standard public sights.

Even within the new monotheism, however, an entrenched tradition of sacral monarchy, long found throughout the ancient world, was difficult to resist. A sacral monarch was himself seen as a god, or sometimes as a special representative of the gods for carrying out a divine mission. The people imagined their flourishing to depend on their leader as mediator between the divine and human. Peace, conquest, protection, health, prosperity, even bountiful harvests depended on his sacral leadership. "Constantine saw himself as a sacral king, on whose relationship with the right worship of God the Father and God the Son depended not only the prosperity of his people but also the balance of creation generally."[17] The Christian faith could unite "with an empire's force of political, military, and economic expansion in order to create a genuine world empire."[18]

By the end of the fourth century, Christianity became the state religion of the Roman Empire. With the exception of Julian the Apostate, all subsequent emperors publicly professed Christianity. And in one person's long lifetime, Christians went from persecuted to persecutors. The melding of political power and Christianity always has this dark side in every single instance throughout history. Attempts to make earthly powers the kingdom of heaven—"as in heaven, so on earth," as Eusebius would have it—have failed with absolute consistency and always will.

Further Reading

Fowden, Garth. *Empire to Commonwealth: Consequences of Monotheism in Late Antiquity.* Princeton University Press, 1993.

Kreider, Alan. *The Patient Ferment of the Early Church: The Improbable Rise of Christianity in the Roman Empire.* Baker Academic, 2016.

Lenski, Noel, ed. *The Cambridge Companion to the Age of Constantine.* Cambridge University Press, 2006.

Potter, David. *The Roman Empire at Bay, AD 180–395.* Routledge, 2004.

Notes

1. David Potter, *The Roman Empire at Bay, AD 180–395* (Routledge, 2004), 314.

2. *Codex Justinianus* V.5.2, as quoted in Stephen Williams, *Diocletian and the Roman Recovery* (Methuen, Inc., 1985), 162.

3. Making the buried, and thus preserved, church at Dura Europos (see chap. 6) such a rare treasure.

4. Potter, *Roman Empire at Bay*, 337.

5. Garth Fowden, *Empire to Commonwealth: Consequences of Monotheism in Late Antiquity* (Princeton University Press, 1993), 87.

6. Lactantius, *De Mortibus Persecutorum* (*On the Deaths of the Persecutors*) 34.

7. Noel Lenski, "The Reign of Constantine," in *The Cambridge Companion to the Age of Constantine*, ed. Noel Lenski (Cambridge University Press, 2006), 68.

8. H. A. Drake, "The Impact of Constantine on Christianity," *The Cambridge Companion*, 126.

9. Lenski, "Reign of Constantine," 62.

10. See Fowden, *Empire to Commonwealth*.

11. Fowden, *Empire to Commonwealth*, 87.

12. Eusebius, *The Life of Constantine*, ed. and trans. Averil Cameron and Stuart George Hall (Clarendon, 1999), 28.

13. Eusebius, *Life of Constantine*, 28.

14. See Nadya Williams, *Cultural Christians in the Early Church: A Historical and Practical Introduction to Christians in the Greco-Roman World* (Zondervan Academic, 2023), 155.

15. Potter, *Roman Empire at Bay*, 358.

16. Potter, *Roman Empire at Bay*, 351.

17. Fowden, *Empire to Commonwealth*, 82.

18. Fowden, *Empire to Commonwealth*, 82.

9

---•---

A North African House Divided—Again

(Carthage and Arles, 314)

The Background

Just months after Diocletian launched the Great Persecution in 303, forty-nine North African Christians—men, women, and young people—were rounded up in their hometown of Abitinia and sent to Carthage for trial. Their own bishop was not among them—he actually had submitted to Diocletian's imperial edict of 303 (see chap. 8) and had turned over copies of the Scriptures to authorities. But the Abitinian Martyrs, as they are called, had refused to stop gathering for worship—something that was explicitly forbidden in the edict—and so caught the unwanted attention of informants and persecutors.

While awaiting trial in prison, the Abitinians vigorously denounced all who, like their own bishop, had submitted to the imperial command. They claimed that *traditores* (literally "those who turned over" Scripture) "merited lasting damnation and un-extinguishable fire," and that no one who so much as "maintained communion with *traditores* would participate in the joys of para-dise."[1] The Abitinians who survived brutal torture were summar-ily executed. Their example was as powerful and memorable as their denunciation of fellow Christians was divisive and influential. Another North African schism appeared imminent, similar to the one Cyprian had opposed back in the mid-third century.

The debates started almost immediately, even while the Great Persecution raged. No one really doubted that a traditor was no longer fit for leadership in the church. The overwhelming question was how to assess the sacraments they had once administered. Did all their baptisms still hold true? Two competing camps emerged. To one group, sacraments that had been administered by those who became traditores were still valid because they claimed the church almost everywhere recognized only one baptism.

According to the other group, a baptism that had been admin-istered by a traditor was invalid and the person had to be baptized anew. This more hardline group further reasoned that any church leader who had been consecrated by one who became a traditor was illegitimate. Anyone who was consecrated by someone who was consecrated by someone who was . . . you get the idea. The stain from the traditor's hand was transmissible, indelible, and even retroactive. "Sin had left a crimson stain," but only rebaptism might be able to "wash it white as snow," to butcher the nineteenth-century hymn "Jesus Paid It All."

The crisis came to a head in 311 when an archdeacon named Caecilian was consecrated as bishop of Carthage. A group of bishops from Numidia, the region to his west, rejected the choice. The consecration was a bit rushed, seemingly to prevent the Nu-midian bishops, who were in the rigorist camp, from attending.[2] They accused Caecilian of once turning away people who were trying to bring food to the Abitinian Martyrs in jail. The contro-versy would get very personal. Even before the Great Persecution broke out, Caecilian had alienated a rich Christian woman named Lucilla by rebuking her for kissing martyr bones in reverence. Lucilla allegedly gave gifts to seventy or so Numidian bishops, who then convened as a local council that presumed to depose Caecilian and consecrate Majorinus, a member of Lucilla's own household, as bishop in his stead. Caecilian and many others refused to recognize this local council, and Carthage was left with two bishops. A Numidian deacon named Donatus, long active within the rigorist party, succeeded Majorinus in 313, and the movement would adopt his name. Donatists and Caecilianists faced off. In the words of Optatus of Milevis, a later fourth-century North African bishop, "Altar was set up against altar."[3] The people of Carthage and the church leadership in Rome maintained support for Caecilian, while the bishops of Numidia sided with the Donatists.

The Moment

Unable to solve the problem locally, the Donatists appealed to Emperor Constantine in 313. Such an appeal was not particularly unusual, as emperors were long seen as the agents of Pax Deorum ("peace with the gods"), or now Pax Dei ("peace with God").[4] "Both Roman emperors and their subjects assumed it to be both a right and a duty of emperors to ensure proper worship of divinity."[5] And this was not even the first time that Christians had appealed an internal dispute to an emperor.[6]

If Constantine initially saw Christianity as a great unifier, he soon realized, to his dismay and eventual disgust, that Christians could be a fragmented and divisive lot. He appointed a group of bishops as a court to respond to the Donatist question. As he so poignantly put it, "When certain men began wickedly and perversely to disagree among themselves in regard to the holy worship and celestial power and catholic doctrine, I wished to put an end to such disputes among them."[7] A group of about twenty bishops from Italy and Gaul met in Rome. After three days of discussion, they decided against the Donatists.

The Donatists rejected that decision, protesting that it had been reached by too few bishops and with scant consideration of all of the facts. They again appealed to Constantine, emphasizing that Caecilian had been ordained by a traditor named Felix. Following Roman procedure, Constantine set up a special commission to investigate their claims. The emperor then called a larger council at Arles in southern France, and this time representatives of forty-four churches gathered from all over the western part of the empire—from Britain to North Africa, from Spain to Italy.

This was the first time an emperor had called a church council, and it set an "enormous precedent."[8] In order to maximize attendance, Constantine insisted that bishops travel to Arles via the public post road, which was reserved for government business. He even provided "public vehicles" for each bishop and a small entourage of lesser church officials and servants.[9] Traveling this way guaranteed them "higher status and visibility" as they made their way to the council.[10] It made a clear statement of "the benefits that could flow from imperial favor."[11]

Constantine himself attended the council, which opened on August 1, 314. Sitting in the audience as an observer,[12] he refused to intervene, leaving the church to weigh in on its own affairs. At this stage, he was longing for unity in the church, not grasping for power over it. In addition to the immediate issues raised by the Donatist controversy, the council also addressed several other related and unrelated matters.[13]

After deliberation for a number of weeks, the council uncontroversially declared that traditores should be removed from office. But they also put down important stipulations that "random accusations of being a traditor should not be admitted" without public and written documents.[14] The insistence on written documentation was the standard Roman practice of justice and reminiscent of the emperor Trajan's dismissal of anonymous accusations against Christians almost exactly two centuries prior.

The Council of Arles ruled strongly in favor of Caecilian. Baptisms and ordinations by traditores were not to be invalidated retroactively. The commission determined that the charges against Felix came from forged documents. Constantine himself strongly denounced the Donatists, "in whom it is clear as day that their madness is of such a kind that we find them abhorrent even to the heavenly dispensation . . . repudiating the equitable judgement that had been given by the will of heaven."[15] For a time, Constantine threatened to enforce the council's decisions by punishing Donatists, but within a few years he relented, instead turning them over to the judgment of heaven. He "refused to use force to compel belief,"[16] as he had seen how compulsion had failed during the Great Persecution.

The Donatists did not submit to court, commission, council, or Constantine. They saw themselves as the true North African church in the spirit of Cyprian of Carthage. The Donatist church would continue to exist alongside the universal church in North Africa; in the next century they would be one of the major opponents of the North African bishop Augustine of Hippo.

The Mathēma

There is much for us to appreciate about the Donatists. They held the Scriptures in high regard and had a dim view of anyone who would dare to "destroy the testaments and divine commands of Almighty God and our Lord Jesus Christ."[17] They desired the "purity, holiness, and integrity" of the church as the pure bride of Christ, unblemished by unfaithfulness and compromise in a rapidly changing world.[18]

Modern Christians might sympathize with a church unwilling to submit to decrees backed by a central government. They might resonate with a famous question Donatus posed: "What has the

88

emperor to do with the church?"[19] Never mind that it was his appeal to Constantine that started the whole imperial involvement in the first place. And we might well imagine that solidarity with martyrs necessarily puts our cause in the right.

Yet, as with the Novatianists (see chap. 5), grace and forgiveness were in remarkably short supply among the Donatists. Even in antiquity they earned a reputation for being a self-righteous and graceless church. The movement had imbibed more than a small dose of Greco-Roman classical assumptions of human perfection and perfectionism.

"In an abundance of counselors there is safety" (Prov. 11:14). Wisdom here lay in a broader voice of the church. The only group to side with the Donatists was a local gathering of bishops from Numidia, most likely under a gift-bribe. So certain were they of their correctness, the rigorist group seemed willing to do anything to get their way—even producing forged letters when written documents were demanded. Such might call to mind the all-too-common anonymous online attacks and deep-faked videos we see today by zealous Christians who imagine their cause as just and desire quick victories even at the expense of openness and truth. Wisdom can never be in such corners, regardless of how justified some might feel in carrying out dishonest and cowardly acts.

Christians sometimes revel in nostalgia. It is not uncommon to hear Christians today pining for a return to the fourth-century church or to sixteenth-century communities or even imagining themselves as the restoration of the first-century church. Quite often, a bit of historical scrutiny reveals a fundamental myth of a golden age that never really existed.

The Donatists were a nostalgic church. They longed for the days of the suffering church before Christianity became the emperor's faith, imagining it was the pure church. Donatists regarded themselves as "the suffering people of God, destined to undergo persecution and martyrdom for the sake of maintaining the integrity of the Christian community."[20] As we saw in chapter 5 and will see again in subsequent chapters, there is nothing inherently pure or superior about a persecuted church. It is easily possible to honor the blessed martyrs while longing for the church to live at peace and grow, as in Acts 9:31.

Further Reading

Drake, H. A. "The Impact of Constantine on Christianity." In *The Cambridge Companion to the Age of Constantine*. Edited by Noel Lenski. Cambridge University Press, 2006, 111–36.

Frend, W. H. C. *The Donatist Church: A Movement of Protest in Roman North Africa*. Oxford University Press, 2000.

Frend, W. H. C. *The Rise of Christianity*. Fortress, 1984.

Grant, Robert M. *Augustus to Constantine: The Emergence of Christianity in the Roman World*. Barnes & Noble, 1970.

Potter, David S. *The Roman Empire at Bay, AD 180–395*. Routledge, 2004.

Notes

1. W. H. C. Frend, *The Rise of Christianity* (Fortress, 1984), 462.

2. H. A. Drake, *Constantine and the Bishops: The Politics of Intolerance* (Johns Hopkins University Press, 2000), 214.

3. Optatus of Milevis, *On the Schism of the Donatists Against Parmenian* 1.15.

4. Hans Pohlsander, *The Emperor Constantine* (Routledge, 1996), 29.

5. H. A. Drake, "The Impact of Constantine on Christianity," in *The Cambridge Companion to the Age of Constantine*, ed. Noel Lenski (Cambridge University Press, 2006), 117.

6. As, for example, a property dispute between the Christians of Antioch and a deposed bishop, Paul of Samosata, which the Antiochians appealed to the pagan emperor Aurelian.

7. Constantine's Letter Summoning the Council of Arles is in Eusebius, *Church History* 10.5.21–24. Here he is referring to the court at Rome.

8. Averil Cameron, *The Later Roman Empire* (Harvard University Press, 1993), 67.

9. Eusebius, *Church History* 10.5.21–24.

10. Drake, "Impact of Constantine," 118.

11. Drake, *Constantine and the Bishops*, 219.

12. David S. Potter, *The Roman Empire at Bay, AD 180–395* (Routledge, 2004), 408.

13. These included the date for Easter, the minimum number of bishops required for a valid consecration of a bishop, and the marriage of Christian women to non-Christian men.

14. Potter, *Roman Empire at Bay*, 408.

15. Potter, *Roman Empire at Bay*, 409.

16. Drake, "Impact of Constantine," 120.

17. *Acta Saturnini* 18.701.

18. W. H. C. Frend, "Donatism," in *Encyclopedia of Early Christianity* (Routledge, 1990).

19. Optatus of Milevis, *On the Schism of the Donatists* 3.3

20. Frend, "Donatism."

10

A Handsome Heretic at the First Ecumenical Council

(Nicaea, 325)

The Background

In the early fourth century, Arius, a priest in Alexandria, was winning over distant bishops and local dockworkers alike. He was described as "tall and lean." Women and men loved his "beautiful manners" and "aura of intellectual superiority." His gentle voice moved ordinary people.[1] It is said he inspired protest marches in the streets when his controversial teachings were condemned, with supporters singing catchy songs he had written to promote his errant theology. It was the most serious doctrinal controversy the church had faced and perhaps ever will face.

It began sometime after 312 in what some think was a seminar on the book of Proverbs, of all places. Alexander, bishop of Alexandria, was leading a discussion of Proverbs 8, a passage that memorably personifies Wisdom as created by Yahweh "at the beginning of his work, the first of his acts long ago" (v. 22). Arius argued that this and other passages presented Jesus Christ as a being created by God. Christ was a special creation, but he was not God. Arius claimed that the Son was not eternal and that there was a time when he was not. Speculations drawn from Plato nuanced Arius's views, but "put simply, Arius reasoned that because fathers precede sons, there must have been some point at which the Son did not exist."[2] Arius and Alexander went head-to-head after that, with Arius once even protesting in the middle of one of Alexander's sermons.

The notion that the Son was a creation of the Father had been heard in corners of Alexandria before Arius came on the scene.[3] Arius was well-connected, though, in Alexandria and elsewhere, and his confidence and charisma gained disciples. Whereas Donatism (see chap. 9) was a serious issue for the North African church in particular, the views espoused by Arius threatened to divide the church worldwide. And these were no small matters—the very person of Christ and his status as a member of the Godhead were at stake.

In 318, Alexander called together about one hundred bishops from Libya and Egypt to examine Arius's teaching; they ended up condemning his views and excommunicating him. Arius then turned to some influential episcopal friends for help and defense, including Eusebius of Nicomedia and Eusebius of Caesarea. Another small council, about half the size of the one called by Alexander, met in Antioch and likewise condemned Arius's teaching in 324.

The matter suddenly came to the attention of Emperor Constantine that same year, just after he defeated Licinius, his friend turned rival, to become sole ruler of both the eastern and western halves of the empire. Problems in the eastern part of the empire that had been overseen by Licinius were now Constantine's to deal with. He turned immediately to Ossius of Cordoba, who had been his trusted theological adviser at least since the time of

his famous vision in the sky. Ossius was sent to Alexandria to rec-
oncile Alexander and Arius and deliver a letter from the emperor
encouraging unity. Quickly realizing that his intervention would
likely be futile, he advised Constantine to call a general ecumenical council. It was not the first council called by the emperor (see
chap. 9), but it would be the most famous and arguably most important in church history.

The Moment

Constantine wanted a serious turnout. The unity of his entire
empire was at stake after all. He originally chose Ancyra (modern-
day Ankara, the capital of Turkey), a convenient location where
more Roman road systems converged than at almost any other city
apart from Rome itself.[4] A small church synod had already been
held there about a decade earlier. But at the last minute, Constantine switched the venue to Nicaea (modern-day Iznik, in western
Turkey), ostensibly because it had better weather and was more
convenient for himself and others coming from points to the west.

Imperial invitations were sent to as many as 1,800 bishops
throughout the empire and beyond. Somewhere between 250 and
300 bishops came, along with their staff and retainers. According
to church historian Eusebius of Caesarea, they came eagerly: "All
dashed like sprinters from the starting line, full of enthusiasm.
They were drawn by the hope of good things, the opportunity
to share in peace, and the spectacle of that strange marvel, to see
such a great Emperor."[5] And they came from all over:

> There was gathered the most distinguished ministers of God, from
> the many churches in Europe, Libya, and Asia. A single house
> of prayer, as if enlarged by God, sheltered Syrians and Cilicians,
> Phoenicians and Arabs, delegates from Palestine and from Egypt,
> Thebans and Libyans, together with those from Mesopotamia.
> There was also a Persian bishop, and a Scythian was not lacking.[6]

The famous Nicholas of Myra was indeed present, even if stories of his involvement and actions long assumed mythic proportions well before he became known as Santa Claus.

Many of the bishops were simple pastors[7] (apparently one was an actual sheepherder), and most probably could not have handled the expense on their own. Once again, as he did at the Council of Arles (see chap. 9), Constantine opened the imperial coffers to cover travel expenses for the council. Many of the bishops were also confessors, meaning they had suffered for their faith in past times of persecution (see chap. 5); some of these, like one who was missing an eye, even bore the marks on their bodies.

It was clear from the outset that Constantine desired unity, unanimity, and harmony above all else. Division must end, and quickly. "For to me," said Constantine, "internal division in the Church of God is graver than any war or fierce battle, and these things appear to cause more pain than secular affairs."[8] Although he came to realize the seriousness of the issue itself, his initial letter to Alexander and Arius had dismissed it as "small and utterly unimportant" and "some futile points of dispute."[9] He began with hopes for an easy solution.

In late May or early June of 325, the council opened at the imperial palace in Nicaea. The views of those in attendance ranged widely. At opposite poles were Arius's ardent defenders and determined detractors. But the majority of those who gathered were at first neither utterly in favor nor diametrically opposed to Arius per se. Arius, who was about sixty-five years old at this time, was not a bishop but exerted a great deal of influence on some speakers. The deliberations lasted about a month. There were some memorable moments, including an apparent turning point when Arius's friend Eusebius of Nicomedia delivered a speech in favor of Arius that suddenly and inadvertently solidified the resistance to his teachings. When Eusebius affirmed that the Son was a creature, there were angry outbursts: "You lie!" "Blasphemy!" "Heresy!" "Eusebius was shouted down and we are told that his speech was snatched from his hand, torn to shreds, and trampled underfoot."[10]

Constantine himself, Eusebius of Caesarea tells us, proposed the crucial and clinching word in the debates—*homoousios* ("of the same substance"), meaning Christ was of the same substance as the Father and thus coeternal with the Father. The term itself had a long history before Nicaea, and Arius had likely already denounced it ahead of the council.[11] Constantine was apparently sensing the growing consensus and was hoping to solidify it with a focal term. Among several different proposed creeds, one suggested by Constantine was largely adopted. This version remains today, with some modifications over time, as the Nicene Creed, one of the church's most important doctrinal statements.

The vote on Arius's teaching was overwhelming—all but two voted against him. His teachings were condemned, and he and his two supporters were sent into exile at imperial (not ecclesiastical) command.

The Mathēma

Arius had an awful lot going for him: eloquence, charm, powerful friends, and even the initial sympathy of the emperor himself (who was looking for ways to spot and build consensus at the council more than anything else, it appears). Nonetheless, the gathered and collective voice of the "one, holy, catholic, and apostolic Church" soundly rejected Arius's teachings. Contrary to some popular beliefs, the council was not a mere tool of imperial politics.

Arius would soon return, though, and his views actually would catch on in the court of Constantine and some of his successors for decades to come. The matter was far from over. It was an Arian, in fact—Eusebius of Nicomedia, the old friend of Arius—who famously baptized Constantine on his deathbed.

Arianism was more conducive to that longed-for unity and harmony than were the "rigid supporters of Nicene doctrine."[12]

One young deacon at the council, Athanasius, the secretary of Alexander, was perhaps the most significant of those supporters. He would later succeed Alexander as bishop and face an intense and costly struggle against Arius and Arianism for the rest of his life. Arius played it well and was able to get "the upper hand at Constantine's court" by painting bishop Athanasius as "intransigent and unwilling to compromise."[13] Although gifted in many ways, Athanasius seemed to lack the broadly winsome charm that is the hallmark of so many false teachers. He was incapable of unity and harmony at the expense of compromise, and was thus exiled multiple times. His intransigence is summarized well in his famous nickname *Athanasius contra mundum* ("Athansius against the world").

False teachers throughout time have amassed fervent followings owing to personal ties, charm, and charisma. Donatus, whom we met in the previous chapter, was likewise described as "charismatic, eloquent, tireless."[14] At the same time, some of the most important defenders of truth and orthodoxy appear so utterly unlikeable—we will encounter one such church leader, Cyril of Alexandria, in chapter 14. God often works with the most flawed, most unlikely, even most unlikeable of vessels.

Further Reading

Grant, Robert M. *Augustus to Constantine: The Emergence of Christianity in the Roman World.* Barnes & Noble, 1970.

Jones, A. H. M. *Constantine and the Conversion of Europe.* University of Toronto Press, 1978.

Lenski, Noel, ed. *The Cambridge Companion to the Age of Constantine.* Cambridge University Press, 2006.

Pohlsander, Hans A. *The Emperor Constantine.* Routledge, 1996.

Potter, David S. *The Roman Empire at Bay, AD 180–395.* Routledge, 2004.

Van Dam, Raymond. *The Roman Revolution of Constantine.* Cambridge University Press, 2009.

Notes

1. David S. Potter, *The Roman Empire at Bay, AD 180–395* (Routledge, 2004), 411.

2. H. A. Drake, "The Impact of Constantine on Christianity," in *The Cambridge Companion to the Age of Constantine*, ed. Noel Lenski (Cambridge University Press, 2006), 123.

3. Potter, *Roman Empire at Bay*, 414.

4. Mark W. Graham, *News and Frontier Consciousness in the Later Roman Empire* (University of Michigan Press, 2006), 107–10.

5. Eusebius, as quoted in Drake, "Impact of Constantine," 126.

6. Eusebius, *Life of Constantine* 3.7. Quoted in Justo González, *The Story of Christianity: The Early Church to the Present Day* (Prince Press, 2006), 162–63.

7. A. H. M. Jones, *Constantine and the Conversion of Europe* (University of Toronto Press, 1978), 131.

8. Quoted in Potter, *Roman Empire at Bay*, 419.

9. Quoted in Potter, *Roman Empire at Bay*, 412.

10. Gonzáles, *Story of Christianity*, 164.

11. Christopher Stead, *Philosophy in Christian Antiquity* (Cambridge University Press, 1994), 166.

12. Raymond Van Dam, *The Roman Revolution of Constantine* (Cambridge University Press, 2009), 273.

13. Drake, "Impact of Constantine," 130.

14. H. A. Drake, *Constantine and the Bishops: The Politics of Intolerance* (Johns Hopkins University Press, 2000), 213.

11

War, Apocalypse, and the Great Slaughter of Christians

(Sassanian Persian Empire, c. 340–379)

The Background

The two superpowers of the Sassanian Persian and Roman Empires were embroiled in war—again. Something was different this time, though: One empire had become Christian. And now Christians in the other empire had some crucial decisions to make. Aphrahat, a church leader and theologian in the Sassanian Persian Empire, turned to apocalyptic passages in the book of Daniel for help in understanding his volatile and uncertain times. He was not the first Christian to do so—and, of course, he would not be the last.

In a sermon titled "On War," Aphrahat envisioned Daniel's fourth kingdom—that is, the iron legs and feet of the grand statue described in Daniel 2—as the pagan Roman Empire, which had passed away with the conversion of the emperor Constantine. The fourth beast of Daniel 7, which he also interpreted as pagan

Rome, "exceedingly terrible and strong and mighty, devouring and crushing and trampling with its feet anything that remained," was falling. The newly Christian Roman Empire heralded the second coming and the universal kingdom of Messiah, "Who will bring to nought the kingdom of this world, and He will rule for ever and ever."[1]

Christians in Aphrahat's flock and throughout the Sassanian Persian Empire suddenly found themselves in a delicate position. Their empire was at war with an empire claiming a Christian identity. As Aphrahat understood Daniel's prophecies, the Christian Roman Empire would ultimately be victorious over the Sassanian Persians because those "clothed with his [Jesus's] armour . . . will not be defeated in war."[2] The loyalties and allegiances of the Christians of Persia were now complicated in unprecedented ways— their empire was led by a "wicked and proud man puffed up with vanity," the fierce and destructive king and evil one prophesied in Daniel 8:23–25. Aphrahat's message to his flock was ultimately one of reassurance.[3]

The number of Christians in the Sassanian Persian Empire had been increasing remarkably since the mid-third century (see chap. 6). Church historian Eusebius records a Persian emissary telling the emperor Constantine that "the churches of God were multiplying among the Persians and that many thousands of people were being gathered into the flock of Christ."[4] These Christians had frequent contact with those of the Roman Empire through councils, bishops, and a variety of informal networks.[5]

Constantine came to see himself as a patron of "Christians both inside and outside the boundaries of his realm."[6] At a dinner with bishops, he once claimed "his flock to be those inside the church regardless of political boundaries."[7] The emperor even wrote a letter to the Sassanian shahinshah Shapur II in which he claimed personal "guardianship over the substantial Christian community" in the Sassanian Persian Empire.[8] His letter amounted to "a statement that reflected the growing Christian identity of the

Roman Empire and spreading imperial notions of a global Christianity with the Roman king as protector."[9] The shahinshah was not amused.

The Moment

Immediately after Constantine's death in 337, Shapur II invaded the Roman Empire. According to one account from around that same time, he soon "began to harass the Christian people, to afflict and persecute the priests and members of the covenant, and to destroy the churches in all of his realm."[10] An ancient account of Persian martyrs preserves an edict in which Shapur II declared that Christians "dwell in our land and yet they are of one mind with Caesar, our enemy, and we fight but they enjoy quiet."[11] Suspicion fell hard on Christians—at first on leaders in the church and converts from the court religion of Zoroastrianism.[12] The list of Persian martyrs shows that ultimately men and women of all social levels met death at the hands of their compatriots.

Zoroastrianism did have "a streak of intolerance" to begin with.[13] Aside from a few exceptions, though, Christians and other religious minorities had dwelled in relative peace and safety within the Sassanian realm up to this moment. But beginning around 340 until Shapur II's death in 372, the Christians of Persia encountered a period of brutal persecution, often referred to as the "Great Persecution" or "Great Slaughter" of Persia.[14] In his firsthand accounts of the violence, Aphrahat lamented that Christians had been "plundered, persecuted and dispersed."[15] He recounts the destruction of churches and "a great massacre of martyrs in the eastern region."[16] The number of those who were martyred at that time remains unknown, but lists published in later centuries record the names of over one hundred martyrs and recount the harrowing and brutal tales of their persecutions.[17]

At issue were questions of allegiance. Since leaders of Christian communities in Persia were responsible to collect the taxes for their communities,[18] taxation served as a tangible indicator of loyalty to the shahinshah. Ancient accounts record a story of one Simeon bar Sabbae, the bishop of Seleucia-Ctesiphon, among the first and most famous of the Persian martyrs. When Shapur II doubled taxes to support the war effort against Christian Rome, Simeon declared that his congregation would no longer pay taxes.[19] He was defending his congregation and was hesitant to support war against fellow Christians. Shapur responded directly: "In your pride and your arrogance, you want to incite your people to rebel against me." Shapur then commanded his officials, "As for Simeon, the head of the sorcerers, bring him to me, for he has rejected my kingdom and chosen that of Caesar by worshipping his god but mocking my god."[20] Despite Simeon's protest that he was loyal to the Persian shahinshah, he was arrested, charged with disloyalty, and executed.

Episodes like this raised serious questions for Sassanian Persian leaders. Christians were suspected of being partisans of Rome[21] or even of being a fifth column—that is, a group of people conspiring with outsiders against their own government. There is no evidence that Sassanians thought of all Christians in Persia as a fifth column, but they indeed "feared that some might be."[22] To be sure, Christians could be (and some were) "spies, turncoats, and traitors" from the perspective of the Sassanians.[23] Bishops were well-known as conduits of information across the frontier.[24] One account, *Martyrdom of the Forty Martyrs from Kashkar*, presents a Persian Christian accusing other Christian bishops of receiving "Roman spies" and revealing "the secrets of your empire to them."[25] After more than three decades, persecution ended with the death of Shapur II in 379. Christians were largely able to live at peace again for a time.

The Mathēma

In the middle decades of the fourth century, Christians in the Sassanian Persian Empire faced a dilemma that no Christians had ever faced before. Plenty of Our People since then have found themselves suspected of being a fifth column. For example, Christians in the Ottoman Empire after the fall of Constantinople in 1453 and in China during the Boxer Rebellion around 1900 were targets of suspicion and persecution for their potential connections to outsiders. It is a situation that Christians around the world know all too well.

While Christians today rightly remember and honor martyrs, we should resist a simplistic narrative that frames Our People merely as helpless and hapless victims. The Christians of Sassanian Persia were in a precarious position and had to make decisions based on what they believed and knew at the time. We can hardly doubt that some aided or were at least sympathetic to Persia's enemy and firmly believed their actions to be godly, justified, and wise. Some, like Aphrahat, were guided by sincere exposition of Scripture. Any Persian Christian who, like him, believed that the Christian Roman Empire was the Messiah's kingdom destined to overthrow the last wicked king (Shapur II) as foretold in Daniel's prophecy could not in good conscience support Shapur's war effort, whether through doubled taxes or other means. It was only in the next century that Christians in Sassanian Persia would begin to carefully and publicly distance themselves from the Roman Empire, as we will discuss in chapter 13.

Aphrahat, known as "the Persian Sage," seemed like a faithful shepherd of God's people in the Sassanian Persian Empire. His major surviving writings, which consist of twenty-three treatises or sermons, are full of pastoral advice and reassurance based on Scripture, which he "interpreted in a literal, historical manner."[26] He well knew the heart of the Christian message and encouraged his flock in many Christian virtues through his writings. He did not seem intent on merely raising up political warriors or politicizing his congregation. And most importantly, Aphrahat was humble. Even though he himself was convinced his interpretation of Daniel's vision was correct, he acknowledged he might well have the timing wrong. He offered the following words of caution toward the end of "On Wars": "These words are not ended" [i.e., this is not the final word].[27]

We too can be wrong in some of our interpretations and applications of Scripture, often in ways that will only be clear in hindsight. One can only imagine what Aphrahat might have to say about some of the far more fanciful interpretations of Daniel that have arisen in the twentieth and twenty-first centuries! This need not be a cause for despair but a caution to remain humble. It is also an encouragement to continue to study the struggles and victories of Our People in ages past. In the end, the message of Daniel remains the same, however meager our (and their) glimpses. Aphrahat concludes "On War" with a solid reminder that God is the Sovereign of all history and some clear encouragement for God's people:

> For even if the forces shall go up and conquer, yet know that it is a chastisement of God; and though they conquer, they shall be condemned in righteous judgment. But yet be thou assured of this, that the beast shall be slain at its (appointed) time. But do thou, my brother, at this time be earnest in imploring mercy, that there may be peace upon the people of God.[28]

We might smile at how directly (and wrongly) Aphrahat connected Daniel's prophecy to the struggle between the two superpowers of his day, but his final advice to Christians everywhere—mercy and peace—is timeless, and is needed as much today as in every age.

Further Reading

Barnes, T. D. "Constantine and the Christians of Persia." *Journal of Roman Studies* 75 (1985): 126–36.

Gross, Simcha. "Being Roman in the Sasanian Empire: Revisiting the Great Persecution of Christians Under Shapur II." *Studies in Late Antiquity* 5, no. 3 (2021): 361–402.

Potter, David S. *The Roman Empire at Bay, AD 180–395*. Routledge, 2004.

Smith, Kyle. *Constantine and the Captive Christians of Persia: Martyrdom and Religious Identity in Late Antiquity*. University of California Press, 2016.

Walker, Joel. *The Legend of Mar Qardagh: Narrative and Christian Heroism in Late Antique Iraq*. University of California Press, 2006.

Notes

1. Aphrahat, *Demonstrations* 5.14, in vol. 13 of *Nicene and Post-Nicene Fathers*, Series 2, ed. Philip Schaff (Hendrickson, 1994). See comments at David S. Potter, *The Roman Empire at Bay, AD 180–395* (Routledge, 2004), 469; T. D. Barnes, "Constantine and the Christians of Persia," *Journal of Roman Studies* 75 (1985): 134.

2. Simcha Gross, "Being Roman in the Sasanian Empire: Revisiting the Great Persecution of Christians Under Shapur II," *Studies in Late Antiquity* 5, no. 3 (2021): 378–79.

3. Gross, "Being Roman," 378–79.

4. Quoted in Kyle Smith, *Constantine and the Captive Christians of Persia: Martyrdom and Religious Identity in Late Antiquity* (University of California Press, 2016), 21.

5. Jan Willem Drijvers, "Rome and the Sasanid Empire: Confrontation and Coexistence," in *A Companion to Late Antiquity*, ed. Philip Rousseau (Blackwell, 2012), 451.

6. Drijvers, "Rome and the Sasanid Empire," 445.

7. Elizabeth Key Fowden, "Constantine and the Peoples of the Eastern Frontier," in *The Cambridge Companion to the Age of Constantine*, ed. Noel Lenski (Cambridge University Press, 2006), 382.

8. Garth Fowden, *Empire to Commonwealth: Consequences of Monotheism in Late Antiquity* (Princeton University Press, 1993), 93.

9. Gross, "Being Roman," 375.

10. *History of Simon bar Sabbaʿe*, in Gross, "Being Roman," 365.

11. Gross, "Being Roman," 365. Shapur's edict is recorded in *Acta martyrium*.

12. Gross, "Being Roman," 381; and Susan A. Harvey, "Persia," in *Encyclopedia of Early Christianity* (Routledge, 1990).

13. Joel Walker, *The Legend of Mar Qardagh: Narrative and Christian Heroism in Late Antique Iraq* (University of California Press, 2006), 110.

14. Recent studies have brought into serious question the cause and scale of persecutions in Sassanian Persia at this time. See Smith, *Constantine and the Captive Christians*. For a convincing case that such downplaying has been overdone, see Gross, "Being Roman."

15. *Demonstrations* 14, in Gross, "Being Roman," 369.

16. Barnes, "Constantine and the Christians of Persia," 128.

17. Modern scholars reject stories of 200,000 martyrs recorded by church writer Sozomen, and even numbers in the lower thousands are questioned. See Gross, "Being Roman," 371.

18. Richard N. Frye, "The Sassanians," in *Cambridge Ancient History*, 2nd ed., vol. 12, ed. Alan K. Bowman, Averil Cameron, and Pete Garnsey (Cambridge University Press, 2005), 476.

19. *Martyrdom of Simeon bar Sabba'e*, in Gross, "Being Roman," 364.

20. Gross, "Being Roman," 365.

21. Frye, "The Sassanians," 474.

22. Gross, "Being Roman," 384.

23. Gross, "Being Roman," 384.

24. Gross, "Being Roman," 386.

25. Gross, "Being Roman," 385.

26. Robert J. Owens, "Apraates (Syriac Aphrahat)," in *Encyclopedia of Early Christianity* (Routledge, 1990).

27. Craig E. Morrison, "The Reception of the Book of Daniel in Aphrahat's Fifth Demonstration, 'On Wars,'" *Hugoye: Journal of Syriac Studies* 7 (2007): 80.

28. Aphrahat, *Demonstrations* 5.25.

12

Priscillian of Ávila and the First Church Dispute to End in Execution

(Spain and Rome, 380s)

The Background

We often enjoy stories that pit valiant heroes against duplicitous villains, defenders of truth against sinister detractors, and stalwart champions of orthodoxy against cynical heretics. However, the early church chronicler Sulpicius Severus does not present such clear-cut divisions in this disturbing moment when he writes, "There followed portentous and dangerous times of our age, in which the churches were defiled and everything was disturbed by an unaccustomed evil."[1]

Church leaders from all sides, secular officials, and even two Roman emperors contributed to a bizarre disaster worth remembering. At the center of the story is Priscillian of Ávila, an ascetic and charismatic layman from Spain, who was ordained as a bishop under contested circumstances amidst controversy over his practices. Condemned at two small local church councils, he ultimately appealed his case to the emperor. To the shock and disgust of even his most ardent foes, the emperor had Priscillian executed along with some of his closest and most loyal followers, including a noblewoman and several men.

Among the many howlers in Dan Brown's ill-informed blockbuster *The Da Vinci Code* is the claim that millions of women were killed by the church as witches. The truth is that the church has never executed anybody, woman or man—the state has. But Priscillian and a mixed handful of followers were a Christian state's first victims over what was essentially an ecclesiastical dispute. Unfortunately, their case was brought before a new emperor who had assassinated the previous ruler and seized the throne. Eager to establish his Christian orthodoxy, the new emperor saw this as an opportunity to choose a side in the dispute and executed the key figures of the opposing faction.

The conflict began in the far western fringe of the empire and soon drew in the major figures of the Western church. It highlighted some crucial local battles within the churches in Spain and Gaul over the nature of the church and the exercise of authority within it. Bishops aligned against bishops, and when both sides did not get clear resolution, they each appealed to the state to intervene, going so far as to bribe secular officials.[2] In the words of Sulpicius Severus:

> And now all things were seen to be disturbed and confused by the discord, especially of the bishops, while everything was corrupted by them through their hatred, partiality, fear, faithlessness, envy, factiousness, lust, avarice, pride, sleepiness, and inactivity. In a word, a large number were striving with insane plans and obstinate inclinations against a few giving wise counsel: while, in the meantime, the people of God, and all the excellent of the earth were exposed to mockery and insult.[3]

The Moment

In the late 370s and early 380s in southwest Spain, small groups of men and women gathering for private Bible studies and retreats began to alarm some area bishops. Their leader, Priscillian, was described by Sulpicius Severus as "a man of noble birth, of great riches, bold, restless, eloquent, learned through much reading, very ready at debate and discussion," who was also "a very vain man, and was much more puffed up than he ought to have been with the knowledge of mere earthly things." He was rumored to have "practiced magical arts from his boyhood," although the details on that are far from clear.[4]

Men and women of all social levels were attracted to Priscillian's peculiar ascetic teachings and practices. He advocated fasting on Sundays, holding private retreats away from church during Advent and Lent, and even going barefoot and practicing vegetarianism. The goal seems to have been "attaining a state of perfection or election."[5] The practices spread beyond southwestern Spain, and though most bishops opposed Priscillian's views, there were a few who advocated for them.

Things reached a critical point when two bishops, Hyginus of Cordoba and Hydatius of Merida, protested Priscillian's teachings. A small council of twelve bishops was called in October 380 at Saragosa, Spain. The canons of the council specifically condemned the Sunday fast, absence from church during Lent, and mixed gatherings of men and women for Bible studies. Priscillian and his followers did not accept the decision of the council. Soon thereafter, two of Priscillian's supporting bishops consecrated him as bishop of Ávila, a place that previously had not been attested as a bishop's seat, presumably to give Priscillian himself more standing in the discussions. The state became involved in the matter when several bishops, including Hydatius, complained to the Roman emperor Gratian of Manichees and pseudo-bishops. In 381, Gratian responded by expelling Priscillian and some supporters from church leadership.

Accusations against Priscillian became more extreme and pronounced. Bishops such as Ithacius of Ossonoba began to accuse him and his followers of magic and sorcery as well as Manichaeism.[6] In his own writings, Priscillian would reject these accusations, affirming that magicians ought to be executed and Manichees ought to be declared anathema.[7]

Though he had been defrocked, Priscillian was still committed to working within church channels, so he traveled to Italy to present his case before the two most important leaders of the Western church at that time: Ambrose, bishop of Milan, and Damasus, bishop of Rome. Priscillian hoped to demonstrate his full embrace of "the Catholic faith according to which we live,"[8] but both Ambrose and Damasus refused to even meet with him. Moving outside of church channels, Priscillian then bribed Macedonius, a state official in charge of public services, to restore his church to him.[9]

Shortly afterward, in 383, Emperor Gratian was killed by Magnus Maximus of Spain, who then seized the imperial throne. The new emperor summoned a council in Bordeaux in 384 to address the controversy over Priscillian. At this council, Priscillian was once again declared unworthy of church office.

As a last resort, Priscillian appealed to the emperor, and Magnus Maximus accepted the case. Priscillian and his close followers were condemned for magic, studying obscene doctrine, organizing nocturnal gatherings with immoral women, and praying while naked. He along with a noblewoman named Euchrotia and several other lay and clerical supporters were beheaded by the order of the emperor. Other supporters were banished.

The shock and outcry were immediate, with Ambrose, Damasus, Martin of Tours, and many other church leaders denouncing the emperor's actions. But not everyone was appalled, including Felix, bishop of Trier, who would not denounce Maximus's decision. Magnus Maximus still seemed quite sure of himself when he later wrote these words to Siricius, who succeeded Damasus as bishop of Rome:

Our arrival found and discovered certain matters so contaminated and polluted by the sins of the wicked that, unless our foresight and attention had quickly brought aid, great disturbance and ruin immediately would have arisen . . . but it was then disclosed how great a crime the Manichees recently had committed, not by doubtful or uncertain rhetoric or suspicions, but by their own confession.[10]

The Mathēma

Writing three decades after Priscillian's death, the church father Jerome posited, "Why do I speak of Priscillian, who has been condemned by the whole world and put to death by the secular sword?"[11] He was quite certain that the worst charges against Priscillian were true and that his disciples still exerted dangerous influence. Priscillian's movement did continue well past his execution; for the next several centuries, pockets of Priscillianists in Spain revered him as a martyr and claimed to follow his teachings. Given that the imperial court likely used torture to extract a confession, it's hard to know the extent to which Priscillian actually held to the views and practices for which he was condemned. Later writers continued to accuse him of witchcraft and sorcery, Manichaeism, and even Gnosticism, despite the latter two heresies being otherwise unknown in Spain in his day.[12]

We do know that Priscillian was convinced enough of his rightness that he tried to appeal through proper church channels by seeking out Ambrose and Damasus.[13] It is evident that he and his followers had a different vision from many other church leaders that was characterized as "charismatic." He had the support of bishops and other clerics until the end and beyond. In the immediate aftermath, Priscillian's most adamant foes faced disaster. Most of the bishops who had relentlessly pursued him either resigned or were forced out of office.[14] The lines between "good" and "bad" remain hard to draw.

Sulpicius Severus faulted all sides, even the self-professed guardians of orthodoxy. Severus faulted Priscillian, of course, for his "wasting disorder" and "depraving influence."[15] Yet, he also faulted Priscillian's accusers for being so zealous in their harassment of Priscillian that they ended up adding fuel to the fire of the movement.[16] He recorded, "And my feeling indeed is, that the accusers were as distasteful to me as the accused."[17] Ithacius, one of the major accusers, "had no worth or holiness about him. For he was a bold, loquacious, impudent, and extravagant man; excessively devoted to the pleasures of sensuality."[18] Ithacius even accused Martin of Tours of complicity with Priscillian, which was a preposterous charge. Sulpicius Severus simply could not countenance that anyone had "applied to secular judges."[19] It was "a foul and unheard-of indignity, that a secular ruler should be judge in an ecclesiastical cause."[20]

Self-professed guardians of orthodoxy today can learn much from this episode. When they attack their opponents viciously, without any apparent love or desire to restore, their presumed antidote can be as dangerous as the disease. Even if they have a good case against the error, they create more problems if they do not show some wisdom and restraint. In the case of Priscillian, many came to regret where their zeal had led them—the destruction of human lives in zealous defense of truth.

Further Reading

Burrus, Virginia. *The Making of a Heretic: Gender, Authority, and the Making of the Priscillianist Controversy*. University of California Press, 1995.

Chadwick, Henry. *Priscillian of Ávila: The Occult and the Charismatic in the Early Church*. Clarendon, 1976.

Mathisen, Ralph W. *Ecclesiastical Factionalism and Religious Controversy in Fifth-Century Gaul*. Catholic University of America Press, 1989.

Van Dam, Raymond. *Leadership and Community in Late Antique Gaul*. University of California Press, 1985.

Notes

1. Sulpicius Severus, *Chronicon* 2.46, as quoted in Ralph W. Mathisen, *Ecclesiastical Factionalism and Religious Controversy in Fifth-Century Gaul* (Catholic University of America Press, 1989), 12.

2. Raymond Van Dam, *Leadership and Community in Late Antique Gaul* (University of California Press, 1985), 88.

3. Sulpicius Severus, *Chronicon* 2.51.

4. Sulpicius Severus, *Chronicon* 2.46.

5. Ana Marie C. M. Jorge, "The Lusitanian Episcopate in the 4th Century: Priscilian of Ávila and the Tensions Between Bishops," *E-Journal of Portuguese History* 4, no. 2 (January 2006): 4.

6. Van Dam, *Leadership and Community*, 101.

7. Van Dam, *Leadership and Community*, 101.

8. Van Dam, *Leadership and Community*, 95.

9. Sulpicius Severus, *Chronicon* 2.49.

10. Letter quoted in Mathisen, *Ecclesiastical Factionalism*, 123.

11. Jerome, *Epistle* 133.

12. Van Dam, *Leadership and Community*, 102–3, 105.

13. Van Dam, *Leadership and Community*, 94.

14. Sulpicius Severus, *Chronicon* 2.51.

15. Sulpicius Severus, *Chronicon* 2.46.

16. Sulpicius Severus, *Chronicon* 2.46.

17. Sulpicius Severus, *Chronicon* 2.50.

18. Sulpicius Severus, *Chronicon* 2.50.

19. Sulpicius Severus, *Chronicon* 2.47.

20. Sulpicius Severus, *Chronicon* 2.50.

13

A Persian "King of Kings" Calls a Church Council

(Sassanian Persian Empire, 410)

The Background

Few rulers in history have inspired such contradictory assessments as the Sassanian Persian shahinshah Yazdgerd I. To fellow Zoroastrians (and to later Muslim/Arabic writers) he was simply "the Sinner" or "the Impious One." He "changed the traditions of the Sassanian dynasty, agitated the earth, oppressed the people and was tyrannical and corrupt," as one writer put it.[1] The coins he issued, not surprisingly, give a far more positive assessment by using a title that had never before been seen on Sassanian Persian currency: "Yazdgerd, who maintains peace in (his) dominions."[2] To Jews he was a new Cyrus, the Lord's anointed to deliver the children of Israel. Christians knew him as "the victorious and illustrious king," a "Second Constantine," and king "whose rule, by the grace of God, makes peace reign in all the universe and whose benevolence earns the exaltation of the churches and the flocks of Christ in all of the east."[3]

It was Yazdgerd's kind treatment of religious minorities within his realm, particularly Jews and Christians, that provoked such disgust and praise. Although the "Great Slaughter" of Persian Christians ended with the death of Shahinshah Shapur II back in 379 (see chap. 11), hostilities could and did break out briefly in the decades that followed. Several leading bishops were subsequently martyred, leaving the church fragmented and in chaos. Imagine their joy in the early fifth century when Yazdgerd announced to the Christians of Persia, "There was previously a great persecution directed against you, and you walked in secret; now the King of Kings has granted you complete peace and tranquility."[4] Like King Cyrus of old, he offered God's people far more than simple toleration; he actively protected and assisted them. He even ordered that churches destroyed during previous times of persecution were to be "magnificently rebuilt."[5] Gone were the days when a prominent Christian leader in Sassanian Persia could imagine the shahinshah as an evil king or the veritable "man of sin" who would appear just prior to the second coming of Christ (see chap. 11).

This enthusiastic support from a pagan Zoroastrian king helped establish "the Church of the East," a commonly used title for the church throughout the Sassanian Persian Empire and even farther eastward. Yazdgerd worked closely with two Christian bishops: Mar Marutha of Maypherqat from Syria in the eastern Roman Empire and Mar 'Ishak (Isaac) of Seleucia-Ctesiphon in Persia from the Sassanian Empire.[6] Marutha served as a diplomat to the Sassanian royal court. He developed a friendship with Yazdgerd, reportedly because his additional skills in medicine once helped heal the shahinshah. 'Ishak would serve as head bishop of the Church of the East, a position known as *catholicos*. One Persian Christian summarized the relationship between the shahinshah and the bishops this way: "Thanks to the access which the *catholicus* Isaac has to the King of Kings, who has been pleased to establish him, as head of all the Christians of the East, and particularly since the arrival here of Mar Marutha, by the favour of the King of Kings, peace and tranquility are granted to you."[7] The most visible and immediate fruit of this partnership was a major church council, known as the Council of Seleucia-Ctesiphon or the Council of Mar 'Ishak, that assembled in Persia in 410.

The Moment

Some bishops from the Roman Empire had earlier sent a letter of advice and encouragement to their counterparts in the Sassanian Persian Empire. 'Ishak and Marutha translated the letter from Greek into Persian and presented it to Yazdgerd, who enthusiastically supported the idea of a council and immediately sent out invitations throughout his realm. One Persian Christian later reflected on Yazdgerd's actions by quoting Proverbs 21:1, which says, "The king's heart is a stream of water in the hand of the LORD; he turns it wherever he will."

Forty Christian bishops, known as the "vigilant guardians of the faith,"[8] traveled to Yazdgerd's capital city of Seleucia-Ctesiphon, which had a vibrant Christian community in the early fifth century. They came from throughout the realm, ranging from Mesopotamia to Samarqand (in eastern Uzbekistan). The city stretched out on both sides of the Tigris River, not far from modern Baghdad. A cathedral in Veh-Ardashir, an upscale suburb, served as the venue. 'Ishak officiated, with support from Marutha, who served as a "guest of honor."[9] Yazdgerd himself actually attended the council, just as Constantine had done at the Council of Nicaea.

The council convened with a statement and gesture of the fundamental unity of Christians on both sides of the frontier. Marutha read aloud the letter from the Western bishops, and a Persian writer described the response of the Persian bishops: "Though physically they [i.e., bishops in the Roman Empire] are far removed from us, they have fully revealed to us the strength of their love for us and the anxiety (caused by) their separation from us."[10]

All forty bishops who gathered at Seleucia-Ctesiphon gladly accepted the letter's advice, which emphasized three main points:

1. Each city and its jurisdiction should have only one bishop.
2. Christmas and Easter should be celebrated on the same day as by Christians in the West.
3. The "steadfast admonitions, chaste laws, upright rules, glorious canons, and enlightening ordinances" of the Council of Nicaea should be maintained.[11]

Although it was a gathering of a Persian church led by a Persian bishop and called by a Persian King of Kings, they affirmed their commitment to "one, holy, catholic, and apostolic Church." They knew that Christians flourish when connected to fellow Christians everywhere through shared teaching and practice.

The bishops' discussions and decisions were summarized in the twenty-two canons of the council, which all bishops affirmed "of their own free will."[12] These addressed issues including the ordination and conduct of bishops, prohibitions against pagan divination, rules governing councils, hospitality for strangers, and worship and liturgy. The leaders further committed to praying for long life and strength for their "victorious and illustrious king."[13]

The oversight of Yazdgerd was clear, and unity was key. Concerning the appointment of church leaders, the shahinshah declared:

Everyone that you shall choose, whom you shall know to be fit to govern and direct the people of God, who shall have been established by the bishops 'Ishak and Marouta [Marutha], will hold

117

valid office. No one must separate himself from these: whoever opposes them and flouts their will shall be reported to us, and we shall tell the King of Kings, and the malice of such an one shall be punished, whoever he be.[14]

The Mathēma

It is an age-old adage that leaders who can proclaim freedoms have the ability to take them away. For all the benefits that surely came with it, the Persian Christians' connection with their state would always be a delicate balancing act, as it has been for many Christians through the centuries. Christians of the Church of the East would draw timeless guidance from this moment as "a study of the promise and perils of non-Christian rule."[15] At the same time, these brothers and sisters were negotiating their relationship with Christians in the empire to their west. They knew that they were all part of the "one, holy, catholic, and apostolic Church," but they had to resist the control the Byzantine Church might try to exert over them. One part of the church should not lord it over others.

Several years after 'Ishak's death, Yazdgerd learned that a shipment of pearls coming from India and China had been stolen by pirates. Even though his own nephew had informed him of the theft, Yazdgerd was suspicious of the reported details. So he turned to the Christian *catholicos*, Mar 'Ishak's successor Mar Ahai, "to ascertain the truth of these allegations and report on them." There was a clear reciprocal relationship between the Church of the East and the shahinshah—trust for one and oversight by the other. Mar Ahai had been put in place "with agreement of the fathers and Yazdgerd."[16] And Ahai's successor, Mar Yabalaha, became *catholicos* when Yazdgerd "ordered him to be appointed."[17] There are obvious benefits and potential dangers lurking here.

While affirming fundamental unity through Nicaea and heeding brotherly advice from Western church leaders, the Christians of

Persia also knew they could not simply be subordinates or extensions of a Western church. For one, they knew the importance of "self-consciously marking themselves off from Rome" as they were "automatically suspect" because of "presumed and indeed demonstrable links with their rival empire."[18] We already saw in chapter 11 how the Christians of Persia once paid a steep price for their association with the Roman Empire when they were suspected of being a fifth column.

Not everything was simply about their own safety, though. They were a Persian church, a Church of the East, and did not need to slavishly follow a Western model or submit to leadership from the West. In 424, just over fifteen years after the Council of Seleucia-Ctesiphon, another Persian synod, the Council of Dadiso, clearly rejected Western oversight of the Church of the East: "Now, by the word of God, we decree that the Easterns will not be permitted to carry complaints against their patriarch before the Western patriarchs; and that every cause which cannot be determined in the presence of their patriarchs shall be left to the judgement of Christ."[19] Even as they embraced the bonds of faith with their imperial neighbors, the Church of the East would not be mediated by the church in the Roman Empire.

Christians have often faced and will continue to face challenges of political identity. Yet God grants moments of peace and safety, the benefits of which can lead to flourishing and growth. Yazdgerd's efforts that culminated with the Council of Seleucia-Ctesiphon "organized a Christian Persian church that grew in number, and many in the royal family and the nobility, especially the women, gravitated toward this religion."[20] The Church of the East persists up to our day. Like Christians through the ages, we too can feel the timeless hope and longing in the ancient prayer of Christians at the Council of Seleucia-Ctesiphon, who petitioned for "liberty and peaceful existence to the congregations of Christ" that "the servants of God" may be permitted "publicly to exalt Christ during this earthly life, or at their death."[21] Their example can still inspire us today.

Further Reading

Daryaee, Touraj. "History, Epic, and Numismatics: On the Title of Yazd-gerd I (Rāmšahr)." *American Journal of Numismatics* 14 (2002): 89–95.

McDonough, Scott. "A Second Constantine?: The Sasanian King Yazd-gard in Christian History and Historiography," *Journal of Late Antiquity* 1, no. 1 (Spring 2008): 127–40.

Walker, Joel. "From Nisibis to Xi'an: The Church of the East in Late Antique Eurasia." In *Oxford Handbook of Late Antiquity*. Edited by Scott Fitzgerald Johnson. Oxford University Press, 2012.

Notes

1. Touran Al-Jahiz, as quoted in Touraj Daryaee, "History, Epic, and Numismatics: On the Title of Yazdgerd I (Rāmšahr)," *American Journal of Numismatics* 14 (2002): 91.

2. Daryaee, "History, Epic, and Numismatics," 93.

3. Daryaee, "History, Epic, and Numismatics," 91–92; and Scott McDonough, "A Second Constantine? The Sasanian King Yazdgard in Christian History and Historiography," *Journal of Late Antiquity* 1, no. 1 (Spring 2008): 129–30.

4. "Religious Peace in Persia: The Synod of Seleucia, 410," in *Creeds, Councils and Controversies: Documents Illustrative of the History of the Church A.D. 337–461*, ed. J. Stevenson (Seabury, 1966), 256.

5. "Religious Peace in Persia," 256.

6. "Mar" is a Syriac honorific title for high clerics, meaning something along the lines of "Most Reverend."

7. "Religious Peace in Persia," 256.

8. Bar Hebraeus, *Chronicon Ecclesiasticum*, vol. 2, ed. Joannes Baptista Ab-beloos and Thomas Joseph Lamy (Maisonneuve, 1877), 48–52.

9. Joel Walker, "From Nisibis to Xi'an: The Church of the East in Late Antique Eurasia," in *Oxford Handbook of Late Antiquity*, ed. Scott Fitzgerald Johnson (Oxford University Press, 2012), 1002.

10. "The Synod of Mar Ishaq," trans. M. J. Birnie, https://www.fourthcentury.com/wp-content/uploads/2009/06/thecouncilofmarishaq.pdf.

11. "The Synod of Mar Ishaq."

12. *Chronicle of Se'ert* 66, trans. Anthony Alcock, https://archive.org/details/AlcockChronicleOfSeertET.

13. "The Synod of Mar Ishaq."

14. "Religious Peace in Persia," 256.

15. McDonough, "A Second Constantine?," 127.

16. *Chronicle of Se'ert* 69.

17. *Chronicle of Se'ert* 71.

18. Garth Fowden, *Empire to Commonwealth: Consequences of Monotheism in Late Antiquity* (Princeton University Press, 1993), 122.

19. "The Synod of Dadiso, 424," in *Creeds, Councils and Controversies*, 259–60.

20. Touraj Daryaee, "The Sasanian Empire (224–651 CE)," in *Oxford Handbook of Iranian History*, ed. Touraj Daryaee (Oxford University Press, 2012), 205.

21. "The Synod of Mar Ishaq."

14

Mobs and Murder in Alexandria

(Egypt, 415)

The Background

It was Lent in the year 415. A mob of Christian extremists swarmed through the streets of Alexandria, Egypt.[1] Made up of agents of Bishop Cyril, they had been sent into the midst of a high-profile dispute between the bishop and Orestes, the Christian governor. They found one of the city's most venerable and famous intellectuals, Hypatia, riding through the streets. The mob tore her from her carriage and unleashed their fury upon her in a horrific act of murder that shocked Romans throughout the empire.

For many Christians today and through time, stories of violence from the church's early centuries are expected to follow a standard plotline of Christians as helpless victims and devout pagans as bloodthirsty perpetrators. Indeed, this scenario played out many times in those early centuries, and it is important to remember and celebrate the faithful martyrs. However, by the late fourth and early fifth centuries, Roman violence was no longer one-sided.

The fifth-century church historian Socrates Scholasticus, our most reliable and important source on this harrowing moment, records, "The Alexandrian public is more delighted with tumult than any other people: and if any time it should find a pretext, breaks forth into the most intolerable excesses; for it never ceases from its turbulence without bloodshed."[2] With a population from 300,000 to 500,000 people in the fourth and fifth centuries,[3] Alexandria witnessed a surge of civic unrest and riots driven by rival political and religious factions.

The Christian Roman emperor Theodosius I had banned pagan sacrifice in 381, and over the following decade Alexandria was wracked by conflicts between Christians and pagans. By the end of that decade and into the next, brutal atrocities were being committed by pagans and Christians alike.[4] By 392, a veritable street war had broken out, with monks and priests assaulting pagan temples and pagans making "forays among the Christians, capturing, torturing, and even crucifying them."[5] The civic order of the city teetered on the brink.

Theodosius responded to the emergency by issuing "a blanket amnesty to the pagan rioters," declaring "the Christians killed in the violence to be martyrs," and disbanding the pagan cults in the city entirely.[6] The imperial decree registered, and a relative calm settled over Alexandria for two decades.

The Moment

In 412, tensions returned with the appointment of Cyril as bishop. A significant faction supported a different candidate for the office, and Cyril's place was not immediately secure. His tendency toward harsh, even cruel reactions against rivals soon became apparent. His uncle and predecessor as bishop, Theophilus, had been known for "harsh and authoritarian conduct" that earned him the epithet "the church's Pharaoh,"[7] but Cyril quickly began to match that reputation.

Factions could be seen fighting in the street again. In response, Cyril took aim at the Novatianist churches (discussed in chap. 5), forbidding them to worship because they sided with his rival. Cyril soon clashed with Alexandrian Jews, who had had a significant presence in the city for nearly seven centuries and made up as much as 20 percent of its population.[8] The Jews vehemently— and, according to some accounts, violently—responded to Cyril's measures of intimidation, prompting him to launch an attack on the entire Jewish community. Consequently, numerous Jews were either killed or forced to leave the city. These despicable actions only fueled further violence, and Alexandria staggered on the brink of chaos once again. Cyril and Orestes clashed bitterly with each other over how to rein in the carnage, and their rift became irreconcilable. Different factions gravitated toward one or the other. In one memorable scene, Cyril approached Orestes brandishing a copy of the Gospels in his hand and demanding reconciliation, to no avail.

In his own bid to reestablish order in the city, Cyril called upon five hundred aggressive monks from Nitria, an isolated settlement thirty miles to the south. Cyril had lived among these monks before he became bishop, and he "hoped they would intimidate the governor into an agreement."[9] He also called upon Alexandria's *parabalani*, a semi-clerical order of charitable aid workers whose role was somewhere between retainers and henchmen. Described as "paid workers under his control,"[10] they came to act essentially as Cyril's "personal militia"[11] and were "fundamentally loyal to their ecclesiastical superior."[12]

Monks and *parabalani* alike quickly embraced their roles. One of the monks from Nitria, Ammonius, struck Orestes with a stone and seriously injured him. Ammonius was immediately arrested by the political authorities and tortured so intensely that he died. Cyril then brazenly declared a church funeral for Ammonius and proclaimed him a martyr, renaming him Saint Thaumasius ("the Wonderful"). Through these and other acts, Orestes saw Cyril baldly flouting his own authority as the emperor-appointed agent of order.

One of the most respected public figures of her day, the elderly Hypatia, was drawn into the center of the fray. She was well-known in the city as a Neoplatonist philosopher, teacher, and public lecturer. Her former students, most of them Christians, had gone on to prominent positions throughout the empire, including that of bishop. She herself was not a Christian; however, contrary to many modern interpretations, she was not a "devout pagan" either.[13] "Esteemed by the ruling elite, sympathetic toward Christians, indifferent to pagan cults, neutral in the religious fights and altercations, she lived in Alexandria for many years enjoying the city rulers' respect and her disciples' love."[14] Political officials, including Orestes, regularly consulted her because of her established reputation for wisdom and moderation.

Ancient sources note Cyril's jealousy of the sway Hypatia held among Alexandrian elites. Her association with Orestes put her squarely on one side of the conflict. Rumors about her began to spread, and the bishop apparently did nothing to discourage them. Some believed that he actively encouraged the rumors as they took on a life of their own. One such rumor claimed Hypatia had caused the rift between bishop and emperor, and thus she was the root cause of the mayhem. Another suggested she was actually an enthusiastic pagan who wielded black magic and had cast a spell over Orestes, the people of God, and the whole city.[15]

A gang of *parabalani* set out to confront Hypatia. They found her riding along the streets of the city, "unprotected and unexpecting," and they viciously attacked.[16] Brandishing shattered roof tiles and oyster shells, they tore the elderly woman from her chariot, shredded her clothing, gouged out her eyes, dragged her body through the streets, and burned her remains.

As word of the atrocity spread far and wide, the Roman world reeled in shock. Most historians today have little doubt that

Cyril instigated the deadly moment by fanning the flames of popular anger[17] in such a way that Hypatia could be murdered.[18] All the ancient sources agree that Cyril created the climate and that it was "men in Cyril's employment" who "assassinated Hypatia."[19] Socrates Scholasticus strongly condemned the whole affair, noting that it "brought no slight opprobrium upon Cyril and the whole Alexandrian church. Indeed nothing is farther from the spirit of Christianity than murders, fights, and similar things."[20]

Emperor Theodosius II immediately ordered an investigation of her death. Sanctions were brought against Cyril, but he paid "outrageous bribes" to avoid harsher penalties[21] and actually remained in office until he died in 444. Imperial laws soon sanctioned the *parabalani* for sowing terror in the city.[22] Their power was curtailed, and they were temporarily placed under the control of the governor rather than the bishop.[23] Orestes was removed from his position and never heard from again. Public violence in Alexandria ended abruptly, and the city was generally free of it for most of the rest of the century.

The Mathēma

This is not an easy moment to stomach let alone process. Do we claim Christians as Our People only when they were persecuted victims? It borders on dishonest to ignore unflattering moments by confining them safely to the past and only remembering moments we like so as to claim outright affinity with early Christians.

Where Cyril of Alexandria is remembered by Christians today, he is almost always viewed fondly as a major doctor of the church and teacher of orthodoxy. His voice and his writings were crucial at the Councils of Ephesus (431) and Chalcedon (451). Amidst a series of famous and intense theological debates, Cyril would provide a robust and influential defense of Jesus Christ as the divine Word made flesh—that is, one person having two natures. He played a crucial part in the battles over orthodoxy.

Yet, we do a disservice to Cyril's humanity if we remember him solely as a theologian whose ideas are compelling and accurate. Like all church fathers, he was not a mere collection of propositions, a lifeless figure with doctrines etched upon it. No, he was a real person with influential strengths and significant weaknesses. His and others' actions against Jews, against Hypatia, and against his adversaries in general are indefensible, even if they are conveniently overlooked by many.

While praised by most church historians even today, Cyril was perceived quite differently by his contemporaries.[24] One of the most brutal assessments came from Theodoret, an ardent theological foe, who declared when Cyril died, "At last and with difficulty the villain has gone . . . the Lord has lopped him off like a plague and taken away the reproach from Israel." Theodoret went on to suggest that the undertakers "lay a very big and heavy stone upon his grave, for fear he should come back again."[25] Contrast such an assessment with Arius, the charming arch-heretic adored by many of his contemporaries (see chap. 10). The truth of one's ideas is hardly contingent upon having a pleasant personality. Often, truth and orthodoxy are carried by those with glaring and inexcusable faults. Thankfully, though, we do not depend upon the character of women or men or even famous church fathers. Centuries after this moment, another African church controversy inspired the famous hymn "The Church's One Foundation," which continues to remind us that the foundation remains "Jesus Christ her Lord."

This episode might cause us to reflect in another way. How thin can be the veneer of civility and "civilization," even among professing Christians! These were Christians enflamed into mob action and even driven to murder by their political commitments, which they perceived as noble and just. Their cause, they were assured, was God's cause. Perhaps we are not so different from them, for might we too be capable of such actions under the same circumstances?

Further Reading

Bowersock, G. W. "A Terrorist Charity in Late Antiquity." *Anabases* 12 (2010): 45–54.

Brown, Peter. *Power and Persuasion in Late Antiquity: Towards a Christian Empire*. University of Wisconsin Press, 1992.

Dzielska, Maria. *Hypatia of Alexandria*. Trans. F. Lyra. Harvard University Press, 1995.

Haas, Christopher. *Alexandria in Late Antiquity: Topography and Social Conflict*. Johns Hopkins University Press, 1997.

Watts, Edward J. *Hypatia: The Life and Legend of an Ancient Philosopher*. Oxford University Press, 2020.

Notes

1. G. W. Bowersock, "A Terrorist Charity in Late Antiquity," *Anabases* 12 (2010): 45.

2. Socrates Scholasticus, *Ecclesiastical History* 7.13.

3. Edward J. Watts, *Hypatia: The Life and Legend of an Ancient Philosopher* (Oxford University Press, 2020), 15.

4. Watts, *Hypatia*, 56–59.

5. Maria Dzielska, *Hypatia of Alexandria*, trans. F. Lyra (Harvard University Press, 1995), 81.

6. Watts, *Hypatia*, 59.

7. Dzielska, *Hypatia*, 84.

8. Watts, *Hypatia*, 109.

9. Watts, *Hypatia*, 2.

10. Watts, *Hypatia*, 117.

11. Bowersock, "Terrorist Charity," 50.

12. Timothy E. Gregory, "Parabalani," in *Oxford Dictionary of Byzantium*, vol. 3 (Oxford University Press, 1991).

13. Dzielska, *Hypatia*, 63.

14. Dzielska, *Hypatia*, 46.

15. Maria Dzielska, "Hypatia," in *Late Antiquity: A Guide to the Postclassical World*, ed. G. W. Bowersock, Peter Brown, and Oleg Grabar (Belknap Press of Harvard University, 1999).

16. Watts, *Hypatia*, 3.

17. Dzielska, *Hypatia*, 97.

18. Watts, *Hypatia*, 117.
19. Dzielska, *Hypatia*, 104.
20. Quoted in Watts, *Hypatia*, 112.
21. Watts, *Hypatia*, 117.
22. Bowersock, "Terrorist Charity," 49.
23. Watts, *Hypatia*, 117.
24. Dzielska, *Hypatia*, 84.
25. Theodoret, *Letters* 180.

15

Heresy Invades Post-Roman Britain

(Southern Britain, 429)

The Background

There's a well-known adage among archaeologists and historians that "the absence of evidence doesn't imply the evidence of absence." However, in the case of early medieval Britain, it's been tempting to think it does. Roman rule in Britain formally ended in 410, and for nearly the next two centuries, there's almost no direct evidence—archaeological or written—of the Christian church's presence. One rare and illuminating moment emerges from this darkness, and it involves the sudden spread of a heresy on the island and the larger church's immediate response to it. Amidst the collapse of Roman civilization and the looming threat of barbarians, there still existed a fervent desire for faithful Christian teachings.

The earliest evidence dates Christianity's arrival in Britain to the second century. Around the year 200, the North African bishop Tertullian noted that Christ already had subjugated "haunts of the Britons—inaccessible to the Romans."[1] How Christianity reached those shores so early is unknown, and it remained in the shadows for the entirety of the third century. By the fourth century, the picture becomes much clearer. It must have been an established church in Britain that sent bishops to the Council of Arles in 314 (see chap. 9) and the Council of Arminium in 360. Over the course of the fourth century, Christianity became firmly rooted.[2] Villas, mosaics, and wall paintings discovered at Frampton, Hinton St. Mary, and Lullingstone famously memorialize its presence in this century.

While Christianity was spreading, fourth-century Britain was beset by calamity and crisis.[3] Its towns began an inexorable decline, and in the so-called Barbarian Conspiracy of 367, several distinct barbarian groups united, invaded the island, and commenced pillaging and killing. The central Roman government came to the rescue, though, and cities and forts were recovered and restored.[4]

In 410, everything suddenly changed. *The Gallic Chronicle of 452* puts it succinctly: "In the sixteenth year of [Roman emperor] Honorius [i.e., 410]: The British provinces were devastated by an incursion of the Saxons."[5] This time, the Roman government could not—or at least did not—come to their aid, and never would again. The emperor Honorius wrote to the cities of Britain, telling them to be "watchful of their own security"; in other words, they were now completely on their own.[6] This was effectively the end of Roman Britain. Saxon pressure increased, and local Romano-British leaders were forced to organize their own regional defense; any kind of central rule on the island would be gone for centuries to come.

Very soon thereafter, a new heresy called Pelagianism began spreading throughout Britain. Its founder, Pelagius, was born in

Britain around 354 but spent most of his active career on the Continent and along the shores of the Mediterranean. He went to Rome in 380, where he attracted attention, both favorable and hostile, due to his emphasis on the essential goodness of human nature. Contending that free will made humans responsible for their own ultimate destiny, he stressed that humans are therefore capable of earning their salvation through their own merits. Pelagius's teachings opposed the teachings of his famous contemporary, Augustine of Hippo, who emphasized the absolute necessity of divine grace. Pelagius was challenged and denounced by many in the Western church and was excommunicated in 418, backed up by the arm of the Roman state.

Agricola, a Pelagianist and the son of a Pelagianist bishop, began spreading the heresy around Britain during this time. The fifth-century theologian Prosper of Aquitaine records that Agricola "corrupts the churches of Britain by the urging of his own dogma."[7] Britain's newfound independence from Roman imperial control, its lack of a central political authority, and its geographic remoteness likely provided opportunity and a "safe haven" for the heresy's spread.[8]

The Moment

In response to the growing threat of Pelagianism, a group of concerned bishops in Britain decided to get help from the Continent. In the late 420s, they sent a commission to report that in their "home territory the Pelagian heresy had seized hold of a broad section of the population," and begged that "aid should be sent to the Catholic faith as quickly as possible."[9]

Exactly what happened next is unclear. One medieval source, *The Life of Germanus* by Constantius of Lyon, claims that a synod was called in Gaul and that many gathered bishops unanimously appointed Germanus of Auxerre and Lupus of Troyes, "two shining lights of the faith" and "apostolic priests," to go to Britain to address the problem.[10] Another account, that of Prosper of Aquitaine, claims that it was actually Celestine, the bishop of Rome, who sent Germanus to bring people back to the Catholic faith at the advice of Palladius, a deacon.[11]

Fundamental differences in these accounts aside, it is clear enough that British bishops sent word to the Continent and that at least Germanus was then appointed for the task. The role of Lupus, if any, remains unclear. There are no other references to this alleged council or synod, and some scholars doubt that it ever happened. Nonetheless, help did come via the church on the Continent.

In 429, Germanus (and maybe Lupus) arrived in Britain. He was "a prominent Gallo-Roman bishop" who was just over fifty years old at the time.[12] His varied background had prepared him for avid defense and for the administrative task before him. He had studied law in Rome and had served as a lawyer for a time. He then became a government official before he was called to the bishopric in north central Gaul in 418. The biography by Constantius of Lyon is filled with the sorts of improbable details that are difficult to substantiate and that often characterize hagiography. For instance, he tells how Germanus once battled a demonic storm on the English Channel and led an army that drove a host of Saxon invaders to drown simply by shouting "Alleluia!" But a solid factual core remains, and his account is a rare and often unique example of narrative from this time.[13]

A meeting was called to debate Pelagianism, and Germanus advocated skillfully and eagerly for orthodoxy. "When this damnable heresy had thus been stamped out, its authors refuted, and the minds of all re-established in the true faith,"[14] the defeated Pelagians were expelled. The *Life of Germanus* also describes a second commission by Germanus some years later to again combat Pelagianism. It is quite likely, though, that this second commission never happened. But what is certain—and has been preserved for us—is that he was sent to Britain at the request of British church leaders and helped defeat the Pelagianists there.

The Mathēma

Civilization (indeed, Western civilization) in Britain was crumbling around the island's inhabitants. They were being invaded and attacked by pagan Saxons. Yet any ideas of saving civilization or reestablishing former political and architectural greatness do not appear in the early sources. What is apparent is a concern for an accurate doctrine of salvation by the grace of God, not by mere human willpower and merit. Christianity was facing a growing threat from paganism with the Saxon domination. And yet, "at a time when one might have feared for the very survival of the Christian religion in Britain . . . thanks to Germanus' expulsion of the Pelagians the faith still endured intact in that part of the world."[15]

Some like to claim that orthodoxy and heresy are a function of politics. Sometimes that is difficult to refute. Leading twentieth-century church historian Robert Markus notes, "Italy, and to some extent other Western provinces, were subjected to the African theological tradition, rounded off in a coherent theological synthesis by Augustine and his episcopal colleagues in Africa, and imposed by government coercion." But, he continues, "Britain was not. It now lay beyond the reach of the emperor's writ."[16] The political connections were now gone, but Christians on both sides of the channel knew the importance of maintaining "one, holy, catholic, and apostolic Church."

"Doctrine divides" is a slogan we often hear, especially when groups of Christians seem to be separating from others and from one another over minor issues. While there certainly is a place for warning against needless division, this key moment reminds us of an important corollary that we do not celebrate enough: "Doctrine unites." It even united Britain with the Continent—no small feat over the medieval centuries!

As to the question of how long Christianity survived in Britain thereafter, sources allow little more to be said. Hints are few and fleeting at best. The famous fifth-century evangelist St. Patrick was born and raised in Britain, where he was captured by Irish pirates and later set out on his famous mission to Ireland. He noted a definite church structure led by bishops, which was clearly still in place at his time.[17] But it remains unclear exactly when Patrick lived in the fifth century and whether his life extended into the sixth. The latest hint of Christianity in Britain is a record of a British bishop named Mansuetus who attended the Council of Tours in 461.[18] Most scholars are convinced that Christianity entirely died out after that. It's a sobering reminder that the light of the gospel can go out when connections to the broader church are not rigorously maintained. Not until the end of the sixth century does Christianity reappear in Britain when it was reintroduced through the famous mission of Augustine of Canterbury under the aegis of Gregory I, bishop of Rome (aka Gregory the Great; see chap. 18).

For some Christians today, the worst possible scenario would be the collapse of Western civilization. This would indeed be catastrophic. However, this unique moment allows us to recognize that for Our People in Britain during the early Middle Ages, the stakes seemed even higher: the loss of orthodoxy.

Further Reading

Barrett, Anthony A. "Saint Germanus and the British Missions." *Britannia* 40 (2009): 197–218.

Cleary, Simon Esmonde. "Britain in the Fourth Century." In *A Companion to Roman Britain*. Edited by Malcolm Todd. Blackwell, 2004.

Markus, R. A. "Pelagianism: Britain and the Continent." *Journal of Ecclesiastical History* 37, no. 2 (April 1986): 191–204.

Wood, Ian. "The Fall of the Western Empire and the End of Roman Britain." *Britannia* 18 (1987): 251–62.

Wood, Ian. "The Final Phase." In *A Companion to Roman Britain*. Edited by Malcolm Todd. Blackwell, 2004.

Notes

1. Tertullian, *Against the Jews* 7.

2. Peter Salway, *Roman Britain: A Very Short Introduction* (Oxford University Press, 2000), 54.

3. Ian Wood, "The Final Phase," in *A Companion to Roman Britain*, ed. Malcolm Todd (Blackwell, 2004), 431.

4. Salway, *Roman Britain*, 60–63.

5. Quoted in Michael E. Jones and John Casey, "The Gallic Chronicle Restored: A Chronology for the Anglo-Saxon Invasions and the End of Roman Britain," *Britannia* 19 (1988): 379.

6. Zosimus, *New History* 6.10.2.

7. Prosper of Aquitaine, *Epitoma Chronicon*, as quoted in Anthony A. Barrett, "Saint Germanus and the British Missions," *Britannia* 40 (2009): 197–218.

8. Wood, "Final Phase," 433, 440. See also Barrett, "Saint Germanus," 200; R. A. Markus, "Pelagianism: Britain and the Continent," *Journal of Ecclesiastical History* 37, no. 2 (April 1986): 191–204.

9. Constantius of Lyon, *Vita Germani* 12, as quoted in Barrett, "Saint Germanus."

10. Constantius of Lyon, *Vita Germani* 12.

11. Barrett, "Saint Germanus," 202.

12. Salway, *Roman Britain*, 68.

13. Barrett, "Saint Germanus," 197.

14. Constantius of Lyon, *Vita Germani* 12.

15. Constantius of Lyon, *Vita Germani* 27.

16. Markus, "Pelagianism," 199.

17. Wood, "Final Phase," 431.

18. Wood, "Final Phase," 437.

16

Massacre and Revenge in Southern Arabia

(Himyar/Yemen, 523–524)

The Background

It was the first time in history that a religious persecution provoked an international incident. All the surrounding political powers of the day got involved—the Byzantine and Sassanian Persian superpowers, the Christian kingdom of Aksum (Ethiopia), the Jewish kingdom of Himyar in southern Arabia, and the two major Christian tribal groupings ("supertribes") in northern Arabia, the Lakhmids and Ghassanids.[1] Christian communities within Sassanian Persia—Monophysite, Nestorian, and Chalcedonian (see introduction)—each responded on their own as well. Some see this key moment as ultimately helping to pave the way for the arrival of Islam about a century later,[2] and memories of it echo in the Qur'an.

The setting was southern Arabia, a region that once contained the legendary land of Saba (Sheba). This ancient land was renowned for its "Queen of the South" who had visited the Israelite King Solomon fifteen hundred years earlier.[3] Romans called the area Arabia Felix ("Happy Arabia") because of its lush greenery, a stark contrast to the desert that covers much of the rest of the Arabian Peninsula. The region had long been connected with Ethiopia to the west and the Mediterranean world to the north through the Red Sea trade routes (see chap. 17). A kingdom known as Himyar flourished here from the mid-fourth century to the latter half of the sixth century.

In the late fourth century, Himyar experienced a major religious transformation. Its ancient traditional polytheism suddenly disappeared at the highest political levels. Between 380 and 384, polytheistic references in royal inscriptions vanished entirely, replaced by monotheistic language.[4] Centuries earlier, a few ethnic Jews had likely made their way here following the Jewish revolts of 70 and 135,[5] but now the ruling ethnic Arabs were being converted to Judaism and the religion was spreading quickly.[6] By the early fifth century, Himyar was a Jewish kingdom.

Simultaneously, Christianity was also growing and expanding. Aksum/Ethiopia, just across the Red Sea, was a major Christian influence. Hints of Christianity's arrival and spread are scattered among stories of bishops and monks bringing Christianity to Himyar from Ethiopia and elsewhere, sometimes with strong Byzantine support. Christianity was represented at all levels of Himyarite society.

Aksum/Ethiopia and the kingdom of Himyar had a long and complicated political history, with the former exerting, or at least claiming to exert, control over southern Arabia. Ethiopians had, in fact, ruled much of southwestern Arabia outright as recently as the late third century, something they seem to have never forgotten. Well after they held any official claim to the area, the Ethiopian king (or *negus*) continued to use royal titles asserting his claim.[7] The strong growth of Judaism in Himyar and Christianity in Ethiopia among the elite of society coincided with clear claims of power outside their borders by both kingdoms. Here as elsewhere, monotheism and imperial claims went hand in hand.[8]

Ethiopia invaded Himyar in 518, and Kaleb, one of Ethiopia's most celebrated kings, placed a Christian negus on the throne of Himyar. When this Himyarite king died in 522, however, his successor, Yusuf Dhu Nuwas ("Joseph the Long Haired"), immediately set out to forcibly reassert an ardent Judaism throughout his realm.

The Moment

Such upheavals in the ruling ideology provoked both random and state-sponsored violence. Apparently, a few Christians and Jews attacked each other's houses of worship. Yusuf, undoubtedly reacting against political influence from Ethiopia and harboring hatred for Christianity, massacred an Ethiopian garrison within his borders and then proceeded to forcibly convert all within his realm to Judaism. He unleashed unprecedented terror on Christians in 523. Accounts of the brutality are vivid, with all sources agreeing on their ferocity; Yusuf himself even bragged about the gory details.

He seems to have delighted in burning Christians alive. In at least one case, hundreds of Christian men and women were burned alive inside a church. Another account records that Yusuf burned alive 427 clerics and nuns, killed 4,252 Christian laypeople, and enslaved 1,297 children.[9] Memories of such brutal fiery moments seem to be enshrined in the Qur'an from well over a century later. Surah 85 ("the Constellations") recounts Christian believers being burned alive en masse in a trench while their tormentors looked on.

Despicable acts and inhuman cruelty run through the ancient sources. Yusuf promised safety to groups of Christians if they would surrender, then ordered their executions as soon as they did.[10] Another source records Himyarites cutting off the hands and feet of Christians one at a time in response to individual questions about their faith.[11] Some accounts claim as many as twenty thousand Christians died, but that number is impossible to substantiate. Surviving stories do, however, show that Yusuf was intent on completely eradicating Christians and Christianity from his kingdom.

Word of such atrocities spread quickly, and an international emergency meeting convened at a site in Mesopotamia known as Ramla. Representatives came from the Byzantine and Sassanian courts as well as from various Christian communities within the Sassanian Empire. A representative of Yusuf was there as well. They were all pleading for Mundhir ibn Numan, a Lakhmid leader and Nestorian Christian from northern Arabia, to intervene—or not to.

The Byzantine emperor Justin encouraged the Ethiopian negus Kaleb to invade Himyar. Kaleb was only too willing and ready to do so, as he already had aspirations of ruling Himyar and wanted revenge for the brutal treatment of Christians.[12] Both motivations ran together, no doubt. In 524, the negus launched a massive invasion force of 70,000 (some sources say as many as 120,000) that sailed directly across the Red Sea to Himyar. According to the later Ethiopian epic *Kebra Nagast*, this was "Kaleb's hour of greatest glory,"[13] and it is commemorated even today as an epic moment in Ethiopian history. Sources differ slightly on whether Yusuf committed suicide or was killed by Kaleb, but in every account, he lay dead and his army was decisively defeated once the Ethiopian army landed and disembarked.

Kaleb memorialized his victory on a carved stone known today as the Marib Inscription, which he erected within the kingdom of Himyar.[14] In it, he invoked Scripture to celebrate his vanquishing of God's enemies. The inscription uses phrases like "seek first the righteousness" and "will be added to you" that echo Matthew 6:33 as the motive and fruits of his conquest.[15] Quoting or paraphrasing from the book of Psalms, the inscription declares, "Let God arise, let his enemies be scattered" (68:1); "I cried to Him with my mouth and shouted to Him with my tongue" (66:17); and "Now they have horses and chariots, while we will be great by the name of God our Lord; they have stumbled and fallen but we have risen" (20:7–8).[16] Negus Kaleb claimed "the glory of David" in defeating Yusuf and defending the beleaguered Christians of Himyar.[17]

The victorious Kaleb sponsored the rebuilding of churches throughout Himyar and helped reestablish the Christian community. Sadly, the cycle of violence did not end with the crushing of Yusuf Dhu Nuwas. As it often does, violence led to more violence. In retaliation, the Christian community launched "a systematic massacre of Jews."[18] The persecution by the Christians became so intense that non-Christians, whether Jew or pagan, "began to tattoo a cross on their hands to escape death."[19]

For a time, southern Arabia became a Christian kingdom directly tied to Aksum/Ethiopia. It would remain so until it was taken over by the Sassanian Persians in 570, who ruled it until it was conquered by Muslim armies more than a half century after that.

The Mathēma

This is at once a harrowing and cautionary tale of religion, politics, and the invocation of Scripture. Many of Our People—men, women, and children—suffered horribly, most of them innocent victims simply caught up in the larger political drama of the time. We grieve with those who are grieving, even though the time and place of their loss are so distant.

Yet, this was not a simple and straightforward instance of brutal persecution of Christians. Political rivalries and commitments also played a significant role in the entire affair. When political systems wholeheartedly embrace monotheism, the outcomes are rarely what many had hoped for. More frequently than not, political ambitions to gain or coerce have resulted in violence and brutality. The few exceptions to this pattern throughout history are indeed noteworthy.[20]

This moment wouldn't be the last time the desire to protect Christians through use of foreign armies went hand in glove with imperial and expansionary impulses. More recent examples can be found in the Russian Tsarist state proposing to protect the Christians of the Ottoman Empire as a cause of the Crimean War. Or the French incursion into Indochina tethered to protecting Christian missionaries there. In all such cases, there are unanticipated and undesirable ramifications for Christians that accompany the protection and good that indeed comes to them. There are always mixed results, as we can often see in retrospect. History is like that.

The tendency to read oneself and one's goals, motives, and aspirations into the Scriptures is also a mainstay through Christian history. On the one hand, is it not perfectly legitimate to see God's enemies as the ones who persecute his people? The Psalms and other parts of Scripture are indeed full of longing for God to avenge his people against persecutors. "Vengeance is mine," declares the Lord (Rom. 12:19). Is it too much to imagine that God would simply use his own people as his instruments?

It is hard to imagine outright, though, that Kaleb's success was that which was "added unto" him for supposedly "seeking first the kingdom and righteousness of God." He was convinced that he carried out his mission "under biblical authority."[21] He even fashioned himself an Old Testament leader going forth against the Amalekites, whom God had called his people to exterminate.[22] He was convinced that he was the leader of the Christian true Israel against a false Israel.[23] An illegitimate triumphalism is always a temptation even as we might rejoice in the defeat of the persecutors of God's people. Hindsight reveals the violent places to which such belief led Kaleb and his supporters in their own brutality against innocent non-Christians.

That seemingly noble dream, Christian political rulership, is ever fleeting and is never truly realized in the ways we might imagine. Christians often long for heaven on earth. The massacre and revenge at Himyar could help us more faithfully, wisely, and carefully assess the ongoing Christian quest for "the kingdom of God and his righteousness."

Further Reading

Bowersock, G. W. *The Throne of Adulis: Red Sea Warfare on the Eve of Islam*. Oxford University Press, 2013.

Moffett, Samuel Hugh. *A History of Christianity in Asia, Vol. 1: Beginnings to 1500*. HarperSanFrancisco, 1992.

Robin, Christian Julien. "The Judaism of the Ancient Kingdom of Himyar in Arabia: A Discreet Conversion." In *Diversity and Rabbinization: Jewish Texts and Societies Between 400 and 1000 CE*. Edited by Gavin McDowell, Ron Naiweld, and Daniel Stökl. Cambridge University Press, 2021.

Notes

1. G. W. Bowersock, *The Throne of Adulis: Red Sea Warfare on the Eve of Islam* (Oxford University Press, 2013), 86–87.

2. Bowersock, *Throne of Adulis*, 6.

3. 1 Kings 10; 2 Chronicles 9; Matthew 12:42; and Luke 11:31.

4. Christian Julien Robin, "Judaism of the Ancient Kingdom of Himyar in Arabia: A Discreet Conversion," in *Diversity and Rabbinization: Jewish Texts and Societies Between 400 and 1000 CE*, ed. Gavin McDowell et al. (Cambridge University Press, 2021), 167, 182.

5. Robin, "Judaism of the Ancient Kingdom of Himyar," 220.

6. Bowersock, *Throne of Adulis*, 87.

7. Bowersock, *Throne of Adulis*, 64, 95.

8. Bowersock, *Throne of Adulis*, 77–79; see also Garth Fowden, *Empire to Commonwealth: Consequences of Monotheism in Late Antiquity* (Princeton University Press, 1993).

9. Maxime Rodinson, *Muhammad*, trans. Anne Carter (The New Press, 1980), 31.

10. Robin, "Judaism of the Ancient Kingdom of Himyar," 226–27.

11. Samuel Hugh Moffett, *A History of Christianity in Asia, Vol. 1: Beginnings to 1500* (Harper San Francisco, 1992), 278.

12. Bowersock, *Throne of Adulis*, 96–97.

13. Fowden, *Empire to Commonwealth*, 114.

14. Bowersock, *Throne of Adulis*, 98.

15. Bowersock, *Throne of Adulis*, 100.

16. Bowersock, *Throne of Adulis*, 101–2.

17. Bowersock, *Throne of Adulis*, 102.

18. Robin, "Judaism of the Ancient Kingdom of Himyar," 169.

19. Moffett, *A History of Christianity in Asia*, 279.

20. "What is also observable is that a religion never durably keeps a hegemonic position; in the most monolithic of societies, seeds of dissent swiftly sprout. Total conversion is therefore a goal that one tries to achieve but that

is never completely reached." Robin, "Judaism of the Ancient Kingdom of Himyar," 217.

21. Bowersock, *Throne of Adulis*, 102.

22. See Exodus 17:8–16.

23. Yonatan Binyam, "The Conflicts Between Christian Aksum and Jewish Himyar in Pre-Islamic Arabia," Coproduced Religions, 2023, https://coproduced-religions.org/resources/case-studies/the-conflicts-between-christian-aksum-and-jewish-himyar-in-pre-islamic-arabia.

17

---•---

Saints, Snakes, and Scriptures in Aksum

(Ethiopia, Late Fifth to Early Sixth Centuries)

The Background

One of the greatest eras of global missions, spanning from the second half of the fifth century onward, demonstrates that the Great Commission rarely operates independently. Other factors often play a crucial role in motivating and facilitating Christian missionary activities. For instance, as discussed in chapter 6, captives of war and forced resettlement played a significant role in spreading and strengthening the faith in Sassanian Persia. Additionally, doctrinal divisions and subsequent political persecution led Christians to seek refuge and share their faith in distant lands during the mid-fifth century and beyond.

Two persecuted groups, Nestorians and Monophysites, produced the greatest missionaries of the premodern world. Recall that, for whatever their disagreements with subsequent church councils, these two groups affirmed the creed of the Council of Nicaea (325) and thus professed doctrinal essentials of God as creator, the Trinity, the Lord Jesus Christ as God incarnate, Christ's sacrificial death for us on the cross, and his resurrection, ascension, glorification, and second coming (see introduction). Not all heresies are created equal. In chapter 20 we will read more about a memorable and far-reaching Nestorian mission to China, but for now we will see how one of the most enduring Monophysite missions transformed the villages and countrysides of East Africa.

The ancient Aksumite kingdom—roughly modern-day Ethiopia and Eritrea—was a vibrant, confident powerhouse in the political and religious history of late antiquity. Known as "one of the four great kingdoms in this world," along with Persia, Rome, and Sileos (i.e., China),[1] its king went by the title of negus, meaning "king of kings."[2] A high-end luxury trade integrated the Aksumite kingdom with the Mediterranean and Black Sea regions as well as Arabia, India, and China.[3] It was the second country to declare itself a Christian state (Armenia was the first—see chap. 7), even before Rome did. Recent radiocarbon analysis confirms that the kingdom produced the earliest complete illuminated manuscripts of the Gospels as well as one of the earliest copies of Scripture known to exist.

A little over two decades after the conversion of the Roman emperor Constantine, the Aksumite negus Ezana embraced Christianity. He carved in stone a declaration that his kingship and victories were gifts of the Christian God.[4] Royal-sponsored churches followed, and his coinage displayed the symbol of the cross.[5] The traditional story of Ezana's conversion around the year 330, as told by the church historian Rufinus, is full of adventure. Two young Christian Roman boys, Frumentius and Aedesius (who himself told the story to Rufinus), were returning from a sea voyage to India when their ship was captured by Ethiopians, who slaughtered everyone else on board. The boys were sent as slaves to the royal court. Years later they were called to teach Ezana, who was at that time the young heir to the throne; he embraced their Christian faith, and together the three of them spread the gospel among the Ethiopian royalty.

This initial evangelization touched only the nobility, though. Changes in funerary monument styles eloquently attest to the conversion of elites, but there is no sign of Christianity outside of these small circles. Christianity was known in only two cities: the port city of Adulis and the inland capital at Aksum. The rest of the kingdom—the general populace in village and countryside—remained stalwartly pagan.

The Moment

Almost two centuries after Ezana's conversion, a Byzantine writer, merchant, and adventurer known as Cosmas Indicopleustes ("Indian voyager") traveled around the Red Sea and Indian Ocean and visited the Aksumite kingdom in 525. His treatise *Christian Topography* reveals a very different picture of Christianity here. "Everywhere" in the country, he writes, there were now "churches of the Christians and bishops, martyrs, monks and recluses, where the gospel of Christ is proclaimed."[6] Ethiopian gold coins with Christian inscriptions would soon appear with the legend "may this be pleasing in the countryside."[7] Christianity now registered broadly in material culture as attested in the archaeological record.[8] The earliest details remain somewhat elusive, but it is clear that the kingdom experienced a second evangelization that was rather different from the first.[9]

According to vivid Ethiopian traditions, this second evangelization was the work of "the Nine Saints," Monophysite monks who came from a variety of places in the Roman world, including Italy, Constantinople, Antioch, Asia Minor, Caesarea, and Cilicia. Several decades after the Council of Chalcedon in 451, they left the Roman Empire under persecution for their Monophysite confession.[10] The Aksumite kingdom provided a haven—a negus with the mysterious name of MHDYS had already embraced Monophysitism "immediately after the Council of Chalcedon of 451" and placed his kingdom "squarely among the Monophysites in the Christian East."[11] The Nine Saints arrived in the late fifth century to begin a long and fruitful ministry in unreached rural regions.

Most stories about these saints come from oral hagiographies that were not written down until centuries after they lived but were preserved in powerful "cultural memory."[12] As always, with hagiography it can be challenging to disentangle historical facts from fantastic tales (see chap. 15). For example, in one story the sun slows down to allow Garima, one of the Nine, to write out an entire copy of Scripture complete with illuminations in a single day. Another story tells how one of the saints remained standing upright for forty-five years straight. The Nine Saints appear frequently in artwork and have long been symbols of Christian

The Aksumite Nine Saints

Ethiopia. "Their names are to be heard still in church dedications and local tales":[13] Afse, Alef, Aregawi, Garima, Guba, Liqanos, Pantalewon, Sehma, and Yemata. Most historians today suspect there must have been many more Syrian and Egyptian monks in Aksum, but some of the major sites associated with the Nine have long had monasteries dedicated to them that survive to the present day.[14] Many stories ring true.

The ministry of the Nine Saints presents a certain type of paradox that is common in the history of monasticism. As monks, the Nine Saints would have generally sought out isolated and remote regions for meditation and prayer. The places they settled, though, were "at once isolated, yet central."[15] The monasteries might have been hard to access, but they were visible for miles around. So, while the monks might have lived in remote locations, they were always connected to society, which explains their great influence, especially in rural regions. Stories also present some of the Nine Saints as political advisers, even to kings. They are credited with building churches and fashioning the liturgy that became standard to Ethiopian worship.[16] It is undeniable that monks and monasteries from this period were "key agents for the Christianization of the countryside."[17]

Driving out paganism is a recurring theme in the stories of the Nine Saints. Both historical accounts and archaeological evidence indicate that Christian sites were frequently established near or directly on top of former pagan sites. A common motif in these stories is confrontations with snakes, which are sometimes depicted as dragons and are often associated with pagan snake cults and shrines.[18] Serpents featured prominently in Ethiopian tales, and there's even a story about one of their earliest rulers who transformed into an evil serpent king before eventually being overthrown and killed. Snake cults appear to be part of pre-Christian paganism throughout the kingdom, especially in the countryside, and the victory of Christianity is celebrated in some stories as the eradication of the snake cults and winning over the snake worshipers.[19] The rugged and hard-to-access site of Debre Damo was the location for one of the most famous serpent stories. One of the Nine, Abuna Aregawi, was taken up to the site by a serpent.[20] Here he wrestled with a ferocious serpent.[21] Even in places where the stories border on the fantastic, the eradication of pagan cults and the spread of Christianity remain evident.

From the time of their arrival, the monks dedicated themselves to translating, copying, and disseminating Scripture. Monophysite Christianity was already multilingual—Greek, Syriac, Coptic. To these was now added Geez, a Semitic language of Ethiopia related to Hebrew and Arabic. Where before the second evangelization only some passages from the Psalms were available in Geez, now all of Scripture as well as other church writings were translated into the language. In fact, the earliest surviving copies of several important early Christian writings—*Book of Enoch*, *Book of Jubilees*, and *Ascension of Isaiah*—are known only in Geez.[22]

Recent discoveries have verified what Ethiopian tradition has long affirmed—that the Garima Gospels, three ancient illuminated Geez manuscripts of the four Gospels, were produced around the time of the Nine Saints.[23] Critical Western scholars long contended that the Garima Gospels could be no older than the tenth or eleventh century. Recent radiocarbon dating has shown, however, that they indeed date back to around the year 500, lending credence to stories of the Nine Saints. The Gospels derive their name from Abba Garima, one of the Saints, and are now believed to have been copied out at the very monastery he established.[24] One of the texts is the earliest surviving Gospel book and contains "intact portraits of all four evangelists."[25] The Gospels are major "literary monuments of early Christian Mediterranean culture,"[26] and they eloquently declared Christianity in the Aksumite hinterlands through the second evangelization.

The Mathēma

At its core, Christianity is a universal vision for all peoples, yet up until the fifth century, Romans largely "remained uninterested in mission to populations outside the privileged bounds" of the Roman cultural world.[27] Even if we cannot be certain of all the earliest details, the gospel and the Scriptures were carried under duress into areas that the bearers likely would never have dreamed of going otherwise. Whether through the direct missionary efforts of the exact Nine Saints named in this chapter or through a greater number of unknown monks from the Mediterranean world, all of the Aksumite kingdom was transformed by the Good News. Their story is hardly remembered in the West, partially because it does not fit with the Western civilization narrative to which we have tethered church history and partially because the missionaries themselves usually have been dismissed as heretics (see introduction).

The second evangelization affirms a powerful truth we have seen elsewhere in this book: Orthodoxy was consistently defended and promoted by an imperial power across these early centuries. Clarity of theological language seems necessarily tied to heavy-handed empire and imperial control (see chap. 10). At the same time, a significant driving force behind these missions was the exclusion and exile of certain Christians by these very same empires. It appears that God used central imperial power both to solidify the teachings of the faith and to expand the gospel beyond the empires. Both worked together for good to the glory of God and the advance of the church worldwide.

Celebration of God's sovereignty in history must not be restricted to instances where he uses our preferred means or conforms to our expectations. It can be challenging to recognize how a heavy-handed empire on the one side and Christians persecuting Christians on the other can somehow both be a "God thing." And yet how marvelous are his ways that these too can play a role in his grand design to call all nations unto himself.

Further Reading

Finneran, Niall. "Hermits, Saints, and Snakes: The Archaeology of the Early Egyptian Monastery in Wider Context." *International Journal of African Historical Studies* 45, no. 2 (2012): 247–71.

McKenzie, Judith, and Francis Watson. *The Garima Gospels: Early Illuminated Gospel Books from Ethiopia.* Ioannou Center for Classical and Byzantine Studies, 2016.

Pankhurst, Richard. *The Ethiopians: A History.* Blackwell, 2005.

Phillippson, David W. *Ancient Churches of Ethiopia.* Yale University Press, 2009.

Notes

1. Garth Fowden, *Empire to Commonwealth: Consequences of Monotheism in Late Antiquity* (Princeton University Press, 1993), 12; and Stuart Munro-Hay, *Ethiopia, the Unknown Land: A Cultural and Historical Guide* (I.B. Tauris, 2008), 236.

2. G. W. Bowersock, *The Throne of Adulis: Red Sea Warfare on the Eve of Islam* (Oxford University Press, 2013), 64.

3. Robert O. Collins and James M. Burns, *A History of Sub-Saharan Africa* (Cambridge University Press, 2007), 68.

4. Bowersock, *Throne of Adulis*, 65.

5. David W. Phillippson, "Aksum: An African Civilization in Its World Context," *Proceedings of the British Academy* 111 (2001): 39.

6. Cosmas Indicopleustes, as quoted in Richard Pankhurst, *The Ethiopians: A History* (Blackwell, 2005), 37.

7. Niall Finneran, "Hermits, Saints, and Snakes: The Archaeology of the Early Egyptian Monastery in Wider Context," *International Journal of African Historical Studies* 45, no. 2 (2012): 256; and David W. Phillippson, *Ancient Churches of Ethiopia* (Yale University Press, 2009), 31.

8. Finneran, "Hermits, Saints, and Snakes," 256.

9. Stuart Munro-Hay, *Ethiopia, the Unknown Land: A Cultural and Historical Guide* (I.B. Tauris, 2008), 237.

10. Babu calls them "non-Chalcedonian exiles." See Blessen George Babu, "Cultural Contacts Between Ethiopia and Syria: The Nine Saints of the Ethiopian Tradition and Their Possible Syrian Background," in *Ethiopian Orthodox Christianity in Global Context*, ed. Stanislau Paulau and Martin Temcke (Brill, 2022), 46.

11. Bowersock, *Throne of Adulis*, 76.

12. Babu, "Cultural Contacts Between Ethiopia and Syria," 45.

13. Munro-Hay, *Ethiopia*, 42.

14. Finneran, "Hermits, Saints, and Snakes," 258.

15. Finneran, "Hermits, Saints, and Snakes," 260.

16. Paul B. Henze, *Layers of Time: A History of Ethiopia* (Palgrave MacMillan, 2000), 39.

17. Finneran, "Hermits, Saints, and Snakes," 261.

18. Munro-Hay, *Ethiopia*, 299.

19. Finneran, "Hermits, Saints, and Snakes," 260, 262.

20. Henze, *Layers of Time*, 38.

21. Finneran, "Hermits, Saints, and Snakes," 260.

22. Richard Pankhurst, *The Ethiopians: A History* (Blackwell, 2005), 37.

23. Maria Bulakh, "Early Ge'ez Phonology as Reflected in Abbā Garimā," *Journal of Near Eastern Studies* 83, no. 1 (April 2024): 77.

24. Judith McKenzie and Francis Watson, *The Garima Gospels: Early Illuminated Gospel Books from Ethiopia* (Ioannou Center for Classical and Byzantine Studies, 2016), vii.

25. McKenzie and Watson, *Garima Gospels*, 1.

26. Gianfrancesco Lusini, review of *The Garima Gospels: Early Illuminated Gospel Books from Ethiopia* by Judith McKenzie and Francis Watson, *Rassagna di Studi Etiopici* 3rd series, vol. 1 (2017): 211.

27. Fowden, *Empire to Commonwealth*, 100n7.

18

Pope Gregory the Great Launches Church-Sponsored Missions

(Lombard Italy, 591)

The Background

Protestants, even those who describe themselves as "traditional," sing very few hymns from the first millennium of the church. The few they do sing, such as "Be Thou My Vision," are almost always ancient or medieval poems first introduced as hymns by modern hymnologists striving to connect their churches to early Western Christianity. One hymn, however, stands as a true medieval remnant: "O Christ Our King, Creator, Lord." Martin Luther described this hymn as *optimus hymnus*, "the best hymn of all."[1] It was written by Pope Gregory I (r. 590–604), the greatest of the early medieval bishops of Rome and one of the finest men to ever hold the office. In the second line of his hymn, he addresses Christ as "Savior of all who trust thy Word."

Throughout his papacy, Gregory showed an unprecedented desire to have that Word proclaimed to those outside the faith, which was fueled by an unwavering confidence that it would ultimately bear fruit. He essentially orchestrated "almost the first example since the days of Paul" of church-sponsored missions.[2] It might come as a surprise that the church waited over five hundred years to sponsor deliberate missionary activity. And the first attempt was not exactly a rousing success—at least not initially.

In Gregory's day, Italy was in shambles as barbarians and plague devastated the peninsula. Plague even claimed the life of Gregory's predecessor as bishop. Italy had not seen such chaos in a long time, if ever. Because this time was such a "confused and fragmented" situation, the bishop of Rome by necessity began to take on "enormous secular influence and political power."[3] Gregory, once a wealthy Roman urban prefect and envoy to the Byzantine Empire, initially wanted out of the political fray. He retired to a quiet life of meditation for about five years before being summoned into the priesthood and soon thereafter hailed as bishop of Rome. He was so reluctant to take up the papacy that he even secretly tried to persuade the Byzantine Empire to derail the plans to consecrate him. Once he realized he could not avoid his call, though, he embraced the office and, as it turned out, came to permanently redefine it.

One could say that Gregory was also pressured into missions. The barbarian Lombards arrived in Italy in 568, well after the initial period of barbarian invasion and settlement in western Europe back in the fourth and fifth centuries. The Lombards rapidly seized most of the major cities of northern and central Italy, forcing monks, clergy, and laity alike to flee their onslaught.[4] Rome was surrounded, and the See of Saint Peter, the extensive landholdings of the Roman church, was constantly endangered.

The Lombards were different from previous barbarian invaders. Unlike the earlier Goths and Franks, the Lombards initially showed no interest in protecting let alone preserving classical culture. They also had no central religious identity or unity, unlike the Franks who were Catholic and the Goths who were Arian. The Lombards were a mixed group—a few Catholics, some Arians, and a lot of pagans.[5]

The pope preceding Gregory memorably described the Lombards as "an unspeakable race."[6] Gregory also despised them, using much the same language. In one memorable line he bemoans, "Because of my sins . . . I have been made bishop, not of the Romans, but of the Lombards, whose treaties are broadswords and whose friendship is a punishment."[7] One scholar claims that Gregory "preferred a dead Lombard, even if reformed and converted, enjoying his reward in heaven, to a living one."[8] Yet it was to the Lombards that Gregory—and indeed the Western church itself—would launch the first church-sponsored missions effort in over five hundred years.

The Moment

It all started in the Easter season of 590 with a decree by Authari, king of the Lombards. Authari suddenly forbade Lombards from baptizing any children into the Catholic faith. Gregory, just recently installed as bishop of Rome, called on the other bishops of Italy in January of 591 to use all their persuasive power to bring the Lombards into the "right faith": "Preach to them eternal life without end; so that, when you shall come into the presence of the strict judge, you may be able, in consequence of your solicitude, to show in your persons a shepherd's gain."[9] From this point onward, missions to outsiders became a dominant theme of his papacy.[10]

A few months later, Gregory followed up with a bishop just north of Rome: "It has reached us, with errors being imminent in your city, that is Narni, that mortality has utterly run riot. . . . Saluting your fraternity most urgently, we advise that you should on no account delay by warning and exhortation to the Lombards . . . that they might be converted immediately from paganism and heresy to the true and right catholic faith."[11] He encouraged the bishop to preach so vigorously that the Lombards in his area would either move elsewhere or convert to Catholic Christianity. Gregory had high and optimistic expectations for bishops, which became evident when he later expressed disappointment that the metropolitan bishop of Armenia had not yet converted the Sassanian Persian emperor (although he commended him for trying).[12]

Gregory began formulating a new mission strategy for outsiders that would indelibly shape later missions efforts. He would begin by encouraging bishops to do everything within their power to bring pagan (and Arian) Lombards in their regions into the Christian fold. Preaching the Word of God vigorously and persuasively was paramount. Throughout his ministry, Gregory showed a deep sensitivity to the audience and was eager to instruct priests and bishops on how each could best serve as "an interpreter of the Word of God."[13]

Gregory's experience as a political envoy had trained him in how to influence foreign royal courts and nobility, and as bishop of Rome he aimed to do so by means of the Christian faith. Theodelinda, queen of the Lombards, happened to be a Catholic Christian, but her husband, King Agilulf, was not. Gregory corresponded with her often. While there were undoubtedly political, diplomatic, and even economic factors at play in his many interchanges with Theodelinda (as with all his missionary efforts), there is "ample evidence of careful, pastoral approach to Theodelinda."[14] He wrote to encourage her in the faith, warn against schismatic influences, and plead with her to do everything within her power to share the faith with her husband and her people. At first Gregory considered using force in conversion, but he became convinced that outsiders ought to be persuaded, not compelled.[15] He saw some fruit when Theodelinda and Agilulf had their infant son Adaloald baptized into the Christian faith. Gregory encouraged Theodelinda to keep God's commandments so that Adaloald might grow up to do "good deeds before the eyes of God."[16]

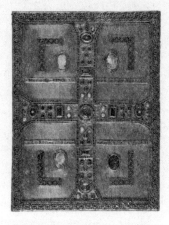

The Gospel Book of Theodelinda, Queen of the Lombards, a gift
from Pope Gregory the Great
© Museum and Treasure of the Cathedral of Monza

Gregory also promoted miracles and stories of divine intervention as means of drawing pagan and heretic Lombards into the
faith. Although he himself "held that conversion was a greater
miracle than raising the dead," he believed in the power of miracles
to convert.[17] Some vivid miracle stories appear in Gregory's own
writings and in a work by medieval biographer Paul the Deacon.
In one account, the souls of monks killed by Lombards return
to sing psalms among their killers with "strong, clear voices."[18]
In another, a mob of heretics is struck blind while attacking a
Catholic church.[19] Despite these promising signs, Christianity did
not make much headway thereafter.

In 594, Gregory raised a telling question in a sermon on Ezekiel:
"How can I . . . see that the city is guarded against the swords
of the enemy, and take precautions lest the people be destroyed
by a sudden attack, and yet at the same time deliver the word
of exhortation fully and effectually for the salvation of souls?"[20]
In the very next year, he sought a more fruitful field and chose
Augustine of Canterbury for what became the famous Gregorian
or Augustinian mission to Britain.[21] It was an almost immediate

success and used some of the same methods and approaches as with the Lombards—preaching, miracles, and political connection. Gregory did not have bishops in place in Britain to work with, so the mission there began by sharing the faith with the pagan King Aethelberht of Kent, whose wife Bertha was a practicing Christian.

The Mathēma

When Gregory died in 604, there was very little to show for his mission efforts among the Lombards. But amidst the frustrations and sometimes bitter disappointments, it seems he never stopped believing that the Lombards would eventually become members of Christ's body.[22] These hopes were realized nearly a century after his death. By the end of the seventh century, the Lombard leaders and most of the people had indeed embraced Christianity. It was a slow and gradual process nonetheless.

Gregory came to see pagans (and heretics) in realms beyond his own in a different light than did most of his contemporaries. His mission methods assumed that the proclamation of the Word of God was the primary means of building the church throughout the world. Whereas most leaders before him (and many thereafter) saw foreign conquest as the preferred means of spreading the Christian faith by forcing outsiders to convert, Gregory instead saw "pastoral opportunity" among outsiders.[23] Ultimately, it was a different sort of conquest that Gregory had in mind as he concluded his *optimus hymnus*:

> Now in the Father's glory high,
> Great Conqu'ror, nevermore to die,
> Us by thy mighty pow'r defend,
> And reign through ages without end.[24]

Gregory's story helps us to appreciate the long history behind certain questions we are still asking today and gives us solid guidance for how to answer them: How can we fulfill the gospel call to share our faith when we feel threatened by—or even loathe—the very people we are called to reach? How do we patiently wait for results, even when they may not come in our lifetime? When is it right to take our mission elsewhere if the fruit seems meager? And how do we discern which tools—political, miraculous, or otherwise—are legitimate in spreading the faith? In the mission work of Gregory, we see some of the earliest attempts to wrestle with these vital questions that remain just as relevant today.

Further Reading

Demacopoulos, George E. *Gregory the Great: Ascetic, Pastor, and the First Man of Rome*. University of Notre Dame Press, 2015.

Fanning, Steven. "Lombard Arianism Reconsidered." *Speculum* 56, no. 2 (1981): 241–58.

Markus, R. A. *Gregory the Great and His World*. Cambridge University Press, 1997.

Richards, Jeffrey. *Consul of God: The Life and Times of Gregory the Great*. Routledge, 1980.

Notes

1. Philip Schaff, *History of the Christian Church*, vol. 7, 5.85 (1910 ed.). Schaff notes that Luther wrongly ascribed this hymn to Ambrose of Milan. The Latin title of the hymn is *Rex Christe, Factor Omnium*.

2. Stephen Neill, *History of Christian Missions*, 2nd ed. (Penguin, 1986), 58. Ian Wood also notes "the insignificance of mission within the Christian tradition before Gregory's pontificate," in "The Mission of Augustine of Canterbury to the English," *Speculum* 69, no. 1 (1994): 14–15.

3. Averil Cameron, *Mediterranean World in Late Antiquity: AD 395–600* (Routledge, 1993), 41.

4. R. A. Markus, *Gregory the Great and His World* (Cambridge University Press, 1997), 99.

5. Steven Fanning, "Lombard Arianism Reconsidered," *Speculum* 56, no. 2 (1981): 241–58.

6. Neil Christie, *The Lombards: The Ancient Longobards* (Wiley-Blackwell, 1999), xviii.

7. Gregory the Great, *Epistles* 1.30. Quotes in this chapter from Gregory's *Epistles* have been translated by the author from the Latin text and informed at points by James Barmby's translation in Nicene and *Post-Nicene Fathers*, Series 2, vol. 12, ed. Philip Schaff and Henry Wace (1895; repr., Hendrickson, 1994).

8. Markus, *Gregory the Great and His World*, 100. See more recent qualifications to such strong claims in George E. Demacopoulos, *Gregory the Great: Ascetic, Pastor, and the First Man of Rome* (University of Notre Dame Press, 2015), 94–95.

9. Gregory the Great, *Epistles* 1.17.

10. R. A. Markus, "Gregory the Great's Europe," *Transactions of the Royal Historical Society* 31 (1981): 24.

11. Gregory the Great, *Epistles* 2.4.

12. Gregory the Great, *Epistles* 1.123; see also *Epistles* 3.67.

13. Claudia Rapp, *Holy Bishops in Late Antiquity: The Nature of Christian Leadership in an Age of Transition* (University of California Press, 2013), 55.

14. Demacopoulos, *Gregory the Great*, 110, 139.

15. Markus, *Gregory the Great*, 82; see Robert Louis Wilken, *Liberty in the Things of God: The Christian Origins of Religious Freedom* (Yale University Press, 2019), 30.

16. Gregory the Great, *Epistles* 14.12.

17. Wood, "Mission of Augustine of Canterbury," 13.

18. Gregory the Great, *Dialogues* 4.22, trans. Odo John Zimmerman (Fathers of the Church, Inc., 1959).

19. Gregory the Great, *Dialogues* 3.29.

20. Gregory the Great, *Homilies on Ezekiel* 1.118, as quoted in Jeffrey Richards, *Consul of God: The Life and Times of Gregory the Great* (Routledge, 1980), 87.

21. Stories of his desire to convert the Angles before his papacy are famous but hard to substantiate.

22. Demacopoulos, *Gregory the Great*, 94.

23. Markus, "Gregory the Great's Europe," 34.

24. Pope Gregory I, "O Christ, Our King, Creator, Lord," trans. Ray Palmer (1858), Hymnary.org, https://hymnary.org/text/o_christ_our_king_creator_lord.

19

The First Holy War and Its Unintended Consequences

(Byzantine and Sassanian Persian Empires, c. 622)

The Background

The Byzantine emperor Heraclius (c. 575–641) was born just as the world was about to end. Or so it seemed at a time when many were engulfed in constant violence amidst "wars and rumors of wars" (Matt. 24:6; Mark 13:7). Seizing political and military power, Heraclius issued a summons to so-called "holy war" against the Sassanian Persian Empire. Those who heeded the call were assured that death in battle would gain them eternal life in paradise—men must go forth and conquer in God's name before the last trumpet sounds. Facing seemingly impossible odds, his forces would wage an apocalyptic holy war against a neighboring superpower empire.

Many of those same things could also be said about his contemporary, Muhammad (c. 570–632). That is hardly coincidental, as we will see. Heraclius's fortunes were fickle, though, and he would cycle between infamous and famous until ultimately he was forgotten.

The tension between the Byzantine (or eastern Roman) and the Sassanian Persian superpowers was long-standing (see chaps. 6, 11, and 13). When hostilities broke out, the Sassanians were usually the initiators of "unprovoked campaigns of aggressive warfare."[1] When the Sassanians began open hostilities once again in 602, the Byzantines were in no condition to repel them, and defense seemed hopeless. The Sassanian shahinshah Khusrau II apparently "had dreams of restoring the whole of the Near East to Persian rule,"[2] something that had not been seen in centuries. He would, for a time, be remarkably successful.

Things were going poorly inside the Byzantine Empire. Heraclius came to power by forcibly deposing the emperor and having his severed head and arm put on display and his corpse dragged through the streets of Constantinople. Yet Heraclius's seizure of the throne did little to halt the empire's decline, at least not for the first decade of his reign. Disaster after disaster struck the Byzantines as the Sassanian forces swept through the eastern provinces, and by 610 they had captured every Roman city east of the Euphrates. They then pushed westward to the sea, advancing to the very doorstep of Constantinople. Along the way they took Antioch and set its churches ablaze.

And yet such disasters paled in comparison to what was to come. In 615, the Sassanians captured Jerusalem itself and slaughtered untold thousands of Christians there. It was what one writer calls a "foretaste of Doomsday."[3] From the Holy City they seized the most revered Christian relic of all, the True Cross—long believed to be the very cross upon which Christ had died—and took it back to Ctesiphon, their capital.

The Sassanians put sympathetic Jews in charge of Jerusalem, then went on to destroy Ephesus and capture Alexandria, Egypt. The Byzantines, surrounded and humbled as never before, begged for peace. Senators in Constantinople put on an extreme display of self-abasement, producing "perhaps the single most humiliating document in all of Roman history."[4] They appeared to have little choice but to wait for the ultimate deathblow.

Apocalypticism was already rampant in the Mediterranean and Near Eastern worlds, but such political and military catastrophes involving Jerusalem brought it to a fever pitch. Surely this was more than a mere episode in the conflict between these two super-powers; no, this must be the "End of Days."[5] The only hope now for the Byzantines was "an imminent, cataclysmic change in the world that would end current oppression or distress and usher in a new era in which the righteous would be vindicated."[6] A new era would rectify all before the final judgment, and as one leading scholar on early Islam notes, "With the Judgment, the righteous would finally be delivered by attaining everlasting salvation in heaven."[7]

The Moment

The Byzantine collapse never came. In what has been described as one of the most "striking and unexpected" political and military reversals in history[8] and "almost miraculous,"[9] Heraclius brought the Byzantines back from the brink. He would be hailed as a David, an Alexander the Great, and a Constantine all rolled into one, a crusading king "come at the imminent end of time."[10]

The odds Heraclius faced were impossibly high. Everything looked hopeless, even well into his reign,[11] as his empire suffered more than a decade of costly setbacks. In desperation, he attempted a gambit in 622, and it paid off shockingly well. Rather than staging a final heroic defense of the city of Constantinople, as might be expected, he suddenly took the war to the heart of the Persian Empire, to the capital Ctesiphon itself.

Heraclius raised the requisite funds through a series of extraordinary austerity measures. He canceled the grain dole at

Constantinople, drastically cut the pay for soldiers and clerics alike, and "borrowed" precious metals from church treasuries. Desperate times called for desperate measures; Heraclius was taking on the forces of the antichrist, after all.[12]

With an unprecedented "religious propaganda drive," Heraclius inspired his soldiers and recruited from among peoples on the Byzantine frontiers and beyond, including Armenians and Arabs.[13] The language of holy war, with its strong apocalyptic tones, was unmistakable. While he did not invent such language per se (it was likely drawn from Armenian Christian national traditions[14]), he was the first to introduce it into the major clash of empires. The seventh- and eighth-century historian Theophanes the Confessor records Heraclius declaring in apocalyptic tones, "The danger is not without recompense; nay, it leads to eternal life. . . . Let us sacrifice ourselves to God for the salvation of our brothers. May we win the crown of martyrdom so that we may be praised in the future and receive our recompense from God."[15] Heraclius's message was able to transcend "the Christological complexities of conciliar theology"[16] and appeal to varied and even competing Christian groups—no easy task. It was a vital and effective unifier for a time, but it came with tremendous and unforeseen cost.

His efforts quickly bore fruit as he found success on the battlefield and began to turn the tide of disaster. But his campaign was not just about victory—there were evils to eradicate and old scores to settle, and Heraclius was remarkably good at doing both. During his campaign to Ctesiphon, he destroyed the "premier fire-temple of the Zoroastrians" in retaliation for the sack of Jerusalem.[17] His crowning achievements were retaking Jerusalem and reclaiming the True Cross from Ctesiphon. Once he restored Byzantine rule throughout the east, he forcibly baptized the Jews of his realm into the Christian faith as revenge for their collaboration with Sassanians at Jerusalem.

On March 21, 630, with great fanfare and ceremony, Heraclius restored the True Cross to Jerusalem. What Byzantine Christian at that time would not have rejoiced at what they saw as the hand of God reestablishing his empire, recovering his Holy City, and restoring the True Cross to its rightful home? It was a crusade and he was a crusader—notice the Latin word *crux* ("cross") at the root of those two words—long before either term existed.

His victory was celebrated by Christians throughout the Byzantine Empire and beyond, from India to Frankish Europe.[18] In the wake of this holy war, surely the dawn of the apocalyptic age of righteousness and justice would soon begin.

The Mathēma

This age of righteousness and justice did not arrive. Heraclius's triumph was remarkably short-lived, and he would soon be forced to watch all his successes evaporate before his eyes. A threat even bigger than the Sassanians suddenly and unexpectedly appeared.[19] Imagine a man who has just scaled a nearly impossible mountain and is standing at the peak while looking down at the valley below with shouts of victory and his arms raised high in triumph . . . only to be suddenly flattened by a meteor from above. That man would be Heraclius. And the meteor? Muhammad's field commander, Khalid ibn al-Walid, who was also driven by an apocalyptic image of the end of the world and a rousing call to holy war. Within just five years of restoring the True Cross to its home in Jerusalem, Heraclius would lose the Holy City and the True Cross to Muslim armies. All the confidence and triumphalism evaporated at once.

As we see throughout this book, apocalyptic fervor has a way of making Christians look presumptuous or naive in retrospect. Sometimes the fallout is far more drastic. Heraclius had coupled an apocalyptic holy war with a political and cultural war. He had baptized his cause du jour, elevating it to the cause of Christ in a holy struggle. He declared his Sassanian enemies were evil and his cause was holy. Those are high stakes indeed.

Inhabitants of the Arabian Peninsula had been well aware of what was going on to their north between Heraclius and the Sassanians. The Qur'an gives its own abbreviated version of the key events:

> The Romans [i.e., Byzantines] have been defeated on the borders of our land [by the Sassanids]. But in a few years after their defeat, they will be victorious. Their fate, in the past as in the future, is in the hands of Allah. Then shall the believers rejoice.[20]

In 622, the same year that Heraclius took the battle into Persian territory, Muhammad fled from Mecca to Medina, an event that came to mark the first year of the Islamic calendar, the year of the Hijra. An unintended consequence of Heraclius's ideology of Christian holy war was that the Muslims "internalized and appropriated" it.[21] Apocalyptic expectations were rampant and ramped up as Muhammad's followers engaged the Mediterranean world with a holy war of their own.[22] A full one-third of the Qur'an itself exudes apocalypse. It is hardly a coincidence that the "doctrine of martyrdom and holy war" emerged in both areas one after another, and Muhammad's movement likely was directly inspired by the propaganda of Heraclius.[23]

Apocalyptic fervor can transform quickly. About five years after Jerusalem fell to the Arab armies, an unknown author circulated a revamped apocalyptic message among Christians: "Therefore, my beloved ones, the end times have arrived. Behold, we see the signs, just as Christ described them for us. Rulers will rise up, one against the other, and affliction will be upon the earth. Nations will rise against nations, and armies will fall upon one another . . . countries will prepare for battle against the Roman Empire."[24] And with the advent of Islam, the Byzantines saw a new apocalyptic foe. It would not be long before the action of one Muslim leader in Jerusalem was proclaimed as "the abomination of desolation standing in the holy place as affirmed by the prophet Daniel!"[25]

"The Antichrist had appeared," no longer a Sassanian shahinshah but a Muslim caliph.[26]

Assuming that our victories are ultimately God's victories carries a serious risk. Despite Christian confidence over the centuries that each moment is the culminating moment in history, so often it has been revealed to be what it is—a mere episode in the history of Our People. History holds important lessons for us that are painful at times but always helpful. Where does the Russia–Ukraine conflict fit into God's timetable of history? In ten years, will the conflict between Hezbollah and Israel still be seen as a signal of the imminent apocalypse? Confidently affirming that "we trust in the name of the LORD" (Ps. 20:7) does not commit God's people to speculating on each moment in history and its place in God's ultimate timetable for humanity.

Further Reading

Fowden, Garth. *Empire to Commonwealth: Consequences of Monotheism in Late Antiquity*. Princeton University Press, 1993.

Howard-Johnston, James. *The Last Great War of Antiquity*. Oxford University Press, 2021.

Sarris, Peter. *Empires of Faith: The Fall of Rome to the Rise of Islam*. Oxford University Press, 2011.

Tesei, Tommaso. "Heraclius' War Propaganda and the Qur'an's Promise of Reward for Dying in Battle." *Studia Islamica* 114, no. 2 (2019): 219–47.

Notes

1. Peter Sarris, *Empires of Faith: The Fall of Rome to the Rise of Islam* (Oxford University Press, 2011), 226.

2. Jonathan Berkey, *The Formation of Islam: Religion and Society in the Near East, 600–1800* (Cambridge University Press, 2003), 50.

3. Maxime Rodinson, *Muhammad* (New Press, 1980), 136.

4. Sarris, *Empires of Faith*, 248.

5. Fred M. Donner, *Muhammad and the Believers: At the Origins of Islam* (Harvard University Press, 2010), 15.

6. Donner, *Muhammad and the Believers*, 15.

7. Donner, *Muhammad and the Believers*, 15–16.

8. Sarris, *Empires of Faith*, 256.

9. Donner, *Muhammad and the Believers*, 25.

10. Garth Fowden, *Empire to Commonwealth: Consequences of Monotheism in Late Antiquity* (Princeton University Press, 1993), 98–99; for the "New Alexander," see Jan Willem Drijvers, "Rome and the Sasanid Empire: Confrontation and Coexistence," in *A Companion to Late Antiquity*, ed. Philip Rousseau (Blackwell), 448; for the "New Constantine," see Samuel N. C. Lieu, "Constantine in Legendary Literature" in *Cambridge Companion to the Age of Constantine*, ed. Noel Lenski (Cambridge University Press, 2006), 316.

11. Sarris, *Empires of Faith*, 24.

12. Sarris, *Empires of Faith*, 258.

13. Sarris, *Empires of Faith*, 250.

14. Sarris, *Empires of Faith*, 251. Heraclius was probably of Armenian descent.

15. Theophanes, *Chronicles*, as quoted in Sarris, *Empires of Faith*, 252–53.

16. Sarris, *Empires of Faith*, 258.

17. Sarris, *Empires of Faith*, 252.

18. Rodinson, *Muhammad*, 266.

19. Walter Kaegi, *Byzantium and the Early Islamic Conquests* (Cambridge University Press, 1997), 75.

20. Qur'an 30:1–3 (trans. N. J. Dawood).

21. Sarris, *Empires of Faith*, 264–65.

22. Stephen J. Shoemaker, *A Prophet Has Appeared: The Rise of Islam Through Christian and Jewish Eyes* (University of California Press, 2021), 28–29.

23. Sarris, *Empires of Faith*, 266.

24. Pseudo-Ephrem the Syrian, "Homily on the End Times" 2–5, in Shoemaker, *A Prophet Has Appeared*, 85.

25. Cyril Mango, *Byzantium: The Empire of the New Rome* (Phoenix Press, 2005), 205.

26. Mango, *Byzantium*, 205.

20

"The Way" Arrives in Tang Dynasty China

(Xi'an, 635)

The Background

Around 1625, an ancient stela was unearthed by workers in Xi'an (Chang'an) in the Chinese province of Shaanxi. The two-ton stone slab was inscribed with almost two thousand Chinese and Syriac characters (mostly Chinese) and told a remarkable and shocking story of Christianity's arrival in China nearly a millennium earlier during the Tang dynasty (618–907). The stela, engraved with the title "A Monument Commemorating the Propagation of Ta-Chin Luminous Religion in the Middle Kingdom," was erected in AD 781 and tells of a certain bishop/monk named Alopen who brought Christianity from the Mediterranean region to China in 635. The discovery quickly drew much attention in scholarly circles, provoking centuries of fascination and lively debate, particularly among Western scholars.[1] Today, no one doubts its authenticity, but most Christians still have never heard of it or the story behind it.

In the late nineteenth century, several ancient Chinese Christian manuscripts were discovered among thousands of others walled up in a secret room in a cave in northwest China. A few of these manuscripts, laying out Christian teaching and revealing further details on this early mission, seem to have been written by Alopen himself. Nothing about this mission, or even about Alopen, survives in any Western source. The stela itself was intentionally buried in the mid-ninth century,[2] likely in an attempt to eradicate any memory of this moment during a time when foreign religions were being persecuted in China. If that was the goal, it certainly succeeded. Without the fortuitous survival and discovery of the buried slab and the hidden texts, we would know virtually nothing about this fascinating moment in the history of Christianity in China, referred to in the texts as *Jingjiao*, "Religion of the Bright Light."

It's possible that Christianity appeared in China before 635, but solid evidence remains elusive. Christianity was well established along parts of the famous Silk Road early on, though, especially toward the West and into Central Asia. Christian merchants along the Silk Road "plied their trades and told their stories."[3] Most were associated with the Church of the East, whose liturgical language was Syriac and whose Christology was in tune with that of Nestorius (see introduction). Alopen's mission in China was part of the expansion of the Church of the East along the Silk Road.

Shortly before Alopen's arrival, the rise of the Tang dynasty had ushered in a dynamic period of Chinese history. When Emperor Tang Taizong (r. 626–645), cofounder and second emperor of the dynasty, came to power, he sent a clear message to his political ministers: They must not be "close-minded" or suspicious of things new or different as the leaders of the previous Sui dynasty had been.[4] The short-lived Sui dynasty (581–618) had managed to reunite China after centuries of fragmentation and conflict but was definitively closed to new or outside ideas. The Tang dynasty began with a spirit of curiosity and openness to outside influences. Emperor Taizong commanded his ministers to "thoroughly investigate" new ideas and then allow them to flourish if deemed acceptable and helpful. Several years before the arrival of Alopen's mission, Emperor Taizong had permitted the construction of a Zoroastrian temple in Chang'an for Persian merchants and their communities. It has been estimated that in Chang'an during the early years of the Tang dynasty there were more than one hundred houses of worship—Buddhist, Taoist, Christian, Zoroastrian, and perhaps even Muslim and Manichaean.[5] It was a rare window of opportunity, and Christianity arrived at the Tang court at a most opportune moment that some would say was outright providential.

The Moment

The Xi'an Stela declares, "When Emperor Taizong began his brilliant reign with glory and farsightedness, there lived in the land of Ta Qin [i.e., eastern Mediterranean region] a man of exceptional virtue [or a bishop] named Alopen. He observed the heavenly signs, took the true scriptures and reached Chang'an in 635."[6]

Alopen and his entourage likely spent months traveling along the Silk Road before reaching the Tang court. Their arrival near Chang'an was anticipated, and Emperor Taizong sent his prime minister, Duke Fang Hiuen-ling, to meet them at the western border of his province and escort them to the palace. The emperor received them warmly, ordered the Christian Scriptures to be translated into Chinese, and even studied them himself. Impressed by the religion's teachings, he proclaimed its rectitude and truth and issued a decree in 638—three years after Alopen's arrival— promoting its dissemination.[7] The decree stated:

> The Greatly-virtuous [i.e., Bishop] Alopen has brought his sacred books and images from that distant part [Ta-Qin], and has presented

them at our chief capital. Having examined the principles of this religion, we find them to be purely excellent and natural; investigating its originating source, we find it has taken its rise from the establishment of important truths; its ritual is free from perplexing expressions, its principles will survive when the framework is forgot; it is beneficial to all creatures; it is advantageous to mankind. Let it be published throughout the Empire, and let proper authorities build a . . . church in the capital.[8]

Other churches and monasteries followed, and the faith can be traced throughout China, in the provinces and regions of Wuchun, Luoyang, Lingwu, Chengdu, Sichuan, Canton, Dunhuang, and Kocho.[9] Alopen was even granted the official title of "Great Master of the Law and Guardian of the Empire."

The gospel message recorded directly on the stela is evocatively memorable:

One Person of our Three-One became incarnate, the illustrious honored one, Messiah, hid away his true majesty and came into the

Early Chinese Christians in a Palm Sunday procession
Public domain

173

world as a man. An angel proclaimed the joy. A virgin bore a sage in Syria. A bright star was the propitious portent, Persians saw its glory and came to offer gifts. He hung, a brilliant sun, which scattered the regions of darkness. The devil's guile, lo, he was utterly cut off. He rowed mercy's barge to go up to the course of light. The souls of men, lo, he has already saved. His mighty task once done, at noonday he ascended to heaven.[10]

Throughout, we can clearly see an emphasis on the Trinity as well as Christ's incarnation, virgin birth, perfect life, struggles with Satan, and ascension.

The emperor's decree contains a potentially telling remark: "The Tao has no eternal name, the Way has no eternal body. The suitable religion will be adapted to the regions and put into effect in such a way that all people will be saved."[11] Such language of adaptation hints at one of the more controversial aspects of Alopen's whole mission effort: contextualization. The Christian manuscripts employ some obvious Taoist, Buddhist, and Confucian idioms. Some of these texts have been described as "Jesus Sutras," and one modern commentator even describes a "Taoist Christianity" expressed in some of them, a sort of dynamic fusion between Christianity and native Chinese belief.[12]

Elements that would appeal to native Chinese sensibilities tend to be emphasized, as would be expected. One manuscript presents the essence of Christianity as serving the heavenly Lord, serving the emperor, and serving one's parents,[13] all of which would fit particularly well with a Confucian ethos of filial piety. The stela itself even commands that a portrait of the emperor be painted on the wall of the monastery.

Equally revealing is what is not emphasized. The crucifixion and resurrection of Christ are downplayed in the stela and the manuscripts, apparently because they would be repugnant in the Chinese context. Perhaps we have here some clues to the demise of Jingjiao in China, for what is Christianity without the offense of the cross?

The Mathēma

Although a number of Emperor Taizong's successors appear to have followed his support and even promotion of Christianity, the moment was not to last. In 845, a little over two centuries after Alopen's mission had arrived, a brutal persecution wiped out much of Christianity in China. The later years of the Tang dynasty and the subsequent Song dynasty were not open to outside ideas and faiths, and the window of opportunity was slammed shut. In 980, the patriarch of Baghdad inquired about Christians in China, and the findings were poignant: "Christianity in China has become extinct. The native Christians have perished and their churches have been destroyed; there was only one Christian left in the land."[14]

Christianity in China was always precariously dependent on the two-edged sword of imperial favor. The emperor gives, the emperor takes away. Here, as in other parts of Asia, Christianity did not have access to real political power.[15] "As in the Sassanian Empire, in China the Church of the East remained dependent on the goodwill of the absolute rulers and was at the mercy of their whims."[16]

Our faith does not give us a clear mandate for which type of relationship with the state is best in the here and now, other than to pray for the peace of the church everywhere. We should not forget that, for all of their obvious drawbacks, state churches elsewhere did indeed help contribute to "precision of theological language."[17] There is no simple formula here. While there were "few dreams of empire among Christians in Asia,"[18] a medieval patriarch of Constantinople would declare, "It is not possible for Christians to have a church and not have an empire. Church and empire have a great unity and community; nor can they be separated from each other."[19] Both modes have had benefits and drawbacks for the church.

The church in China also became disconnected from the church worldwide. Toward the later years of the Tang dynasty, China became cut off and isolated, and any foreign trade, contact, and influence were staunchly discouraged. The church anywhere cannot long exist disconnected from the larger body, the "one, holy, catholic, and apostolic Church."

How should we assess the decline of Christianity here? Some see it as a consequence of syncretism. Although some today embrace such fusions, the results were clearly a mixture that appears to have been detrimental to Christianity in China. Again, can Christianity long exist minus the offense of the cross, even if parts of the message seem more palatable that way?

One recent account claims that the discovery of the Xi'an Stela "changed forever the course of Western perceptions about China and became a cornerstone of modern sinological [Chinese] study as a whole."[20] Yet, this key moment has been ignored or simply forgotten by most Christians. If my nearly quarter century spent teaching a broad cross section of Christian college students and adult Sunday school classes is any indication, this story remains relatively unknown among Christians even still. It's not that there is a lack of information, for talented authors such as Donald Fairbairn, Philip Jenkins, R. L. Wilken, and Samuel Moffett have all written about it and have even published articles in *Christianity Today*. Moreover, this isn't a novel discovery—it's simply that we tend to overlook it.

The burial of the Xi'an Stela, the eradication of Christianity from China, the hiding of manuscripts in a cave—all are clear explanations for why Jingjiao was forgotten in the first place. But scholars have known and debated the stela for centuries now. Judging by the surprise on the faces of people in my Sunday school classes (sometimes the same faces and the same surprise a few years later), it is clear that it is easy to forget such moments when our memory of Christian history remains so tightly tethered to a single Western narrative. Yet the real story of Our People has never been thus contained. A bold mission that bore two hundred years of Christian fruit in China ought to last in our memories. Alopen should take his place alongside the likes of Patrick in Ireland and Amy Carmichael in India.

Further Reading

Baum, Wilhelm, and Dietmer W. Winkler. *The Church of the East: A Concise History*. Routledge, 2003.

Baumer, Christopher. *The Church of the East: An Illustrated History of Assyrian Christianity*. Bloomsbury, 2006.

Gilman, Ian, and Hans-Joachim Klimkeit. *Christians in Asia Before 1500*. University of Michigan Press, 1999.

Keevak, Michael. *The Story of a Stele: China's Nestorian Monument and Its Reception in the West, 1625–1916*. Hong Kong University Press, 2008.

Palmer, Martin. *The Jesus Sutras: Rediscovering the Lost Scrolls of Taoist Christianity*. Ballantine, 2001.

Notes

1. Michael Keevak, *The Story of a Stele: China's Nestorian Monument and Its Reception in the West, 1625–1916* (Hong Kong University Press, 2008).

2. Donald Fairbairn, *The Global Church: The First Eight Centuries* (Zondervan Academic, 2021), 295.

3. David Bundy, "Early Asian and East African Christianities," in *The Cambridge History of Christianity*, ed. A. Casiday and F. W. Norris (Cambridge University Press, 2007), 118.

4. *The Civilization of China*, trans. Dun J. Li Scriber (Scribner, 1975).

5. Martin Palmer, *The Jesus Sutras: Rediscovering the Lost Scrolls of Taoist Christianity* (Ballantine, 2001), 49.

6. Quoted in Christopher Baumer, *The Church of the East: An Illustrated History of Assyrian Christianity* (Bloomsbury, 2006), 181.

7. Baumer, *Church of the East*, 181.

8. Quoted in Baumer, *Church of the East*, 181.

9. Baumer, *Church of the East*, 183.

10. Quoted in Baumer, *Church of the East*, 181.

11. Quoted in Baumer, *Church of the East*, 179.

12. Palmer, *Jesus Sutras*.

13. Baumer, *Church of the East*, 189.

14. Baumer, *Church of the East*, 187.

15. Bundy, "Early Asian and East African Christianities," 118.

16. Baumer, *Church of the East*, 183.

17. Bundy, "Early Asian and East African Christianities," 119.

18. Bundy, "Early Asian and East African Christianities," 144.

19. Barker Ernst, *Social and Political Thought in Byzantium from Justinian I to the Last Paleologus: Passages from Byzantine Writers and Documents* (Oxford University Press, 1961), 194–95.

20. Keevak, *Story of a Stele*, 7.

21

———•———

Christian "Pupil Smiters" of Nubia Save Their Church—Twice

(Sudan, 642 and 652)

The Background

The greatest archaeological recovery program ever launched was in the early 1960s as the nation of Egypt planned construction of the Aswan High Dam.[1] The objective was to excavate, document, and save (and even relocate) as many cultural heritage sites as possible before they disappeared under the dam's reservoir. Discoveries of ancient ruins and monuments from Egypt's age of the pharaohs—as well as news about the massive displacement of Sudanese people—captured the headlines at that time. Many threatened sites in Sudan (ancient Nubia) to the south of Egypt came to light as well. Among the many discoveries archaeologists unearthed were remains of a once thriving Nubian Christianity that had been the central feature of Nubian identity for eight centuries.[2]

Before this, little was known about the long-lost Nubian church. Now it suddenly emerged in vibrant detail. Archaeologists unearthed over one hundred church buildings,[3] including a half dozen cathedrals such as the one at Faras. They also discovered many beautiful frescoes (particularly in the cathedral at Faras), tombs, inscriptions in Greek, Coptic, and Nubian, and abundant material culture that had been buried under the sand for centuries. While the Nubian people and language still exist today, these Christian sites had been long forgotten after they were abandoned when Muslim armies brought an end to Christianity in Nubia in the fourteenth and fifteenth centuries. Many of the remains now lie beneath the 2,030 square miles of Lake Nasser /

Fresco showing Bishop Marianas with the Virgin Mary and Christ, from the cathedral at Faras, Nubia

Photo by LeGabrie, under CC BY-SA 4.0

Lake Nubia and can only be seen in archaeological documentation photos.

Christianity was introduced into Nubia as early as the fourth century, presumably by travelers and traders from Egypt.[4] The earliest Nubian church building discovered during the emergency excavations dates to the middle of the fifth century, but Christianity's progress here was slow until the mid- to late sixth century. At that time, Nubian society at all levels witnessed an "astonishing ideological transformation."[5] The ancient gods were suddenly abandoned, statuary ceased, and notions of divine kingship were discarded. Great ancient temples were remodeled into Christian churches—for example, a thousand-year-old temple became the church at Qasr Ibrim, and a great temple of the goddess Isis on the island of Philae in the Nile became the Church of St. Stephen. Archaeologists also discovered a change in age-old burial practices. Objects that for centuries had been a fundamental part of Nubian funerary culture were no longer placed inside tombs; these now contained only bodies awaiting the resurrection.

Three African kingdoms made up Nubia in the sixth century: Nobatia in the north, Makouria in the center, and Alwa (or Alodia) in the south. Imperial Christian missions came to all of them from the Byzantine Empire in the middle of the sixth century; Makouria had embraced the Christian faith by 542 and Alwa by 580, so by the end of the sixth century essentially all Nubians of all social levels claimed Christianity.[6] As usual, political, diplomatic, and evangelistic missions were inseparably intertwined in the Byzantine efforts,[7] but the tangible fruit of Christianity is unmistakable. Empress Theodora surreptitiously sent Monophysite missionaries here, given her own attraction to their Christology, and Monophysitism (see introduction) would dominate the Nubian kingdoms. Early church writers also describe a competing Chalcedonian mission sent by her husband, Emperor Justinian, but it would ultimately come to nothing, and

181

no "valid literary or archaeological evidence" of Chalcedonian Christianity has ever been found for these early centuries.[8] Christianity, even in heterodox form, served to bind Nubia to the Christian Mediterranean world from the late sixth century onward in a special way. Some of the indicators of this are in language. Greek remained the main language used in the Nubian church over the centuries.[9] The Coptic language used by Monophysites in Egypt was a minority report at best. The royal regalia of the court, church architecture, and official titles also reflect a strong Byzantine influence.

By the early seventh century, the kingdom of Makouria peacefully absorbed the kingdom of Nobatia and ruled northern and central Nubia.[10] Christianity had not been long established, then, when the conquering armies of Islam arrived at the Makourian frontier in 642. They had already taken Palestine, Syria, and Egypt with relative ease by 641, and now they were poised to fold Nubia into the *Dar al-Islam* ("House of Islam"). The Muslim armies clearly did not expect the indomitable resistance they would encounter there. After two unsuccessful and very costly attempts to take Nubia, the Muslims called off the attacks and reached a peace agreement. Not only was the treaty "the only time in the Middle Ages that Muslims exempted a non-Muslim state from conquest,"[11] it was also likely the longest-lasting peace treaty in all of recorded history and allowed Nubian Christianity to flourish for well over five hundred more years.

The Moments

Over the millennia, Nubian archers had earned a reputation as peerless marksmen, and the ancient Egyptians called Nubia *Ta-Seti*, "Land of the Bow." The Muslim invaders who unsuccessfully attacked them in the mid-seventh century would come to know them as *rumat al-hadaq*, "pupil smiters," for their deadly aim.

The Muslim armies came against Dongola, the capital of Makouria, twice in one decade, first in 642 and then in 652. Written accounts of the battles as recorded by later Muslim chroniclers show that "the Arabs' abrupt stop was caused solely and exclusively by the superb military resistance of the Christian Nubians," or the "Nubian Dam," as one recent historian has called it.[12] One of these Muslim chronicles includes a first-person account of the First Battle of Dongola in 642:

> I went personally to Nubia twice during the rule of [caliph] Umar ibn al-Khattab, and I saw one of them [the Nubians] saying to a Muslim, "Where would you like me to place my arrow in you," and when the Muslim replied, "in such a place," he would not miss. They were many in shooting arrows and their arrows did not fall to the ground. One day they came out against us and formed a line; we wanted to use swords, but we were not able to, and they shot at us and put out eyes to the number of one hundred and fifty.[13]

Another account captures the long-term memory:

> When the Muslims conquered Egypt, [general] Amr ibn al-As sent to the villages which surround it cavalry to overcome them. . . . The cavalry entered the land of Nubia like the summer campaigns against the Greeks [i.e., Byzantines]. The Muslims found that the Nubians fought strongly, and they met showers of arrows until the majority were wounded and returned with many wounded and blinded eyes. So the Nubians were called "the pupil smiters."[14]

After the First Battle of Dongola, a tense truce was violated by both sides, and in 652 the Muslim armies renewed hostilities in what would be called the Second Battle of Dongola. The Muslim general Abd Allah ibn Saʿd Abi Sarh attacked with heavy cavalry and trebuchets.[15] The siege engines damaged some buildings, including a church, but the Muslim cavalry ultimately could not prevail against the Nubian bowmen in the field and along the walls. Abd Allah ibn Saʿd Abi Sarh made a truce with the Nubians once he tired of trying to defeat them.[16] The tenth-century historian Ahmad al-Kufi said that "the Muslims had never suffered a loss like the one they had in Nubia."[17] Some much later Muslim sources would try to downplay the general Nubian victory with convenient revisionism, saying they never *really* wanted the territory to begin with, but the pupil smiters were never forgotten.

There was no precedent or parallel in Islamic history for the peace treaty, known as the *baqt*, that followed the Second Battle of Dongola.[18] Combining diplomatic, political, and economic elements, it promised there would be no Muslim invasions and no forced conversion to Islam in exchange for an annual shipment of enslaved peoples from Nubia. The latter was not consistently enforced. However, wheat, wine, textiles, and horses were exchanged in gifts between the sovereign states.[19] The Nubians, for their part, acknowledged Islamic rule in Egypt as the legitimate power with which they had to deal.[20] The *baqt* was in force for over six hundred years, with only a few interruptions through those years. The Nubian Christian archers had managed to defeat Allah's holy warriors and keep them out of Nubia for centuries, allowing a distinctive Christian culture to flourish peacefully on the very frontiers of the *Dar al-Islam*.

The Mathēma

Sudan has been staunchly Muslim since it came permanently into the hands of Arab invaders from the north in the fifteenth century. Christianity, which for centuries was the very core of Nubian culture and identity, disappeared quickly under Muslim rule. Islam had already been making headway in Nubia through merchants and missionaries by this time. After the conquest, the Christian churches were swiftly abandoned and disappeared under the sand, forgotten, and Islam has shaped the identity of the Sudanese/ Nubian peoples to this day.

But for eight hundred years or so, a Christian church flourished in this African kingdom and was able to live at peace here. Over time, Christian Nubia would lose its fierce reputation for being pupil smiters, and its people would instead become "one of the world's most peaceful peoples."[21] They maintained beautiful churches and painted frescoes and produced timeless liturgical prayers and texts.

There has been much debate among Our People about the legitimacy of war and violence by Christians over the centuries. Should Christians ever take up arms or defend themselves? If so, under what circumstances? How would taking up arms fit with Scriptures that seem to advocate nonviolence for Christians, such as Jesus's command to turn the other cheek (Matt. 5:39; Luke 6:29)? These are and will continue to be lively and helpful discussions among Christians.

It's important to note that our knowledge of these key moments comes from Muslim sources recounting the battles. We do not learn of the pupil smiters from any Nubian voices; there is no triumphalist Nubian description or self-glorification. Glorification of violence has no place among Christians. The great Eastern Church writer Basil of Caesarea once warned God's people against praise heaped up for "the magnitude of slaughter."[22] There is never a time to glorify the mere act of violence or killing. Basil notes elsewhere, though, that it is possible to maintain a "perfect love of God" even while serving in the military.[23]

If Our People in Nubia had not defended their homeland, they likely never would have experienced those centuries of thriving. A minority might have remained Christian, as in Egypt, but likely not many. Ultimately, God's people do not place their trust in bows or chariots or horses (Ps. 20:7). As we look back, we can be grateful that in his sovereignty God used the famous Nubian pupil smiters to preserve and defend his people.

Further Reading

Burstein, Stanley. *Ancient African Civilizations: Kush and Axum*. Markus Wienar, 2009.

Faraji, Salim. *The Roots of Nubian Christianity Uncovered: The Triumph of the Last Pharaoh*. Africa World Press, 2012.

Ruffini, Giovanni. *Medieval Nubia: A Social and Economic History*. Oxford University Press, 2012.

Welsby, Derek A. *The Medieval Kingdoms of Nubia: Pagans, Christians and Muslims Along the Middle Nile*. British Museum Press, 2002.

Notes

1. "Victory in Nubia: The Greatest Archaeological Rescue Operation of All Time," *UNESCO Courier*, February/March 1980.

2. P. L. Shinnie, "Christian Nubia," in *The Cambridge History of Africa*, vol. 2, ed. J. D. Fage (Cambridge University Press, 1978), 557.

3. Stanley M. Burstein, "When Greek Was an African Language: The Role of Greek Culture in Ancient and Medieval Nubia," *Journal of World History* 19, no. 1 (2008): 55.

4. Giovanni R. Ruffini, *Medieval Nubia: A Social and Economic History* (Oxford University Press, 2012), 5–6.

5. Robert O. Collins and James M. Burns, *A History of Sub-Saharan Africa* (Cambridge University Press, 2007), 72.

6. L. P. Kirwan, "The Birth of Christian Nubia: Some Archaeological Problems," *Rivista degli studi orientali* 48 (1984): 119–34; see 128–29 for the various missions.

7. Donald Fairbairn, *The Global Church: The First Eight Centuries* (Zondervan, 2021), 284.

8. Kirwan, "Birth of Christian Nubia," 127.

9. Burstein, "When Greek Was an African Language."

10. Ruffini, *Medieval Nubia*, 5–6.

11. Burstein, "When Greek Was an African Language," 55.

12. David Ayalon, "The Spread of Islam and the Nubian Dam," in *The Nile: Histories, Cultures, Myths*, ed. Hagai Erlikh and I. Gershoni (Lynne Rienner Publishers, 1999), 17–28.

13. Al-Baladhuri, as quoted in Shinnie, "Christian Nubia," 565.

14. Quoted in Shinnie, "Christian Nubia," 564.

15. Jay Spaulding, "Medieval Nubia and the Islamic World: A Reconsideration of the Baqt Treaty," *The International Journal of African Historical Studies* 28, no. 3 (1995): 582.

16. Spaulding, "Medieval Nubia," 582.

17. Spaulding, "Medieval Nubia," 582.

18. William J. Adams, "Medieval Nubia," *Expedition Magazine* 35, no. 2 (July 1993).

19. Derek A. Welsby, *The Medieval Kingdoms of Nubia: Pagans, Christians, and Muslims Along the Nile* (British Museum Press, 2002), 70.

20. Spaulding, "Medieval Nubia," 585.

21. Adams, "Medieval Nubia," 5.

22. Basil of Caesarea, *Homily 21*, on Psalm 61:4.

23. Basil of Caesarea, *Letter 106*.

22

A Matter of Matter: John of Damascus Defends Icons

(Umayyad Islamic Empire, c. 730)

The Background

The two earliest Islamic architectural monuments are the Dome of the Rock in Jerusalem (completed in 691–692) and the Great Mosque of Damascus (completed in 715). Both were constructed on land that had been passed between the Christian Byzantine and Sassanian Persian Empires (see chaps. 6, 11, and 13) before coming into Muslim hands. Each heralded the arrival of a decidedly new era in an old world. Blending emerging Muslim architectural and artistic styles with those of the two older empires, these two monuments still stand today as symbols and reminders of the dynamic worlds of late antiquity.

The Umayyad dynasty of Islam, which produced these two monuments, was arguably the last of the ancient empires. With it, we see strong and influential institutions coming together in a confident blend of the various worlds it incorporated. For the first generation of their rule, the Umayyads borrowed much from their Byzantine and Sassanian predecessors. Greek continued as the language of government in the western part of their realm, and coinage and many administrative traditions endured and were incorporated to remarkable degrees. By the late seventh century, a stronger and more assertive Islamic identity was emerging, symbolized by the Great Mosque and the Dome of the Rock. The majority of the inhabitants in the western part of their realm, however, remained Christians by profession. The Muslims considered them *dhimmi* ("protected people") or *ahl al-kitab* ("People of the Book").[1]

One of the greatest Christian theologians, poets, and hymn writers in the history of Our People, commonly referred to as John of Damascus, lived in or near Damascus and Jerusalem under the Umayyads at this key moment and witnessed the construction of both these monuments. He understood that they heralded a self-confident Islamic rule that was there to stay and to which he was now subject. His life and works bear eloquent testimony to flourishing and faithful witness in such changing and unprecedented times. Around the same time, Christians (and Muslims, it turns out) were experiencing deep theological and liturgical conflicts over visual art and worship, specifically regarding the use of icons.

The Moment

The given name of John of Damascus was Yuhana ibn Mansur ibn Sarjun. For our purposes, I will refer to him by his Arabic name Yuhana.

Yuhana was born in Damascus, Syria, into a prominent Arab Christian family that had a history of government service to three empires over three generations. His Christian grandfather had

189

been an administrator under the Byzantines and then the Sassanian Persians, and it's believed that he was the very official who surrendered Damascus (and all Syria with it) to its Muslim conquerors in 635. Yuhana's Christian father followed in the family tradition, serving as the chief financial administrator under the Umayyad Empire. Living in Damascus, the capital of that empire, Yuhana also served for many years as a high-level financial administrator under a succession of Muslim rulers called caliphs.

Somewhere between the ages of forty and fifty, Yuhana retired from public life and went to live in a Christian monastery near Jerusalem, where he would become known as the greatest poet and one of the finest theologians in the Eastern Christian tradition. His hymns still appear in many church hymnals, and two of them in particular, "Come, Ye Faithful, Raise the Strain" and "The Day of Resurrection," are favorite Easter hymns across many Christian communions. He was also a priest and a philosopher, and he even wrote about the natural sciences. Although he wrote in Greek, the Christian generation immediately following him would write in Arabic.[2]

Yuhana is also well-known for his ardent defense of icons at a time when they were deeply controversial in the Byzantine Empire just across the frontier to his west. In 726, amidst tension with the Umayyad Muslims, the Byzantine emperor Leo III suddenly rejected the veneration of images, which at the time were a regular part of Christian worship. Icons of Christ and the saints were then destroyed throughout the Byzantine Empire. Our English word *iconoclasm*, which literally refers to dashing or breaking icons and images, hearkens back to this moment in history. Groups of Christians, many of them monks, came to the defense of icons and were known as *iconodules*—that is, venerators of icons. Iconoclasm won that day, though, and for a time iconodules were suppressed in and throughout the Byzantine Empire.

Safely outside the Byzantine Empire and under Umayyad Muslim rule, Yuhana mounted a spirited defense of icons. While

Byzantine leaders were eager to enforce doctrinal uniformity in their own realm, the Muslim caliph did not perceive Christian theological divergence as a threat. This simple fact helps us understand why Christian groups such as Monophysites and Nestorians (see introduction) flourished within the Muslim realm despite being suppressed by the Byzantines. Yuhana thus enjoyed freedom to compose and proclaim his oppositional views under comparatively benign—to Christians like him anyway—Muslim leaders. His treatises and orations, such as "In Defense of Icons," made their way into the Byzantine Empire. Not long after his death, Yuhana's views were officially condemned by a church council in 754. Such was the opposition against him by fellow Christians that Yuhana himself, in fact, was denounced posthumously as "Saracen-minded" (*Saracen* was a term used at that time to denote Arab Muslim).

From the time he composed them, Yuhana's works would be among the most compelling defenses for icons ever presented. He began by establishing a distinction between worship (*latreia*) and relative honor (*schetike time*). Christians should never *worship* representations, he maintained, but should give *relative honor* to the images for what they represent—that is, God's good creation/ matter. As he so unambiguously says regarding the honor and veneration of images, "Do not despise matter, for it is not despicable. Nothing is [to be despised] which God has made."[3] In responding to the common iconoclastic argument that icons violate the second commandment, Yuhana says, "I do not worship matter, I worship the God of matter, who became matter for my sake, and deigned to inhabit matter, who worked out my salvation through matter. I will not cease from honouring that matter which works my salvation."[4] Icons were a vivid reminder that the Word indeed "became flesh and dwelt among us" (John 1:14).

Many have noted the apparent irony that Yuhana mounted his defense of icons safely under the rule of an Umayyad Muslim caliph who at this exact moment was waging his own campaign against the use of images by Muslims. The caliph did not care about Christian debates or variations from Chalcedonian orthodoxy. Use of images actually was common in the earliest Islamic art, as can still be seen in Umayyad buildings such as a famous palace at Qusayr Amra, Jordan. Although images were not explicitly forbidden in the Qur'an itself, there was a growing resistance to them that coincided with the iconoclastic movements in the Byzantine realm. Christians on both sides of the Byzantine–Umayyad frontier had been coming under accusations of idolatry, particularly from Jewish groups, who had long forbidden use of images as a violation of the second commandment. The distinct iconoclasms among Christians and Muslims can be interpreted as a response to Jewish challenges,[5] especially in areas surrounding the Levant and on the borderlands between realms.

Living under Muslim rule, Yuhana would be one of the first Christian writers to explore Islam and its beliefs as a scholar and theologian, yet he did not compromise his own Christian faith. His critique of Islam in "Heresy of the Ishmaelites" is clear and direct. It's worth noting that Yuhana treated the earliest Islamic teachings more as a heresy than a new religion outright. His sensitive treatment of Islam prompted some Byzantines to accuse him of being too soft toward the Saracens. In 754, shortly after his death, the Council of Constantinople used this argument to denounce his teachings about icons.

The Mathēma

In the year 787, several decades after Yuhana's death, an ecumenical church council called by the Byzantine empress Irene restored image veneration and relative honor to icons. Yuhana's writings, already well-known in the Byzantine Empire, were readily invoked by those in the council's majority. This was the Seventh (and final) Ecumenical Council, and like the First Ecumenical Council of 325, it too was held at Nicaea. The council decreed that icons were necessary for legitimate worship within the church. While there would later be one more brief moment of highly politicized iconoclasm in the Byzantine Empire, the Eastern Orthodox and Catholic Churches both follow the Seventh Ecumenical Council's directive to this day.

Today, even Christian communities that have not embraced Yuhana's teachings on icons often still sing his words at Easter time. Composed at the monastery where he lived near Jerusalem, Yuhana's hymn still encourages Christians worldwide, "Come, ye faithful, raise the strain, of triumphant gladness; God hath brought his Israel into joy from sadness." The Church, the Israel of God, has been redeemed from sin just as Israel of old was redeemed from slavery. Yuhana knew where the believer's eternal hope lies. He was not obsessed with restoring the Byzantine Christian Empire of his fathers in Syria. He did not waste his brief moment on earth raging against the end of Byzantine Christian rule in Jerusalem and Damascus or longing (as far as we know) for the restoration of political rule to Christians in Syria and surrounding lands. Indeed, his famous Easter song celebrates the spiritual and eternal reality of "glad Jerusalem." Setting a solid example for Christians living in changing times everywhere, and with his eyes fixed firmly on eternity, Yuhana continues to encourage believers to celebrate "[Christ's] own peace, which evermore passeth human knowing" and is the true source of the Christian's triumphant gladness.

Further Reading

Donner, Fred M. *Muhammad and the Believers: At the Origins of Islam.* Harvard University Press, 2010.

Kaegi, Walter E. "John of Damascus." In *Oxford Dictionary of Byzantium.* Oxford University Press, 1991.

Karlin-Hayter, Patricia. "Iconoclasm." In *Oxford History of Byzantium.* Edited by Cyril Mango. Oxford University Press, 2002.

Noble, Thomas F. X. "John Damascene and the History of the Iconoclastic Controversy." In *Religion, Culture, and Society in the Early Middle Ages: Studies in Honor of Richard E. Sullivan.* Medieval Institute Publications, 1987.

Notes

1. Fred M. Donner, *Muhammad and the Believers: At the Origins of Islam* (Harvard University Press, 2010), chaps. 4 and 5.

2. Garth Fowden, *Quṣayr ʿAmra: Art and the Umayyad Elite in Late Antique Syria* (University of California Press, 2004), 268–69.

3. John of Damascus, *Treatise on Images*, trans. Mary H. Allies (Thomas Baker, 1898), 17.

4. John of Damascus, *Treatise on Images*, 16–17.

5. Patricia Karlin-Hayter, "Iconoclasm," in *Oxford History of Byzantium*, ed. Cyril Mango (Oxford University Press, 2002), 154–55.

23

"We Render Not Evil for Evil": The Death of Boniface

(Frisia, Northern Europe, 754)

The Background

Sensational stories from history can capture our attention, even if they are not always based in historical fact. One such story is about Boniface, "the apostle to the Germans," and his famous showdown at the mighty Oak of Thor. The story goes that Boniface, a bold and intrepid missionary, literally used an axe to strike straight at the heart of pagan worship. He marched through the midst of a hostile tribe, went right up to their huge sacred tree, and began chopping. After just a few blows, "the oak's vast bulk, driven by a divine blast from above, crashed to the ground" and divided into four equal pieces. This wowed the local pagans, who were immediately converted to Christianity and used the wood to build a small chapel on the site.[1]

The tale seems to be enjoying a renaissance these days among a certain type of culture warrior posting memes on the internet of Boniface with an axe and a tree. The problem with the repeated (and often exclusive) telling of this exciting story is not that it isn't true—most of the basic facts would hold up to historical scrutiny. Rather, it's that this action was quite out of character for Boniface. It should hardly stand as *the* story to memorialize this fascinating man who wore many hats—scholar, missionary, monk, bishop—and would ultimately die a martyr. He likely would be appalled to know that in some quarters he has become a symbol for so-called Christian culture warriors committing brazen, violent acts.

Boniface's true character is on display much more clearly in the less sensational stories about him, beginning with his early years. His biographer, Willibald, tells how from a very young age Boniface, whose given name was Wynfrith, loved books and longed to "join himself to the sacred study of letters," going so far as to oppose his father when he refused to let him pursue an intellectual life.[2] When Wynfrith was five years old, his family hosted some missionary monks, and he was inspired then and there to become a missionary. It might seem a most unlikely pairing—the collection and intense study of books and mission work in remote pagan hinterlands—but that combination would come to define him. His method was careful, slow, and steady, even in the face of frustration and setbacks. He knew what it meant to see no immediate results—or even no results at all.

Historians today rightly reject the term "Dark Ages" for the whole of the Middle Ages. Yet Boniface lived at a particularly bleak moment. Literacy had not suddenly collapsed with the fall of the Roman Empire centuries earlier. Rather, it had limped along in most areas that had once been part of the empire. But during Boniface's lifetime, literacy and book availability on the European continent plunged to their lowest point in more than five hundred years.[3] Only after Boniface was martyred would literacy rebound to previous levels thanks to the efforts of the Carolingian Frankish emperor Charlemagne (see chap. 24).

Though Wynfrith was born in Britain, he dedicated much of his life to ministering on the pagan fringes of the Continent. His passion was for Frisia, a wild region of what is now the Netherlands. The area was outside the bounds of military and political protection from the Frankish kingdom to its south and east. Prior to Wynfrith's mission, several Benedictine missionary monks from Britain had attempted to share the gospel in Frisia, but their efforts had come to little. Hearing of Wynfrith's desires, Pope Gregory II gave him the name Boniface ("doer of good") and commissioned him to preach the gospel to the pagans of northern Europe, which is why he is known as the apostle to the Germans.

Everywhere Boniface went, no matter how wild or remote, he carried his books. He was often found with books of Scripture, writings and sermons of the church fathers, and historical works. And he rejoiced to receive each new volume, as when he wrote to one archbishop, "When I received your gifts and books I lifted up my hands and gave thanks to the Almighty God."[4]

The Moment

Boniface's mission efforts to Frisia saw little fruit over the decades. He also ministered elsewhere on the Continent, in pagan lands as well as in areas of notable pagan/Christian syncretism. He saw more tangible results in these areas, but his desire to see the Frisians brought to Christ never diminished. He was nearly eighty years old when he embarked on his final mission trip. He saw some initial success with this effort, and he and a group of fifty or so missionary monks traveling with him were preparing to baptize a group of new Frisian converts in the Boorne River.

Though violence was not especially common in that specific place at that time, it was always a possibility. Boniface had enjoyed Frankish political support for his more successful mission projects elsewhere, but he was committed to bringing the gospel to the pagan Frisians no matter the cost, even if it risked being outside that protection. As his entourage was setting out for Frisia, Boniface suspected that his death might be approaching, so he instructed, "Provide by thy most prudent counsel everything which must be joined to our use in this our journey; but also lay in the chest of my books a linen cloth, wherein my decrepit body may be wrapped."[5]

The missionaries carried with them chests full of books. Books had always been part of Boniface's mission into remote regions. These were not for distribution, as each was a rare and expensive treasure, but were part of preparing for and carrying out gospel ministry through studying, preaching, teaching, and instructing in the faith. Remarkably, at least three of these books still survive today. They have been directly connected to Boniface himself, and it's likely he had them with him at the moment of his death.[6] The first of these books, the Victor Codex, is a copy of the New Testament from distant southern Italy and contains marginal annotations in Boniface's own handwriting. The second book, known as the Ragyndrudis Codex, is an early-eighth-century copy of a work by the Spanish writer Isidore of Seville that was bound together with other pieces. We will encounter this book again shortly. The third book, the Cadmug Gospels, is a copy of the Gospels reproduced by an Irish monk.

On Wednesday, June 5, 754, as "the morning light was breaking after the rising of the sun," a large group of brigands bent on violence suddenly appeared at Boniface's encampment alongside the Boorne River. "Armed with spears and shields," they "rushed with glittering weapons into the camp." Some of Boniface's party reached for their weapons, but immediately "he rebuked them: 'Stop fighting, lads! Give up the battle! For we are taught by the trusty witness of Scripture, that we render not evil for evil, but contrariwise good for evil.'"[7] The Frisian marauders proceeded to massacre Boniface, all fifty of the missionaries, and the new Frisian converts, strewing their bodies along the river.

The "exultant throng of heathens" then plundered the missionaries' camp and made off with the chests of books, thinking they were treasure. Later, "having broken open the boxes of books, they found volumes instead of gold, and for silver, leaves of divine learning."[8] Since they were bent on looting treasure, they simply flung the books all around in frustrated disappointment. "The books were found a long time after, sound and unharmed, and returned by the several discoverers to the house [cathedral at Fulda] in which even unto this day they are of use for the salvation of souls."[9] Books, of course, can outlive their owners, and long after Boniface's death, his ministry could continue through the witness of the volumes he carried.

Today, a museum in Fulda, Germany, holds Boniface's Ragyndrudis Codex. The book bears what appear to be deep, violent cuts. This seems to support an early eyewitness account from an elderly woman who claimed Boniface held up this volume as a shield while the brigands slashed at him with their swords.[10] It was also a common practice among pagan tribes in that region to desecrate an object by nailing it to a tree, and one recent study of the codex has revealed there is a nail hole through it.

The Ragyndrudis Codex
© 2025, FacsimileFinder.com

The Mathēma

Christianity is and always has been a religion "of the book"—first and foremost the Scriptures, but also sermons, letters, histories, and treatises. This was true even here at one of Europe's darkest moments. Great signs and wonders can never sustain faith on their own. Boniface painstakingly amassed books at a time when they were in extremely short supply because he was convinced that the written word is vital to both proclaimer and receiver of the gospel message. He once wrote that the messenger going "to enlighten the dark corners of the Germanic peoples" would himself "fall into deadly snares if he had not the Word of God as a lamp unto his feet and a light upon his path."[11]

Boniface was defined by his gentle, learned, patient, and peaceful presentation of the gospel. His outright refusal to fight back when attacked has been an inspiration to those who reject using violence for the cause of the faith, even in self-defense. It provides a direct contrast, for example, with the "pupil smiters" of Nubia (see chap. 21), and shows that Christians have never had one definitive response to such issues.

It would be unambiguously inspiring to end this chapter with the death of Boniface. And it would be encouraging to simply conclude with the continuing influence of the texts he gathered for sharing the gospel with ensuing generations. But the story continues. The famous English historian Hugh Trevor-Roper noted that "by the eighth century, the Englishman Boniface had converted the Germans by preaching to them, and Charlemagne had converted the Saxons by knocking them on the head."[12] While that may be a lively juxtaposition, the impact of Boniface's peaceful mission was dulled by what happened next. Violence broke out from Christians wanting to avenge his death, and it was only a matter of days before the Frisians who had attacked Boniface were killed. "The Christians took as spoil the wives and little ones of the superstitious folk, their menservants also and their maidservants, and returned to their own land."[13] While

Christians through time have rightly treasured and celebrated the stories of the martyrs, it would be dishonest to ignore ignoble tales of Christian violence. History cannot be mere hagiography.

Not long after Boniface died, the Frisians did come into the Christian fold. Boniface's own scholarship came to very little. He tried his hand at poetry and even wrote a book on grammar, yet none of his own writings had any lasting influence. He had the most impact through his mission work and in gathering the written works of others, bringing the "best of English evangelism and monastic scholarship to continental Europe."[14] These were absolutely necessary to the advance of Christianity in his day and beyond. He died boldly doing what he was called to do, and he did so with his books on hand. Perhaps a lesson we can learn from Boniface is that the right weapon to use against an unbelieving world may be not a sword but a book. The circumstances of Boniface's death continue to speak volumes about his life.

Further Reading

Aaij, Michael. "Boniface's Booklife: How the Ragyndrudis Codex Became a *Vita Bonifatii*." *The Heroic Age: A Journal of Early Medieval Northwest Europe* 10 (May 2007). https://jemne.org/issues/10/aaij.html.

Aaij, Michael, and Shannon Goodlove, eds. *A Companion to Boniface*. Brill, 2020.

Geary, Patrick. *Before France and Germany: The Creation and Transformation of the Merovingian World*. Oxford University Press, 1988.

McKitterick, Rosamond. "Anglo-Saxon Missionaries in Germany: Reflections on the Manuscript Evidence." *Transactions of the Cambridge Bibliographic Society* 9, no. 4 (1989): 291–329.

Notes

1. Willibald, *The Life of Saint Boniface*, trans. George W. Robinson (Harvard University Press, 1916), 64.

2. Willibald, *Life of Saint Boniface*, 29.

3. Patrick Geary, *Before France and Germany: The Creation and Transformation of the Merovingian World* (Oxford University Press, 1988), 182, 213.

4. Letter 59, *The Letters of Saint Boniface*, trans. Ephraim Emerton (Columbia University Press, 1940), 132.

5. Willibald, *Life of Saint Boniface*, 79.

6. Rosamond McKitterick, "Anglo-Saxon Missionaries in Germany: Reflections on the Manuscript Evidence," *Transaction of the Cambridge Bibliographic Society* 9, no. 4 (1989): 291–329.

7. Willibald, *Life of Saint Boniface*, 82–83.

8. Willibald, *Life of Saint Boniface*, 85.

9. Willibald, *Life of Saint Boniface*, 86.

10. McKitterick, "Anglo-Saxon Missionaries," 291; and Michel Aaij, "Boniface's Booklife: How the Ragyndrudis Codex Came to be a *Vita Bonifatii*," *The Heroic Age: A Journal of Early Medieval Northwest Europe* 10 (May 2007).

11. Letter 22, *Letters of Saint Boniface*, 61.

12. Hugh Trevor-Roper, *The Rise of Christian Europe* (Thames & Hudson, 1965), 120.

13. Willibald, *Life of Saint Boniface*, 8; Aaij, "Boniface's Booklife," 5.

14. Clifford R. Backman, *The Worlds of Medieval Europe* (Oxford University Press, 2003), 112.

24

Charlemagne and the Return of the Open Book to Europe

(Carolingian Frankish Kingdom, 789)

The Background

Imagine two large stacks of books set side by side. The first stack consists of all surviving Latin manuscripts and major text fragments from the entirety of the ancient and the early medieval worlds up to the year 800. The second stack includes surviving Latin manuscripts from the ninth century alone. The first pile would contain fewer than two thousand texts; the second would contain well over seven thousand.[1] This illustrates a very real story of crisis and survival of Christian western Europe in the late eighth century.

Between the late fifth century and the middle of the eighth, large parts of what are now France and Germany were ruled by the Merovingian Frankish dynasty (c. 481–751). The later Merovingian kings are infamously (and unfairly) known as "Do-Nothing

Kings."[2] They faced serious challenges on many fronts, a veritable cocktail of disasters. Fierce internal rivalries fragmented their realm, the Lombards threatened from the south and east, and the Muslims, newcomers to the western European scene, had crossed over the Pyrenees Mountains from Spain and penetrated deeply and destructively into Frankish territory.

Alongside these obvious political and military challenges loomed a subtle threat that was no less sinister. Literacy and book production—of all books, including Scripture—had plunged to an all-time low for the medieval period, threatening the spiritual and intellectual life of Christian western Europe at its core. Literacy rates fell to far below 10 percent, which had been the high-water mark for the Roman Empire; some suggest that literacy had fallen as low as 1 percent. By the late Merovingian period, it could not be safely assumed that bishops and archbishops, let alone parish priests, were able to read or write.[3] Many of them could not, and the written word no longer held a central place in western Europe. The church was in serious trouble, and only a few recognized it.

With the help of the bishop of Rome, one dynamic Frankish family, the Carolingians, deposed the last king of the Merovingian dynasty in 751 and began to tackle the crises. Charlemagne (aka Charles the Great), the most famous and influential of the Carolingian kings, initiated reforms that ended the political threats while halting and even reversing the devastating cultural slide. The second stack of books from the illustration at the outset of this chapter eloquently attests to the direct and tangible results of his efforts.

While some scholars quibble over the actual terminology, many leading historians today continue to hail the "Carolingian Renaissance" of the ninth century, which brought literacy rates back up to the level of the Roman Empire and restored book production, putting the written word at the very center of Carolingian Frankish life. More than a few leading medievalists continue to see this as one of the most important educational and cultural reform moments in Western history, a period in which "culture and particularly education were revived for the express purpose of reforming or rather rectifying the way the church worked and the way the Christian people lived."[4]

The Moment

Western Europeans by and large professed Christianity at this time. At its core, Christianity is a religion of the Book, and Christians are a people of the Book. In other words, "A Christian society cannot be a wholly illiterate society. It has already made a crucial step towards being literate in its acknowledgement of the written law of God and Christ's teaching."[5] For Christians, any meaningful attempt at cultural reform must include the production of books of Scripture and, ideally, other books of theology, literature, and history. Under Charlemagne and his successors, "the written word became a fundamental element of Carolingian culture, and Frankish society in the Carolingian period was transformed into one largely dependent upon the written word."[6] The results were felt throughout Carolingian society—in the church, in law, in government, and more.

Several decades into his long reign, Charlemagne (r. 768–814) responded to this cultural slide with a clear vision and mission. In the 780s he issued the following directives:

> In consultation with my faithful advisors I have decided that it is desirable that all the bishoprics and monasteries that Christ has entrusted me to govern . . . should devote themselves to the study and teaching of literature. . . . We all know that, as dangerous as misspoken words are, even more dangerous are misunderstandings of God's Word. Therefore I exhort you not only to not neglect literature but to strive to master it, with a humble devotion that will be pleasing to God.[7]

> Let schools be established in which boys may learn to read. Correct carefully the Psalms, grammar, calendar in each diocese, because often some desire to pray to God properly but they pray badly because of incorrect books.[8]

Such measures assumed a level of literacy and book production not seen in centuries. For all of this, Charlemagne himself never actually learned to read, although Einhard, his friend and biographer, indicates he certainly gave it the old college try. To accomplish his ambitious vision, Charlemagne recruited leading scholars from throughout the Continent and the British Isles. Men like Alcuin of York (from England), Peter of Pisa (from Italy), Paul the Deacon (from Italy), Einhard himself (from the Frankish kingdom), Theodulf of Orleans (actually a Visigoth from Muslim Spain), Paulinus of Aquileia (from Italy), and others from Ireland and Germany would be his guiding lights.

Charlemagne's central aim was clear—to encourage understanding of the Bible throughout his realm. His movement was driven by "a clear preoccupation with the Bible and the particular types of knowledge and scholarship this generated, for the effort to understand the Bible and Christ's teaching is one of the clear impulses of Carolingian learning and education."[9] All clerics were now required to be educated and to read the Scriptures during services. Through this public act of reading, the written word thus reached virtually everyone within the realm.

As the realm was large, Charlemagne used the *Missi Dominici*, a commission of royal agents made up of bishops and counts (church and state) for administration and accountability. The *Missi Dominici* would travel about his realm to enforce his laws and report any issues directly back to the king. Charlemagne himself would even show up unannounced in churches throughout his realm to make sure that his reforms were being followed, and he would reward and punish accordingly. A biographer known as Notker the Stammerer records several such colorful stories of Charlemagne's sudden appearance.

Charlemagne's efforts not only resulted in literacy rates rising to where they had been at the height of the Roman Empire but also spurred marked improvement in book production. By all accounts, it is certain that "there was more literacy about in Charles's reign than in any previous early medieval one."[10] The results were felt wherever literate church leaders preached and teachers instructed. The attitude in Europe toward books and the written word would change permanently and decisively.

The Mathēma

In addition to the two stacks of books we imagined at the outset of this chapter, there is another very tangible way to illustrate the success of the Carolingian Renaissance. During the later Roman Empire and even very early in the medieval era before literacy and book production collapsed, artists depicted books as open and having plain leather covers. Such openness and plainness declared the book's everyday use, as the few surviving manuscripts from this era also attest. But when literacy and production plummeted, books—both as physical objects and in art—generally came to be depicted as closed and usually had ornate covers (see the photo on page 158). In fact, by the year 700, artists essentially stopped portraying books as open objects.[11]

The changing iconography of the book tells a story through the art alone. Christians always instinctively knew books were precious, but during the period when books were read infrequently and illiteracy prevailed, their value was expressed in external form. Books were even imbued with near talismanic qualities. They went from "an open and readable codex" to exclusively an object of veneration and beauty, essentially "a jewel-box of mysteries" and "a closed reliquary, glowing with gems, rigidly presented for the veneration but not the comprehension of the faithful."[12]

Once literacy and book production rates recovered under Charlemagne and his successors, books reverted to their artistic roots within the Carolingian realm. They were once again depicted as open, indicating they were to be read rather than merely admired or carried in processions. This shift in perception marks a reorientation back to the written word as the cornerstone of culture and society. Ornate covers did not disappear—we still see them today, in fact. But now there would be greater emphasis on what was actually between the covers, "the greater splendour of the contents."[13]

As books go, so goes the culture. Christianity can truly flourish only when books are central, recognized, and utilized as open and practical resources. It almost goes without saying that sermons and homilies drastically improved when ministers could actually read well. Since reading was generally done publicly and aloud in the ancient and medieval worlds, the results were felt far beyond the newly literate being trained in Carolingian schools.

While the preservation and proclamation of God's Word was the driving force behind the Carolingian Renaissance, secular

Saint Matthew with an open book, early ninth century
Public domain

texts multiplied as well. Most ancient and early medieval Latin texts that still survive today—whether works by Virgil, Cicero, and Plautus or by the North African church father Augustine of Hippo or books of Scripture—would be among the second stack of books from our illustration earlier in the chapter. In fact, 90 percent of all Latin works "that we know nowadays exist in their earliest form" in a manuscript from that ninth-century corpus.[14] Without Charlemagne's efforts, "much of the ancient Roman cultural achievement would be entirely lost."[15] The Scriptures led the way, but Western intellectual culture, both sacred and secular, was preserved.

Back in 2011, Stanford University held a symposium titled "Teaching Humanities for the Twenty-First Century." A former director of Stanford's Introduction to the Humanities (IHUM) Program gave a sobering assessment of the state of reading among incoming students at one of America's most elite institutions. The biggest challenge to teaching humanities, he claimed, was that incoming students had never read a complete work more demanding than the Harry Potter series. A twin challenge was to find a way to encourage students to want to read more challenging books at some point in their lives once they completed their humanities requirement.[16] More recent reports suggest that the problem has only gotten worse since then.[17] Are we reading any books?

Reading books certainly seems increasingly countercultural in the West. While people today might speak disparagingly of the Middle Ages as "Dark Ages," we might well be entering a particularly low moment in the history of reading. In the Middle Ages, even the illiterate majority benefited from the written word through books being read aloud and communally. In our modern age of predominantly private reading, no one benefits but the immediate reader, who is apparently becoming less common. Extended public reading of Scripture has long been uncommon in evangelical churches, yet Our People have always been a people of the Book. Christians today, probably more so than in many centuries, have a mandate to set the cultural example as readers of books. The Carolingian Renaissance can serve as an inspiration and example to us to "take up and read."[18]

Further Reading

Barbero, Alessandro. *Charlemagne: Father of a Continent.* Trans. Allan Cameron. University of California Press, 2000.

Geary, Patrick. *Before France and Germany: The Creation and Transformation of the Carolingian World.* Oxford University Press, 1988.

McKitterick, Rosamond. *The Carolingians and the Written Word.* Cambridge University Press, 1989.

Nelson, Janet. *King and Emperor: A New Life of Charlemagne.* University of California Press, 2019.

Petrucci, Armando. *Writers and Readers in Medieval Italy.* Trans. Charles Radding. Yale University Press, 1995.

Notes

1. Elina Screen and Charles West, eds., *Writing the Early Medieval West* (Cambridge University Press, 2018), 2. Bernard Bischoff once suggested up to fifty thousand manuscripts from the ninth century might have existed at one time. See Rosamond McKitterick, *The Carolingians and the Written Word* (Cambridge University Press, 1989), 163.

2. Patrick Geary, *Before France and Germany: The Creation and Transformation of the Carolingian World* (Oxford University Press, 1988), 180, 223–26.

3. Geary, *Before France and Germany*, 181–82, 211–13.

4. Alessandro Barbero, *Charlemagne: Father of a Continent,* trans. Allan Cameron (University of California Press, 2000), 220.

5. McKitterick, *Carolingians and the Written Word,* 272.

6. McKitterick, *Carolingians and the Written Word,* 2.

7. Quoted in Clifford R. Backman, *The Worlds of Medieval Europe* (Oxford University Press, 2003), 130.

8. Quoted in Rosamond McKitterick, *The Frankish Kingdoms Under the Carolingians, 751–987* (Longman, 1983), 145. In his *Life of Charlemagne,* Einhard records that girls were also included in these schools.

9. McKitterick, *Carolingians and the Written Word,* 165–66.

10. Janet Nelson, *King and Emperor: A New Life of Charlemagne* (University of California Press, 2019), 10.

11. Armando Petrucci, *Writers and Readers in Medieval Italy,* trans. Charles Radding (Yale University Press, 1995), 29.

12. Petrucci, *Writers and Readers*, 29–30.

13. McKitterick, *Carolingians and the Written Word*, 151, 164.

14. Brian Tierney and Sidney Painter, *Western Europe in the Middle Ages, 300–1475*, 5th ed. (McGraw-Hill, 1992), 146.

15. Peter Heather, *The Restoration of Rome: Barbarian Popes and Imperial Pretenders* (Oxford University Press, 2013), 339.

16. Orrin Robinson, concluding remarks at the symposium "Teaching Humanities for the Twenty-First Century," September 16, 2011, Stanford University.

17. See Rose Horowitch, "The Elite College Students Who Can't Read Books," *The Atlantic*, November 2024, https://www.theatlantic.com/magazine/archive/2024/11/the-elite-college-students-who-cant-read-books/679945/.

18. The famous line from Augustine of Hippo, *Confessions* 8.12.

25

"Faith Is a Thing of Will":
Alcuin of York Rejects
Compulsion in Faith

*(Aachen, Carolingian Frankish
Kingdom, 796)*

The Background

The Franks had waged war with the Saxons on and off for decades.
When the Saxons were finally conquered, Charlemagne incorporated them into his growing Carolingian kingdom. Around 785,
Charlemagne then aimed a series of brutal laws at them, known
as the First Saxon Capitulary. Several specific laws stand out from
the list:

> 4. If anyone, out of contempt for Christianity, has disdained the
> holy Lenten fast and has eaten meat, he shall be punished by
> death. . . .

8. If, hereafter, any member of the Saxon people hides among them, wishing to conceal himself unbaptized, and has scorned coming to baptism and wished to remain a pagan, he shall be punished by death. . . .

18. On the Lord's Day no meeting or public judicial assemblies shall be held, unless perhaps in a case of great necessity or when war compels it, but all shall go to church to hear the word of God. . . .

19. All infants shall be baptized within a year, and we have decreed that if anyone refuses to bring his infant to baptism within the course of a year, without the advice or permission of a priest, if he is of noble lineage he shall pay 120 solidi to the treasury; if a freeman, 60 [solidi].[1]

By these and other measures, Charlemagne attempted to force unconverted (or ambiguously converted) Saxons into the Christian fold. One of his contemporaries called it a "baptism with the sword,"[2] and a modern biographer describes it as "ferocious" and initiating "a reign of terror."[3] So harsh was Charlemagne's approach toward the Saxons that historians still debate whether his real intent was to force faith upon them or to eradicate them altogether.[4]

Charlemagne's own relationship with the Saxons had been tumultuous for years. About ten years before issuing these laws, it was recorded in the Frankish Royal Annals that he had resolved to "wage war on the perfidious and treaty-breaking people of the Saxons . . . until they had either been overcome and subjected to the Christian religion or totally exterminated."[5] The assumption that people could be forced into true faith was even shared outside the royal court. Lebuin, an English monk and missionary who labored on the Continent, had himself warned the Saxons, "If you will not accept belief in God . . . there is a king" who will "enter your country, conquer, lay it waste."[6] Whether threat, warning, or promise, that attitude was shared broadly.

These were not mere empty threats or words or laws simply "on the books." After pledging allegiance to Charlemagne in 774, the

Saxons had been baptized en masse. A few years later, however, they rebelled and declared themselves pagan once again. Following this declaration, they proceeded to burn down churches and kill priests. In response, Charlemagne had 4,500 Saxons beheaded on Easter morning in 782 before making his way to Easter Mass later in the day.[7] Styling himself a "King of Israel," he was apparently intent on eradicating the Saxon "Amalekites."[8]

General (and often brutal) caricatures and stereotypes of the European Middle Ages aside, such measures cannot be explained or understood as mere reflections of the "barbarity of the times."[9] The Frankish wars with the Saxons dated back to the reigns of Charlemagne's father and grandfather, Pippin the Short and Charles Martel. But in those days, exacting tribute from the Saxons was deemed a sufficient tool for securing peace. By brutally forcing them to convert to Christianity, Charlemagne was embarking on a new path.

The Moment

Serious concerns began to arise within Charlemagne's inner circle. It was not common for the king's advisers to rebuke him outright, but one close adviser named Alcuin did just that in 796, more than a decade after the First Saxon Capitulary appeared. Alcuin was advising Charlemagne on how to deal with a different pagan people group, the Avars, and his advice clearly challenged the king's earlier treatment of the Saxons. Rather than forcing or compelling the Avars to convert, he urged Charlemagne to teach and comfort them as "the first fruits of the faith."[10]

In one particular letter to Charlemagne, Alcuin's advice and rebuke echo several works by Augustine of Hippo from four centuries earlier. Augustine's own thoughts on this matter were not consistent over his career. Nevertheless, Alcuin drew from Augustine's book *On the Catechizing of the Uninstructed* and warned the king, "First the faith must be taught, then the sacrament of baptism undertaken, and finally the gospel precepts are to be related; if any of these three is neglected, the listener's soul will not be able to achieve salvation."[11] Calling it a tradition of resistance to forced or intimidated conversion might be a stretch, but there was nonetheless a clear thread here going back centuries.

Drawing directly from Augustine's *On the Free Choice of the Will*, Alcuin contends that "faith is a thing of will, not of necessity. . . . A man can be led to faith, not forced; he can be forced to baptism, but it will not help in faith."[12] He then admonishes the king, "If the same pains had been taken to preach to [the Saxons] the easy yoke and light burden of Christ as had been done to collect tithes, and to punish the slightest infringement of the laws on their part, then they would no longer abhor and repel baptism."[13]

Following his conquests, Charlemagne imposed strict tithes on the Saxons. Alcuin demurred. "It may be questioned whether tithes were anywhere exacted by the apostles; and if we ourselves, born and bred in the faith, do not care to give tithes, how much more must the fierce barbarians, lately converted, resent their exaction."[14] In that same year, Alcuin also wrote to Bishop Arno of Salzburg, again emphasizing that preaching and teaching, not force, are the means to true faith. Alcuin urged Arno to "be a preacher of piety, not an exactor of tithes," for "tithes, men say, . . . have destroyed the faith of the Saxons." He argued that the babe in the faith "should be nurtured with the milk of apostolic piety" rather than the force of tithe decrees and arms.[15]

To Alcuin, conquest itself was not the problem. He actually wanted and presumed a strong and expanding *Imperium Christianum* ("Christian empire"). He himself was perfectly content and even joyful with his new conquests of pagan peoples, assuming that they paved the way for converting them. But he contended that to demand conversion, force baptisms, and exact strict tithes was wrong and was even counterproductive to the spread of the gospel and establishing people in true faith.

Serious questions about forced conversion were circulating at this time. In 796, the same year as Alcuin's letters, a council of bishops from the Frankish realm gathered at a military camp on the Danube to discuss the merits (or lack thereof) of forced conversions and baptisms. It's likely that each of these bishops had been appointed to their office by Charlemagne himself. And even if they hadn't been, their continuation in office depended on the king's favor. Though Alcuin himself was not among them, those who gathered clearly shared his concerns. The bishops condemned the forceful, threatening methods Charlemagne had employed in Saxony.[16] Bishop Paulinus of Aquileia presided over the gathering, which strongly advocated for a softer program of evangelization and Christian teaching for the newly conquered Avar territory, as opposed to "baptism by the sword." A majority of the bishops aligned with Alcuin and Augustine in their thinking.

Charlemagne actually heard and heeded the challenges, rebukes, and advice of Alcuin and the collected bishops. The Second Saxon Capitulary, issued just a year later, conspicuously lacks the language of force and compulsion in matters of faith. In fact, not even a tithe is mentioned. One historian suggests that what we are observing here is a "royal learning curve."[17]

The Mathēma

It is wrong to downplay the moral responsibility of medieval Christians by simply saying that the Middle Ages was a brutal time in general. Charlemagne's contemporaries rebuked him, and that rebuke drew on Augustine's teachings from four centuries earlier. Alcuin and the Frankish bishops understood that the king was morally responsible, and the king did too. To suggest otherwise is to adopt a sort of patronizing condescension toward the medievals that says they can somehow be excused because they supposedly did not know any better. The medievals cannot be excused; they did know better.

Alcuin of York and the gathering of Frankish bishops played important roles in this key moment. They all held their king in extremely high regard. Alcuin even referred to him as "King David." To do the right thing by calling out the wrongdoing of their king was risky, even dangerous, and took a large measure of courage. But in this instance, Charlemagne actually accepted and learned from their criticisms.[18] Likewise through subsequent eras, the Western Christian church cannot be excused for being forceful or harsh in its attempts to spread the true faith. They (and we) too have known better.

Receiving and responding to criticism is a mark of any healthy institution. Wise counselors are called to give wise counsel even at personal cost or risk, and wise leaders will heed and consider their voices. The church works best when its leaders (and for better or worse, Charlemagne was a leader of the church in his day) are held accountable in giving and taking and responding to criticism and learning from it. It should come as no surprise that the Saxon and Avar peoples ultimately responded better to the king's new approach than to the harsh measures he initially tried to enforce.

At this time, no one—neither Alcuin nor the bishops at the Council on the Danube—was advocating for anything even remotely like a wall of separation between church and state. Such arguments would not emerge for centuries. Alcuin rejoiced when pagans were conquered by the Frankish kingdom, believing it would make their conversion through the church's teaching efforts easier. His opposition was not to the union of church and state but rather to the specific methods the *Imperium Christianum* was using to convert and lead pagans.

The thread that runs through all of this is a clear recognition and acknowledgment of freedom of conscience, even during those so-called Dark Ages. The fact that faith cannot be coerced is not some modern concept invented by John Locke or discovered by modern architects of liberal democracy. The voices of Alcuin and other medievals affirm that even during those centuries Our People knew and understood what Robert Wilken refers to as "liberty in the things of God." In our own day, as some strident groups of American Christians publicly embrace the idea of enforcing the faith politically once again, we do well to listen to those medieval voices of caution.

Further Reading

Barbero, Alessandro. *Charlemagne: Father of a Continent*. Trans. Allan Cameron. University of California Press, 2000.

Davis, Jennifer R. *Charlemagne's Practice of Empire*. Cambridge University Press, 2015.

McKitterick, Rosamond. *The Frankish Kingdoms Under the Carolingians, 751–987*. Longman, 1983.

Nelson, Janet. *King and Emperor: A New Life of Charlemagne*. University of California Press, 2019.

Wilken, Robert Louis. *Liberty in the Things of God: The Christian Origins of Religious Freedom*. Yale University Press, 2019.

Notes

1. "Capitulary on the Saxon Territories," quoted in *The Medieval Record: Sources of Medieval History*, 2nd rev. ed., ed. Alfred J. Andrea (Hacket Publishing, 2020), 122–23.

2. Richard E. Sullivan, *Heirs of the Roman Empire* (Cornell University Press, 1960), 70.

3. Alessandro Barbero, *Charlemagne: Father of a Continent*, trans. Allan Cameron (University of California Press, 2000), 47, 243.

4. Barbero, *Charlemagne*, 47; Janet Nelson, *King and Emperor: A New Life of Charlemagne* (University of California Press, 2019), 197.

5. *Annales Qui Dicuntur Einhardi*, ed. G. H. Pertz (Hanover, 1826), 41.

6. Barbero, *Charlemagne*, 45.

7. Clifford R. Backman, *The Worlds of Medieval Europe* (Oxford University Press, 2003), 117.

8. Barbero, *Charlemagne*, 47. See 1 Samuel 15 on the destruction of the Amalekites.

9. Barbero, *Charlemagne*, 47.

10. Alcuin of York, Epistle 113, as quoted in Rolph Barlowe Page, *The Letters of Alcuin* (The Forest Press, 1909), 52–53.

11. Alcuin, Epistle 111, as quoted in Alexander Scott Dessens, "*Res Voluntaria, Non Necessaria:* The Conquest and Forced Conversion of the Saxons Under Charlemagne" (master's thesis, Louisiana State University, 2013).

12. Alcuin, Epistle 111.

13. Alcuin, Epistle 111.

14. Alcuin, Epistle 110.

15. Alcuin, Epistle 107.

16. Barbero, *Charlemagne*, 244.

17. Jennifer R. Davis, *Charlemagne's Practice of Empire* (Cambridge University Press, 2015), 414.

18. Barbero, *Charlemagne*, 244.

26

Theodulf of Orleans Exalts the Only Truly "Good and Gracious King"

(Angers, Carolingian Frankish Empire, 820?)

The Background

More than three centuries had passed since the West had seen an imperial coronation. Kingdoms and dynasties came and went, but no emperor had been crowned since the last emperor of the Western Roman Empire back in 475. The long spell ended on Christmas Day in 800 when Charlemagne, the most powerful monarch in all of Europe, was crowned emperor by the bishop of Rome in the Basilica of St. Peter. The gathered crowd immediately hailed Charlemagne, enthusiastically chanting multiple times, "To Charles, the most pious Augustus, crowned by God, the great and peace-giving Emperor, life and victory."[1]

Before this coronation, Charlemagne was "King of the Franks and the Lombards and patrician of the Romans." Now he was "Charles the most serene Augustus, crowned by God great and pacific Emperor governing the Roman Imperium, who on account of the mercy of God [is] King of the Franks and Lombards."[2]

Theodulf, the bishop of Orleans and a close adviser to Charlemagne, was present at St. Peter's Basilica on that auspicious day, fervently praising his newly crowned emperor. As it turns out, he would again be among the crowd sixteen years later when Charlemagne's son Louis was crowned emperor by another bishop of Rome at the cathedral in Reims.[3] Theodulf was a man who knew well the pomp and ceremony of glorious coronations and was as intimately acquainted as anyone of his day could possibly be with the majestic splendor of the imperial court.

Theodulf's path to the courts of emperors was a winding one. He was a Visigoth who was born in Spain around 760, and he grew up there under Muslim rule. Sometime between 778 and 782, he fled Spain in the midst of unrest. Charlemagne's military challenge had provoked insurrection in the city of Saragossa, and the Muslim emir punished the local Christian inhabitants. Many Christians fled the emir's rule, and Theodulf was likely among them.[4] Theodulf made his way into the Frankish kingdom, where his talents quickly attracted the attention of Charlemagne. Theodulf has been described as "a man of unusual charisma, fiercely intelligent and charmingly self-possessed. . . . Rather quickly, Theodulf had become an intimate of the emperor, who delighted in and deeply trusted Theodulf's deft intellect, political poise, innate sophistication, and keen wit."[5]

Charlemagne awarded him a place in his court and appointed him as bishop of Orleans. Theodulf established himself as both the "most gifted theologian"[6] and the "finest poet"[7] of his generation. His intellectual and theological reputation was firmly established with his impressive challenge to the Seventh Ecumenical Council (787), which had declared veneration of icons essential to worship (see chap. 22).[8] He also prepared a corrected edition of the Latin Vulgate that would endure as one of the most important editions used in later medieval centuries. Today, Theodulf is remembered in many churches each year on Palm Sunday when we sing his majestic hymn "All Glory, Laud, and Honor," which is considered the "crown of Theodulf's poetry."[9]

The Moment

The exact date when Theodulf composed his famous Palm Sunday hymn, which celebrates Christ's triumphal entry and symbolic coronation, remains uncertain. However, a strong case can be made for the year 820, when Theodulf was living in Angers in western France. Several details support this date. Notably, the hymn's lesser-known second half, which is omitted from modern hymnals, describes sacred processions through Angers, mentions the city's parish churches, and culminates in a mass gathering at the Cathedral of St. Maurice.[10] This section of the hymn "certainly implies a real procession, real singing, and a real celebration, in which the author of the verses being sung must have shared."[11] Theodulf was by this time no longer a bishop, and he was not in Angers by choice.

Within a few years of Charlemagne's death in 814, Theodulf had fallen out of favor with Louis, Charlemagne's only surviving son and successor. By 817, Louis had deposed Theodulf as bishop, and the following year he ordered him confined to a monastery in the city of Angers. There Theodulf was permitted to worship and do some limited teaching under watchful imperial eyes until his death in 821. An old and oft-told story says that Louis himself once happened to be passing near Theodulf's cell window and heard him singing "All Glory, Laud, and Honor." Deeply impressed by the hymn, Louis freed Theodulf from confinement and restored him as bishop of Orleans. It makes for a touching tale, but sadly it lacks any solid historical support.

The official reason given for Theodulf's punishment was his support of a revolt led by Louis's nephew, Bernard of Italy. Bernard did indeed attempt an insurrection, confessed to it, and was condemned to having his eyes removed—then died three days later from the botched operation. Most historians today, though, seriously doubt that Theodulf had anything to do with Bernard's revolt. Rather, it likely served as a convenient excuse to remove him from office after he ran afoul of the new administration. Apparently, the personality, character, and skills that had ingratiated Theodulf with the old administration made enemies of men not as skilled as he.[12] Theodulf has been described as "wickedly satirical,"[13] having a "caustic wit"[14] and a tongue with a "sharp edge."[15] Not everyone appreciated this about him.

Louis was insecure as a leader, especially in his early reign, and apparently felt threatened by "extraordinary, self-reliant personalities" like Theodulf.[16] When Theodulf disagreed with Louis's plan to divide up the empire in a dynastic arrangement with his sons, he likely put himself on a collision course with the emperor, who perceived the challenge as insubordination.[17]

Theodulf's friend Modoin ascribed the bishop's sudden downfall to the fact that others envied his genius. Theodulf remained adamant up to his death that he was falsely charged, and in letters to his friends he "protested that he was innocent of all charges, and had been unjustly deposed."[18] The false accusation hit him hard, for he himself prized justice and had once even written a book on that topic titled *Ad Iudices* ("To the Judges") in which he pleaded for judges to resist bribes, partiality, and pride.

Theodulf had once placed great confidence in Carolingian political leadership. The year before Charlemagne's coronation, he wrote a poem that portrayed Charlemagne as the "avenger of all wrongs," the "weapons of bishops, the hope and defence of clergy."[19] In the year of Charlemagne's coronation, Theodulf argued that St. Peter himself had "handed to Charlemagne the earthly keys," and thus it was "the duty of the king to govern the church, the clergy, and the Christian people."[20] Theodulf even praised the emperor's son Charles, who was his presumed successor before his untimely death in 811, as "the great salvation, o hope, o glory of the kingdom."[21]

However, by 820 things were very different, and it is not hard to imagine Theodulf's disenchantment with Carolingian politics. His own experiences and observations of the rough and tumble of political life convinced him that the state was using the church to overstep its bounds. As his hope in temporal powers diminished, his fear of the government's overreach of the church increased. Reversing his earlier claims that Charlemagne held the keys to Christ's kingdom, "Theodulf was most aggrieved by the credible threat of complete secular ascendancy over the Church, and the imbalance of jurisdiction concerned him."[22]

Theodulf realized the perfect king was not to be found in any Carolingian court. He longed for a king who did not accuse wrongly or exercise dominion from fear, insecurity, or paranoia. Theodulf's hymn of explicit praise to Christ the King contained an implicit rebuke of the leaders around him. Even as he wrote his famous hymn, his eyes were on eternity and the celebration of Christ's coronation as the true Redeemer and King.

In 822, Louis repented for the way he had treated courtesans such as Theodulf in the early years of his reign. He even publicly confessed and performed penance,[23] which helped earn him the title Louis the Pious, as he often is known today. But his actions were too late to be of any temporal comfort for Theodulf, who by that time had already entered the eternal courts of heaven.

The Mathēma

Theodulf's hymn caught on. Surviving medieval manuscripts show that it was already being sung in churches during the ninth century, and its use has continued right up to the present day.[24] It is thus another rare example of a true medieval church song survival (see chap. 18). Today we have few hymns that come close to it in capturing both the exuberance and majesty of Christ's triumphal entry and coronation as eternal King. One wonders if it would even be possible for anyone to compose a convincing coronation hymn today in our egalitarian and democratic modern world. Theodulf was positioned in a way that no one is today, and actually precious few were even in his own day. Such songs can capture something deep and abiding yet which even the best hymn writers in our own age would hardly be able to muster. This is one reason that we need songs from all ages of the church. The song also reminds us that as much as we might embrace and express thankfulness for the benefits of the democratic modern world in which we live, such governments are not and will never be the great hope for humanity they have so often been hailed as. We will, in fact, live under the rule of a truly good and gracious King of Kings for all eternity.

Theodulf's hymn reminds us that the failures of our political world should prompt our longing for another world. The imperfections of our earthly rulers make us long for the truly good and gracious King who never fails and who reigns yesterday, today, and for all eternity. Charlemagne himself was far from a perfect king (see chap. 25), even if Theodulf was enamored with him for a time. The rulers of earth will always leave God's people longing for something more—more good, more gracious, more just, more worthy of *all* glory, laud, and honor. Theodulf brilliantly takes us back to Christ's triumphal entry while pointing us ahead to his eternal reign.

Theodulf was a man who experienced marked highs and wretched lows. He knew firsthand the majesty of kings and emperors as well as the temperamental cruelty and injustice that so often come with earthly power. He would come to see that glory, laud, and honor are due only to the "good and gracious King" whom he longed to see from amidst the cunning of his own topsy-turvy political world. Both now and through eternity we can sing with Theodulf, "To Thee now high exalted, our melody we raise."[25]

Further Reading

Freeman, Ann. "Theodulf of Orleans: A Visigoth at Charlemagne's Court." In *L'Europe héritiére de L"Espagne Wisigothique*. Edited by Jacques Fontaine and Christine Pellistrandi. Casa del Velázquez, 1992.

Greeley, June-Ann. "Raptors and Rebellion: The Self-Defence of Theodulf of Orleans." *Journal of Medieval Latin* 6 (2006): 28–75.

McKitterick, Rosamond. *The Frankish Kingdoms Under the Carolingians, 751–987*. Longman, 1983.

Noble, Thomas F. X. *Charlemagne and Louis the Pious*. Pennsylvania State University Press, 2009.

Notes

1. Janet Nelson, *King and Emperor: A New Life of Charlemagne* (University of California Press, 2019), 384. Author's translation from the original Latin.

2. Nelson, *King and Emperor*, 387.

3. June-Ann Greeley, "Raptors and Rebellion: The Self-Defence of Theodulf of Orleans," *Journal of Medieval Latin* 6 (2006): 31.

4. Ann Freeman, "Theodulf of Orleans: A Visigoth at Charlemagne's Court," in *L'Europe héritière de L'Espagne Wisigothique*, ed. Jacques Fontaine and Christine Pellistrandi (Casa del Velázquez, 1992), 185–94.

5. Greeley, "Raptors and Rebellion," 70.

6. Robert Louis Wilken, *The First Thousand Years: A Global History of Christianity* (Yale University Press, 2012), 338.

7. Freeman, "Theodulf of Orleans," 185.

8. This work, the *Libri Carolini*, is considered "the most ambitious and original theological work produced at the time." Alessandro Barbero, *Charlemagne: Father of a Continent*, trans. Allan Cameron (University of California Press, 2000), 84.

9. F. J. E. Raby, *A History of Christian-Latin Poetry*, 2nd ed. (Clarendon, 1953), 175.

10. Freeman, "Theodulf of Orleans," 194n66.

11. Freeman, "Theodulf of Orleans," 193.

12. Peter Godman, *Poets and Emperors: Frankish Politics and Carolingian Policy* (Clarendon, 1987), 97; Greeley, "Raptors and Rebellion," 46.

13. Barbero, *Charlemagne*, 125.

14. Greeley, "Raptors and Rebellion," 28.

15. Rosamond McKitterick, *The Frankish Kingdoms Under the Carolingians, 751–987* (Longman, 1983), 162.

16. Greeley, "Raptors and Rebellion," 71.

17. Freeman, "Theodulf of Orleans"; and Thomas F. X. Noble, *Charlemagne and Louis the Pious* (Pennsylvania State University Press, 2009), 206.

18. Freeman, "Theodulf of Orleans," 193.

19. Janet Nelson, *King and Emperor: A New Life of Charlemagne* (University of California Press, 2019), 370.

20. Barbero, *Charlemagne*, 98.

21. Greeley, "Raptors and Rebellion," 29.

22. Greeley, "Raptors and Rebellion," 65.

23. McKitterick, *Frankish Kingdoms*, 135.

24. Chris Fenner, "Gloria laus et honor," Hymnology Archive, March 12, 2019, https://www.hymnologyarchive.com/gloria-laus-et-honor.

25. When the church today sings the majestic "All Glory, Laud, and Honor," there is one little line that we can rejoice has dropped out, along with the stanza it introduces: "Be thou, O Lord, the rider, and we the little ass."

27

Cyril of Thessaloniki:
Global Linguist,
Diplomat, Missionary

*(Baghdad, Khazaria, Moravia,
Venice, 850s and 860s)*

The Background

In the mid-nineteenth century, a few Slavic people groups began celebrating "The Day of the Slavonic Alphabet," commonly known as Cyrillic. Today, this beloved holiday, which is observed on May 24, is a joyous celebration of Slavic culture and language in nations such as Bulgaria, Macedonia, Serbia, and Russia. But in 2017, Russian president Vladimir Putin provoked an international incident when he assured the president of Macedonia that the Cyrillic alphabet had emerged from "Macedonian soil."[1] One Russian minister took issue with that claim, countering that their alphabet actually came from Byzantium. This in turn prompted Bulgaria's prime minister to cancel a meeting with the Russian minister. It was not the first time the alphabet's origins had been disputed, as the person it takes its name from, Cyril of Thessaloniki, has stirred strong emotions across the centuries.

Few figures in church history have been co-opted as a symbol for so many disparate and even conflicting causes as Cyril has been. He and his brother Methodius, who have been heralded as the "Apostles to the Slavs," were the first to bring Christianity to these people groups. Modern and often competing nationalist myths exalt the brothers as the "Founding Fathers of Slavic Culture" and "symbols of primitive unity of a Slavic world which was subsequently deeply divided."[2] Over the past two centuries, some Eastern Orthodox Christians have used the brothers to illustrate the deep conflict between the Eastern and Western halves of the church that well predated the Great Schism in 1054. Conversely, some Roman Catholics (including Pope John Paul II) have declared the brothers as "precursors of the ecumenical movement"[3] and "patrons of reconciliation with the Orthodox Churches."[4] Some Protestants have embraced the brothers as proto-Reformers, early heroic defenders of having Scripture and worship in vernacular languages in the face of the Western church's stubborn insistence on using Latin only.

Whenever a human being is exalted (or reduced rather) to a symbol, historical reality is often ignored. Cyril's primary medieval biographer would be surprised to see him remembered almost exclusively as "Apostle to the Slavs." This anonymous biographer emphasized Cyril's interaction with Muslim scholars in Baghdad, Turkic Khazars in Central Asia, and heterodox Venetians in Italy. Cyril's famous linguistic and translation work was indeed a boon to Slavic Christians, but the faith was already well established in Slavic Moravia when he and Methodius arrived there. In their mission to that region, they essentially came alongside an indigenous church.[5] Cyril did famously invent an alphabet known as Glagolitic, which underlies all subsequent Cyrillic scripts, but he was hardly the father of Slavic culture and identity.

While there were various tensions between the Western and Eastern halves of the church in Cyril's day, his missionary efforts were strongly supported by a church that was still united. Cyril's use of Slavonic language for worship and for translating Scripture was supported by Carolingian Frankish church councils as well as bishops of Rome. The Papal See generally viewed his Slavic translations of Scripture and liturgy as "an important initiative for the spiritual and moral edification of the Slavs and the edification of the Slavic clergy."[6] A few later popes would dissent, but Cyril himself had firm and unambiguous papal encouragement.

Thankfully, in the case of Cyril, the truth can be even more inspiring and meaningful than legend, especially for those who truly value it. When we get to Cyril's historical core, we find a remarkable scholar, librarian, monk, cleric, teacher, philosopher, diplomat, philologist, linguist, and global missionary whose education and gifts prepared him to stand before rulers, be they king, khan, caliph, emperor, duke, or pope.

The Moments

Cyril was born in Thessaloniki, Greece, in 826 or 827, and his given name was Constantine. He was the son of a high-ranking Byzantine officer. As a young intellectual prodigy, he received a premier Byzantine secular education (what some have called "outside learning"). His curriculum consisted of ancient Greek literature (Homer is singled out), grammar, geometry, philosophy, rhetoric, arithmetic, astronomy, music, and "other Hellenic arts."[7] One of his teachers was Leo the Mathematician (also known as Leo the Philosopher), a Byzantine intellectual light who was also something of an engineer and developed a system of beacons to warn of Muslim raids.

Another of Cyril's teachers was Photius, an influential scholar, politician, and diplomat who was controversially exalted to the position of Patriarch of Constantinople. In addition to Greek,

Latin, and Slavic, Cyril apparently also learned Hebrew, Samaritan, and a language called *Ros'sky* (perhaps Syriac).[8] One of Cyril's disciples, Clement of Ohrid, would later eulogize Cyril: "Blessed is your tongue of many languages."[9] Cyril's broad education and linguistic gifts prepared him for vital global roles beyond what he could have imagined.

Western medieval theologians distinguish between "contemplative life" and "active life." Although Cyril initially desired the contemplative life of a scholar, he came to defy such categories. After all, he was a librarian who once chopped down and burned a cherry tree that was being used for pagan rituals; he was a teacher who was sent on multiple diplomatic missions; and he was a linguistic and philological scholar who debated the faith with Muslims and Jews in imperial courts. Long before the idea of "civic humanism," Cyril was using his learning to serve both his church and his state.

His public career began at age twenty-four when he was called from his scholarly work to go to the court of the Abbasid Muslim caliph al-Mutawakkil. The caliph sought a scholar to engage in theological debates, particularly concerning the Holy Trinity, and the Byzantine emperor, recognizing Cyril's intellectual prowess, selected him for this task. At the royal Abbasid court in Samarra, just north of Baghdad, Cyril debated the leading scholars of Islam (*ulema*) on the Trinity, Christian ethics, and even taxation. His knowledge astounded his interlocutors.

Ten years later, the Byzantine emperor sent Cyril to the court of the Khazars, a Turkic people far to the east near the Caspian Sea. Along the way, Cyril shared the gospel with a Samaritan, who believed and was baptized, and he also delivered "edifying words" to a group of threatening Magyars.[10] In Khazaria, he met with the *khagan* or khan ("king of kings") and his court for diplomatic and faith discussions. A variety of faiths were practiced among the Khazars, including Christianity, Judaism, Islam, and a shamanistic religion called Tengrism. Cyril debated Muslim and Jewish scholars on the Holy Trinity, Mary's ability to give birth to God, the validity of the New Testament, icons, and the eating of pork and rabbit. Cyril's medieval biography notes that many Khazars promised Cyril they would convert to Christianity. It's also likely that he helped negotiate an alliance between the Byzantines and Khazars against the nearby Rus' people (see chap. 28).

Cyril's Moravian mission began with a request from Duke Rastislav for "a teacher who can explain to us in our language the true Christian faith, so that other countries might emulate us."[11] Frankish and perhaps Irish missionaries had already been active among the Slavs for some time. By the mid-ninth century, Frankish Christianity had a clear presence in important places in Moravia.[12] The Byzantine emperor again called on Cyril, who had already created a language known as Old Church Slavonic for use in Slavic Scripture translation and liturgy. Before he and Methodius departed for Moravia in 863, Cyril also invented Glagolitic, which better captured the specific nuances of Slavonic sounds than any existing alphabet. It is unlikely that Rastislav or the Byzantine emperor anticipated the brilliant innovations by Cyril or the scale of his linguistic and translation work.[13] Cyril's alphabet and the Slavonic liturgy would have a lasting impact in nearby Bulgaria as well as other areas.

A few years later, Pope Nicolas I invited Cyril and Methodius to Rome to discuss their mission work. On the way to Rome, they stopped in Venice, where Cyril debated a group of bishops, priests, and monks. This particular group had adopted a belief called "trilingualism," which claimed that liturgy and sacred writings were only to be written in the three "holy" languages—Hebrew, Greek, and Latin. All other languages were deemed "not worthy of praising God."[14]

Cyril's response to the trilingualists was simple but memorable: "For we know many peoples who have knowledge of books and praise God in their own language, it is known that there are: Armenians, Persians, Abkhazians, Iberians, Sougdians, Goths, Avars,

Turks, Khazars, Arabs, Egyptians and many others."[15] By recognizing the vibrant reality of global Christianity in the first millennium, he understood what many in our own day have ignored or forgotten: Christianity is and has always been a global faith.

The Mathēma

If we remember Cyril as an example rather than a mere symbol, there is much to appreciate and inspire. No one in his day, of course, dreamed that a millennium after his death he would be co-opted as a symbol for nationalist and sectarian causes. One need not connect to partisan causes to be memorable and inspiring.

Cyril's life clearly models the potential of even secular learning for use in the service of the church and in spreading the faith. One major scholar writes, "I hope to have destabilized the image of Cyril as the apostle of the Slavs he became in later Slavonic texts and modern historiography, and to have offered in its stead a Byzantine diplomat whose life was used to present an *exemplum* of the compatibility of 'outside' learning and faith in missionary activity."[16] His skills in debate, grammar, and rhetoric were clearly used "to refute opponents of the orthodox faith," whether Muslim, Jewish, or trilingualist.[17]

Cyril shows the value of a broad, deep education beyond the straightforward study of theology in preparation for gospel ministry. A friend of mine—who was a professor in an undergraduate biblical and religious studies department—perhaps took this too far. He would annoy some departmental colleagues by persuading young aspiring ministers of the gospel to not major in Bible or theology but instead pursue an undergraduate degree in English, history, philosophy, or another discipline well outside of his own department. But maybe Cyril would have approved.

Cyril preferred the contemplative life of a scholar. The same was apparently true of John Calvin and is true of many pastors I know today. They would prefer retreating to their study or the library over the often messy life of active public ministry. We can be thankful for all the ministers of the gospel who holistically submit to their call and not just their impulses!

It is a mantra today that young people should "follow their passion" to their specific vocational aspirations. Cyril's life serves as a caution to an exclusive diet of this prevalent advice. His education, talents, and gifts blessed many people. He studied broadly and diligently, built up an astounding amount of knowledge, and was useful in ways far different from and well beyond his expectations. He was a man "skillful in his work" (Prov. 22:29) who did indeed stand before kings of distant lands before he died in Rome in 869.

Further Reading

Betti, Maddalena. *The Making of Christian Moravia (858–882): Papal Power and Political Reality*. Brill, 2014.

Cooper, Henry R. "The Bible in Slavonic." In *The New Cambridge History of the Bible*. Edited by Richard Marsden and E. Ann Matter. Cambridge University Press, 2012.

Curta, Florin. *Eastern Europe in the Middle Ages (500–1300)*, vol. 1. Brill, 2019.

Ivanova, Mirela. "Re-Thinking the *Life of Constantine-Cyril the Philosopher*." *Slavonic and East European Review* 98 (2020): 434–63.

Shepard, Jonathan. "Spreading the Word: Byzantine Missions." In *Oxford History of Byzantium*. Edited by Cyril Mango. Oxford University Press, 2002.

Notes

1. Introductory example borrowed from Mirela Ivanova, "Re-Thinking the *Life of Constantine-Cyril the Philosopher*," *Slavonic and East European Review* 98 (2020): 434.

2. Maddalena Betti, *The Making of Christian Moravia (858–882): Papal Power and Political Reality* (Brill, 2014), 9.

3. Florin Curta, *Eastern Europe in the Middle Ages (500–1300)*, vol. 1 (Brill, 2019), 180–82.

4. Betti, *Making of Christian Moravia*, 39.

5. Robert Louis Wilken, *The First Thousand Years: A Global History of Christianity* (Yale University Press, 2012), 346.

6. Betti, *Making of Christian Moravia*, 48.

7. Ivanova, "Re-Thinking," 442; Curta, *Eastern Europe in the Middle Ages*, 183–84.

8. Ivanova, "Re-Thinking," 443–45.

9. Curta, *Eastern Europe in the Middle Ages*, 211.

10. Curta, *Eastern Europe in the Middle Ages*, 184.

11. Betti, *Making of Christian Moravia*, 75.

12. Curta, *Eastern Europe in the Middle Ages*, 179.

13. Jonathan Shepard, "Spreading the Word: Byzantine Missions," in *Oxford History of Byzantium*, ed. Cyril Mango (Oxford University Press, 2002), 238.

14. Curta, *Eastern Europe in the Middle Ages*, 190.

15. Ivanova, "Re-Thinking," 458.

16. Ivanova, "Re-Thinking," 463.

17. Ivanova, "Re-Thinking," 446.

28

Olga of the Rus' Finds Faith

(Constantinople and Kyiv, 950s)

The Background

Once upon a time, the beautiful princess Olga of the Rus' came to the grand city of Constantinople. The Byzantine emperor was immediately taken by her lovely face, her intelligence, and her wisdom. "You are worthy to reign in this city with me," he exclaimed. But she protested, "I am a pagan, and if you want to baptize me, then baptize me yourself." And so he and the patriarch bishop did, and the emperor served as her baptismal sponsor and thus became her godfather. The patriarch bishop at the court then taught Olga the Christian faith. "Blessed are you among the women of Rus', for you have loved the light and have renounced the darkness," said the patriarch. Olga showed great respect for the patriarch bishop and absorbed his Christian teaching like a sponge. She was given the Christian name Helen, after the mother of Constantine the Great.

The emperor then made his intentions crystal clear: "I want to take you as my wife." But Olga strongly rebuked him. "How can you want to marry me? And having baptized me yourself and called me your daughter! Among Christians that is against the law, and you yourself know it!" The emperor then realized that she had cleverly foiled his plans. Thus, Olga skillfully avoided the advances of the Byzantine emperor himself, and she returned to her home kingdom with many gifts and blessings from her new godfather.[1]

Sorting fact from fiction in many such stories as recorded in the *Russian Primary Chronicle* (or "Tale of Bygone Years") is a perennial challenge for those who study Russian history. Some of the central features do indeed ring true, as we will see. Other parts do not hold up to historical scrutiny, in particular the pure fiction of a pursuing potentate. The actual Byzantine emperor at the time of Olga's real visit to Constantinople in the 950s, Constantine VII, had been married to his wife Helen for at least three decades at this point, and together they took Olga under their wings as godparents, with no sign of foul play. But if the main point of this amusing hagiography is to showcase the true-to-life wisdom and shrewdness of the historical Olga, it certainly succeeds.

Olga was the only known female ruler of the kingdom of the Rus', serving for a time as regent for her young son Sviatoslav following the brutal murder of her husband Igor in 945. In the previous century, the Rus' (also known as Varangians or eastern Vikings) had migrated from Scandinavia and settled in what is modern-day Belarus, Russia, and Ukraine. They first settled in Novgorod, but then a group of them went farther south and seized Kyiv, making it the center of the Rus' kingdom and bringing together East Slavs and Varangians under a common ruler.

Olga's visit to Constantinople in the 950s was not the first contact between the Rus' and the Byzantines. About a century earlier, in 860, the Rus' had attacked the city with two hundred ships in a brutal siege that forced the Byzantines to sue for peace. Nor was Olga the first among the Rus' to convert to Christianity. Immediately after the peace treaty with the Byzantines, some Rus' converted to Christianity and petitioned the Byzantines to send an archbishop to Kyiv.[2] The era initiated by the peace treaty is heralded as the real beginning of the first great age of Byzantine missions. Yet Christian presence among the Rus' at this time is hard to trace. The arrival of an archbishop did not result in a national conversion, and precious little fruit seemed to come at all from Olga's conversion.

The Moment

Discerning what is certain about Olga's visit to Constantinople seems like a good place to start. Although there will always be some quibbling over details, Francis Butler has helpfully outlined five things from Olga's story in the *Russian Primary Chronicle* that stand up to historical scrutiny:

1. She traveled to Constantinople.
2. She was baptized.
3. The emperor was her baptismal sponsor.
4. She was given the name Helen.
5. Helen was the name of St. Helen, the mother of Constantine the Great.[3]

Of all the colorful figures appearing in the *Primary Chronicle*, Olga comes across consistently as the wisest and most shrewd, a true "woman of words."[4] In her historical setting, powerful women were "able and expected to use their intellectual and verbal abilities, which were not regarded as inferior to those of men."[5] Time after time, Olga distinguished herself by wisdom and "through intelligence and verbal dexterity."[6]

After her baptism, Olga embraced the faith and sincerely desired to grow in it. The introductory tale is not the only place we see her hunger for knowledge and her great respect for the patriarch bishop who taught her the basics of her newfound faith. One

Byzantine court official records that she was "fittingly honored" for her "religious conviction."[7] Evidence points to the "genuineness of her faith and the significance of her conversion."[8]

It was common for foreign leaders to take a Christian name when they were baptized. For example, a converted Khazar princess named Tzitzak was rechristened Irene, and Boris of Bulgaria took the name Michael. The Christian name was usually chosen in honor of a sponsor.[9] In Olga's case, the name Helen/a did double duty: It connected her back to Helena, the mother of Constantine the Great, and also to Helen Lecapena, the wife of Constantine VII,[10] with whom Olga enjoyed a vital "spiritual relationship."[11]

Conversions of political leaders outside the Byzantine Empire always raise political questions for modern scholars. To what extent did Byzantine missions help spread Byzantine political influence, and to what extent did embracing Christianity help surrounding kingdoms gain the political and military support of the Byzantines? The Byzantine emperor saw himself as uniquely "chosen by God" to "spread the Word," and this has been seen as a "political prop" designed to impress upon foreigners the "uniqueness of the emperor's relationship with God."[12] The Byzantines invariably paired missions with political patronage. The Rus', however, did not seem to get fully on board, and the stories of Olga's resisting the emperor's advances could well have historical roots in her shrewd resistance against Byzantine political patronage.[13]

The Byzantine emperor and empress honored Olga with a very important title and position. They appointed her *Zoste Patrikia*, a chief attendant to the empress, second only to the empress in the imperial court. At least twice they hosted her for special banquets that are described in fascinating detail in the Byzantine *Book of Ceremonies* compiled in part by Constantine VII himself. A reception was held for Olga at which she was able to ask questions of the empress. Then she "conversed about all she wished" with the emperor and his family.[14] There was "apparent closeness of her relationship with the empress and the imperial family."[15] The general scene is "suggestive of a godmother receiving a goddaughter in the intimacy of her family."[16] There certainly would have been political discussions but also clearly a mentoring in the faith.

Just before returning to her pagan kingdom, Olga consulted again with the patriarch bishop. When she arrived home, though, she was able to make no headway in spreading the faith among the Rus'. When her son Sviatoslav came of age and became prince, he did not embrace his mother's faith. He feared that if he converted, "my retainers will start to laugh at this."[17] However, when Olga died in 969, her pagan son at least honored her request to hold no traditional pagan burial feasts at her funeral. Her fervent faith defied age-old Varangian burial traditions.

The Mathēma

There is a far more celebrated Russian conversion story than Olga's. In 988, about two decades after Olga's death, her grandson Prince Vladimir I embraced the Christian faith. His conversion story is remembered to this day as the birth of Orthodox Russia and is celebrated for both its national implications and its humorous and sublime detail. Casting about for a faith to embrace, Vladimir called for representatives of major nearby religions to present their case to him so he could decide among them: Muslims, Jews, German Latin Catholics, and Byzantine Catholics. Islam did not particularly impress him because Muslims practiced circumcision and were forbidden from eating pork and drinking alcohol, the latter of which Vladimir claimed was "the joy of the Russes."[18] He looked suspiciously at the Jewish delegation because they too insisted on circumcision and forbid eating pork, plus the Jews did not even control Jerusalem, their original home. For reasons that are unclear, the German Catholics simply failed to impress Vladimir. A Byzantine orator gave a brilliant speech complete with visual aids but did not move him much either.

Vladimir's boyars (i.e., elite aristocratic advisers) persuaded him to send ten emissaries to observe these various communities at worship. They reported Muslim worship distasteful and thought German Catholic liturgy lacked beauty. But when the emissaries witnessed worship in the Hagia Sophia in Constantinople, they reported, "We knew not whether we were in heaven or on earth. For on earth there is no such splendour or such beauty, and we are at a loss how to describe it. We only know that God dwells there among men, and their service is fairer than the ceremonies of other nations. For we cannot forget that beauty."[19] Anyone who has listened to the fairly recent reconstruction of ancient singing in the Hagia Sophia can at least get a sense of that truly amazing acoustic experience.[20] And this doesn't even capture the added combination of scents, architecture, and decoration!

More pragmatic reasons have also been proposed for Vladimir's conversion. Perhaps the Byzantine emperor Basil II was hoping to secure an ally against possible uprisings within his realm, or maybe Vladimir wanted Basil's sister Anna as a bride.[21] But most people either miss or ignore a briefly mentioned but potentially vital detail about something else that likely helped to push Vladimir over the edge to Christianity.[22] Even after the boyars delivered their resplendent report about worship in the Hagia Sophia, Vladimir still withheld a final decision. "Then the boyars spoke [to Vladimir] and said, 'If the Greek faith were evil, it would not have been adopted by your grandmother Olga who was wiser than all other men.' Vladimir then inquired where they should all accept baptism."[23]

The abiding memories of a grandmother's wisdom and faith helped shape the course of history. Olga's faith, which had seemed like a dead end among her people, did not die with her. Vladimir was eleven years old when his grandmother died and would have been among the "grandsons and all the people" who mourned her.[24]

Too often historians reduce all motivations, including religious, to either politics or economics. And while it's true those are driving factors in the complicated mixture of human motivations, they don't give the full picture. Yes, the Byzantine emperor's desire to make powerful, protective alliances with surrounding kingdoms colored the medieval church's mission to convert the Slavic, Bulgarian, Rus', Polish, and Hungarian peoples and their leaders. But history defies such simplistic reductions, for God ultimately brought about his ends through a simple spiritual mentorship and the life and legacy of a faithful Christian grandmother.

Further Reading

Butler, Francis. "Ol'ga's Conversion and the Construction of Chronicle Narrative." *Russian Review* 67, no. 2 (April 2008): 230–42.

Butler, Francis. "A Woman of Words: Pagan Ol'ga in the Mirror of Germanic Europe." *Slavic Review* 63, no. 4 (Winter 2004): 771–93.

Cunningham, Mary B. "The Orthodox Church in Byzantium." In *A World History of Christianity*. Edited by Adrian Hastings. Eerdmans, 1999.

Featherstone, Jeffrey. "Ol'ga's Visit to Constantinople." *Harvard Ukrainian Studies* 14, nos. 3–4 (December 1990): 293–312.

Obolensky, Dmitri. "Ol'ga's Conversion: The Evidence Reconsidered." *Harvard Ukrainian Studies* vol. 12–13 (1988/1989): 145–58.

Notes

1. Francis Butler, "Ol'ga's Conversion and the Construction of Chronicle Narrative," *Russian Review* 67, no. 2 (April 2008): 232–33.

2. Jonathan Shepard, "Spreading the Word: Byzantine Missions," in *Oxford History of Byzantium*, ed. Cyril Mango (Oxford University Press, 2002), 232.

3. Butler, "Ol'ga's Conversion," 233.

4. Francis Butler, "A Woman of Words: Pagan Ol'ga in the Mirror of Germanic Europe," *Slavic Review* 63, no. 4 (Winter 2004): 771, 792.

5. Butler, "Woman of Words," 773–74.

6. Butler, "Ol'ga's Conversion," 239.

7. Jeffrey Featherstone, "Ol'ga's Visit to Constantinople," *Harvard Ukrainian Studies* 14, nos. 3–4 (December 1990): 294.

8. Butler, "Ol'ga's Conversion," 237.

9. Butler, "Ol'ga's Conversion," 235.

10. Butler, "Ol'ga's Conversion," 236, 238.

11. Dmitri Obolensky, "Ol'ga's Conversion: The Evidence Reconsidered," *Harvard Ukrainian Studies*, vols. 12–13 (1988–1989), 157.

12. Shepard, "Spreading the Word," 230.

13. Butler, "Olg'a's Conversion," 231.

14. Featherstone, "Ol'ga's Visit," 305.

15. Featherstone, "Ol'ga's Visit," 310.

16. Featherstone, "Ol'ga's Visit," 310.

17. Shepard, "Spreading the Word," 237.

18. *The Russian Primary Chronicle: Laurentian Text*, trans. and ed. S. H. Cross and O. P. Sherbowitz-Wetzor (The Mediaeval Academy of America, 1953), 97.

19. *Russian Primary Chronicle* 987.

20. Sam Harnett, "Listen: The Sound of The Hagia Sophia, More Than 500 Years Ago," NPR Weekend Edition Saturday, February 22, 2020, https://www.npr.org/2020/02/22/808404928/listen-the-sound-of-the-hagia-sophia-more-than-500-years-ago.

21. Mary B. Cunningham, "The Orthodox Church in Byzantium," in *A World History of Christianity*, ed. Adrian Hastings (Eerdmans, 1999), 85.

22. Butler, "Woman of Words," 772.

23. *Russian Primary Chronicle* 987.

24. *Russian Primary Chronicle* 969.

29

Y1K: An Abbot, a Bishop, and End-Times Anxiety

(Fleury, France, and York, England, c. 1000)

The Background

The year 1000 was fast approaching for Western Europeans, and a new millennium was dawning. In the 990s, an archbishop of Canterbury, Aelfric, inserted a checklist into a sermon and listed off recent events that corresponded to biblical prophecies. Disturbing Bible prophecies apparently were being fulfilled before people's very eyes.

> "Nation will rise against nation" (Matt. 24:7). *Check*. In 996—and every year for the next decade—Vikings raided England. Wulfstan, bishop of York, invoked this verse from Matthew in response. Decades before, it had been used when the Magyars threatened western Europe.
>
> "Satan . . . will come out to deceive the nations that are at the four corners of the earth, Gog and Magog, to gather

them for battle" (Rev. 20:7–8). *Check*. The invading Vikings were correlated to Gog and Magog. A generation earlier, in 950, a French bishop had also linked the Magyar and Viking invasions to Gog and Magog.[1]

"You will hear of wars and rumors of wars" (Matt. 24:6). *Check*. In 991, civil wars ended the Carolingian Frankish dynasty.[2]

"And there will be signs in sun and moon and stars" (Luke 21:25). *Check*. In 965 there were reports throughout the Frankish kingdom of fire falling from heaven and of demons appearing.[3] In 968, a Saxon army believed a solar eclipse was a sign the world was ending.[4] In 989, Halley's Comet filled many people with dread and foreboding.[5]

"There will be . . . earthquakes in various places" (Matt. 24:7). *Check*. In the year 1000 an unusual earthquake was said to have shaken the whole earth.[6]

"And many false prophets will arise and lead many astray" (Matt. 24:11). *Check*. Around 995, Abbo of Fleury asked for a council specifically to refute widespread apocalyptic heresies. Many other popular heresies proliferated at this time as well.[7]

"Because lawlessness will be increased, the love of many will grow cold" (Matt. 24:12). *Check*. A homily preached around 970 refers to the "approaching End of the World and that the signs predicted in the Gospels have taken place—'monstrous plagues and strange deaths,' terrible wars prompted by evil, 'various diseases in many places of the world' and a flourishing of evil and a cooling of love towards God."[8]

Not all were caught up in the panic. While some church leaders and laity were searching out signs of the coming apocalypse, others considered it futile or even harmful to do so. There might never have been apocalyptic mass hysteria surrounding the year 1000, as was once believed, but there were indeed serious and widespread apocalyptic speculations in western Europe at this time. As one leading medieval scholar puts it, "The year 1000 was not a year like any other."[9]

Western medieval eschatology assumed a particular framework of universal history. Simply put, six ages of the world corresponded to the six days of creation.[10] The sixth age was the period from the time of Christ until the apocalypse, which would herald the seventh age, a sabbatical rest reminiscent of the seventh day of creation. There were several ways of putting all the pieces together. Combining the one thousand years mentioned in Revelation 20:4–6 with 2 Peter 3:8, which says that "with the Lord one day is as a thousand years, and a thousand years as one day," some imagined that the sixth age would last a millennium and that antichrist would appear at the end of it.[11]

The critical question was (and still is) how to read this reference to one thousand years. Some at that time interpreted these as actual years, and thus the year 1000 represented a literal millennium since the birth of Christ and the close of the sixth age. Augustine of Hippo, who was the original architect of the Six Ages framework, had challenged such apocalyptic speculation centuries earlier, teaching that the time of the end was simply unknowable. He interpreted the thousand years as allegorical and figurative. Augustine's take strongly influenced segments of the Western church thereafter. Thus, the Six Ages model both fueled apocalypticism and guided antiapocalypticism as the year 1000 approached.

The Moments

Two medieval figures who were contemporaries, Abbo of Fleury (c. 945–1004) and Wulfstan of York (d. 1023), both lived through the buildup to and aftermath of the year 1000 and represent the range of responses coming from church leaders at that time.

Abbo of Fleury was a Benedictine monk who lived most of his life in France and in 988 was chosen as abbot of the monastery at Fleury. As a youth, he received a liberal arts education that drew on the best resources of the time, and he developed a peculiar interest in the cycles of planets and in *computus*, which is the art of determining the dates for the movable feast days on the church calendar. He was drawn to such calculations specifically to "refute apocalyptic movements of his day."[12]

A letter Abbo wrote to the king of France in 995 shows that he was experienced in dealing with end-times speculation: "Concerning the end of the world, as a youth I heard a sermon preached to the people in the Paris church to the effect that as soon as the number of one thousand years was completed, Antichrist would arrive, and not long after that, the Last Judgement would follow."[13] Note that this sermon was preached in "the Paris church," likely a reference to the city's main cathedral and thus a mainstream venue for this apocalyptic message.[14] These things were not being done in a corner and were not simply part of anticlerical hysteria, as some have claimed. Word of the end was spreading.

In his letter, Abbo continues, "I resisted as vigorously as I could to that preaching, citing the Gospels, Revelation, and Daniel."[15] Turning directly to the Scriptures, he questioned the literal reading of apocalyptic passages and drew upon the Augustinian tradition to challenge such end-times speculation. That anonymous preacher he heard in Paris was

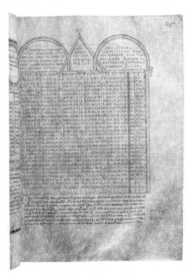

Computus table of Abbo of Fleury
By permission of the President and Fellows of St. John's College, Oxford

247

likely gaining followers. Abbo was deeply concerned and went all out to refute what he deemed a serious error.

Abbo then related another episode that happened soon after he heard the sermon at the cathedral in Paris: "Another error . . . grew about the end of the world" as "a rumor had filled almost the entire world that when the Annunciation fell on Good Friday, without any question it would be the end of the world."[16] Those two days coincided three times in the years leading up to the millennium, in 970, 981, and 992.[17] Perhaps knowing of his earlier challenges to end-times speculators, the abbot of his community commanded Abbo to refute this view also. In 981, Abbo drew on his computus studies to argue that "Christ was actually born twenty-one years earlier" than commonly held; "thus the millennium of Christ's birth had already passed in 979, thereby rendering the year 1000 harmless."[18] Abbo's eagerness to refute apocalypticism led him to propose a radical revision of the dating system itself.

Abbo challenged apocalypticism for the sake of the unity of the church, invoking Scripture and echoing Augustine: "Man simply cannot know the time of the end."[19] He would later request that a church council be convened to combat "heresies about the imminent end of the world."[20] There is no evidence that such a council was ever called, but these episodes indicate that as the millennium approached, apocalyptic speculations were widespread among clergy and laity alike, at least in France.

A very different reading of the signs of the times came from Wulfstan of York, an English bishop who clearly was not convinced of Augustine's framework. Wulfstan was consecrated as a bishop in 996 and over his career served in London, Worcester, and York. He was a major figure in both ecclesiastical and political circles until his death in 1023. He was famous as a moral reformer, through both his sermons and the law codes he helped craft. Some of his most famous sermons powerfully linked the unprecedented catastrophes and immorality happening in England at that time with the approaching end of the world. The Vikings made the first of their annual raids the same year he became a bishop, and Wulfstan interpreted this as a sign of the impending apocalypse and of God's judgment on English immorality.

Among Wulfstan's fifty or so surviving sermons is a series of five that delve into the last days. While the exact dates of these sermons are debated, they can be traced to right around the year 1000 and are clearly inspired by ambient apocalyptic anxiety. In the first of these, he explores the signs of the end in Matthew 24.[21] In the second, he "identifies the Viking attacks as the Gospel sign of the Last Days that 'Nation will rise up against nation.'"[22] In the third, he speaks of the appearance of the antichrist at some point in the future. By the fourth sermon, though, he warns that the antichrist will be appearing "very quickly." In the final sermon of the series, he pulls no punches:

> Now it must of necessity become very evil, because [Antichrist's] time is coming quickly, just as it is written and has long been prophesied: "After a thousand years Satan will be unleashed." . . . A thousand years and also more have now passed since Christ was among people in human form, and now Satan's bonds are very loose, and Antichrist's time is well at hand.[23]

The Mathēma

As it turns out, the world did not end in 1000. Actually, there had been a slight miscalculation. The end of the world would be in 1033. All the literal speculation about the year 1000 had mistakenly assumed the starting date of the sixth age was the birth of Christ when, in fact, the sixth age of the earth began with his death, burial, resurrection, and ascension. And so the apocalypse was pushed forward, as it often is when prophetic speculation fails. Close to our own time, around the year 2000 (Y2K) a variety of apocalyptic speculators came out of the woodwork. More than a few Christians left their churches (including mine at the time) to follow the famous date-setter Harold Camping. And as 2033 approaches, perhaps we will witness a new round of millennial fever—minus the complication of a potential worldwide computer meltdown.

Edgar Whisenant, who wrote the book *88 Reasons Why the Rapture Will Be in 1988* (which, incidentally, made it to number two on the Christian Booksellers Association list in 1988) had to keep updating his rapture predictions.[24] He initially said Christ would return on September 11–13, 1988. When that didn't happen, he changed the date to October 3, 1988, then to September 1, 1989, and finally (at least in print) to 1993. There is nothing new here. Committed devotees "respond to the passing of their doomsday by recalculating, reformulating their expectations, and redoubling their efforts to convince others of its truth."[25]

We might picture medieval Christians as being more impressionable and therefore more susceptible to mass apocalyptic frenzy than people are today. But the evidence from that time instead reveals people who were earnest speculators, skeptical challengers, and everything in between. As we have discussed elsewhere (see chaps. 3, 11, and 19), such apocalyptic moments throughout history call us to exercise caution even amidst our watchfulness.

The Scriptures do not shrink from warning us to be watchful in well-known passages like Matthew 24:36–39, where Jesus says,

> Concerning that day and hour no one knows. . . . For as were the days of Noah, so will be the coming of the Son of Man. For as in those days before the flood they were eating and drinking, marrying and giving in marriage, until the day when Noah entered the ark, and they were unaware until the flood came and swept them all away, so will be the coming of the Son of Man.

We watch and wait for Christ even as we live the call of all Christians, past and present, to live for Christ now. And we plow and thresh in hope (1 Cor. 9:10), knowing that God calls us not to be obsessed with the apocalypse but to live lives of meaning here on earth. We proclaim Christ in word and sacrament, we worship in communities, we build families, we go about our callings in the same way the great cloud of witnesses from past ages did during their own sojourn here on earth.

Further Reading

Cubitt, Catherine. "Apocalyptic and Eschatological Thought in England Around the Year 1000." *Transactions of the Royal Historical Society*, 6th series, vol. 25 (2015): 27–52.

Dachowski, Elizabeth. *First Among Abbots: The Career of Abbo of Fleury*. Catholic University of America Press, 2008.

Landes, Richard. "The Fear of an Apocalyptic Year 1000: Augustinian Historiography, Medieval and Modern." *Speculum* 75 no. 1 (January 2000): 97–145.

Landes, Richard, Andrew Gow, and David C. Van Meter. *The Apocalyptic Year 1000: Religious Expectation and Social Change, 950–1050*. Oxford University Press, 2003.

Madigan, Keith. "Apocalyptic Expectation in the Year 1000." *New Theology Review* 12, no. 3 (August 1999): 5–14.

Notes

1. Catherine Cubitt, "Apocalyptic and Eschatological Thought in England Around the Year 1000," *Transactions of the Royal Historical Society*, 6th series, vol. 25 (2015): 32–33; and Keith Madigan, "Apocalyptic Expectation in the Year 1000," *New Theology Review* 12, no. 3 (August 1999): 6, 9.

2. Richard Landes, "The Fear of an Apocalyptic Year 1000: Augustinian Historiography, Medieval and Modern," *Speculum* 75, no. 1 (January 2000): 128.

3. Landes, "Fear of an Apocalyptic Year 1000," 125.

4. Madigan, "Apocalyptic Expectation in the Year 1000," 9.

5. Tom Holland, *Millennium: The End of the World and the Forging of Christendom* (Little, Brown, 2008), 132.

6. Landes, "Fear of an Apocalyptic Year 1000," 131.

7. Landes, "Fear of an Apocalyptic Year 1000," 132, 142.

8. Cubitt, "Apocalyptic and Eschatological Thought in England," 36–37. *The Blickling Homilies* and *Vercelli Book* exhort in this light.

9. Landes, "Fear of an Apocalyptic Year 1000," 123.

10. See "Of the Six Ages of the World," chap. 22 in Augustine's *On the Catechizing of the Uninstructed*: (1) Creation to Flood, (2) to Abraham, (3) to David, (4) to the Babylonian Captivity, (5) to Christ, and (6) to the Apocalypse.

11. See Landes, "Fear of an Apocalyptic Year 1000," 116–17; and Cubitt, "Apocalyptic and Eschatological Thought in England," 28.

12. Elizabeth Dachowski, *First Among Abbots: The Career of Abbo of Fleury* (Catholic University of America Press, 2008), 230.

13. Quoted in Landes, "Fear of an Apocalyptic Year 1000," 123.

14. Landes, "Fear of an Apocalyptic Year 1000," 124.

15. Quoted in Landes, "Fear of an Apocalyptic Year 1000," 123.

16. Quoted in Landes, "Fear of an Apocalyptic Year 1000," 123.

17. Landes, "Fear of an Apocalyptic Year 1000," 125.

18. Quoted in Dachowski, "First Among Abbots," 55.

19. Quoted in Landes, "Fear of an Apocalyptic Year 1000," 125.

20. Quoted in Dachowski, "First Among Abbots," 141.

21. Cubitt, "Apocalyptic and Eschatological Thought in England," 47.

22. Cubitt, "Apocalyptic and Eschatological Thought in England," 47.

23. Cubitt, "Apocalyptic and Eschatological Thought in England," 27, 48.

24. Wikipedia, "Edgar C. Whisenant," last modified February 16, 2025, 22:45 (UTC), https://en.wikipedia.org/wiki/Edgar_C._Whisenant.

25. Landes, "Fear of an Apocalyptic Year 1000," 102.

30

———●———

Conclusion: "Unto the Ends of the Round World" at 1000

The Gospel of the Kingdom

In Psalm 72:8 we read, "May he have dominion from sea to sea, and from the River to the ends of the earth!" The evocative language of that verse has proven irresistible to modern nationalists on the North American continent that spans from the Atlantic to the Pacific. For example, Canada's official name is "the *Dominion* of Canada," and their national motto—*A mari usque ad mare* ("from sea to sea")—is drawn verbatim from Psalm 72:8 in the Latin Vulgate, which begins with the word *dominabitur*. The Great Canadian Railroad went from sea to sea, after all. Katharine Lee Bates must have also had Psalm 72:8 in mind when she penned her song "America the Beautiful," which culminates with the phrase "from sea to shining sea."[1] Given the tenor of Psalm 72, it is not surprising that many peoples throughout time, not just North Americans, have borrowed its language to express deep national longings.

The king who is speaking in this psalm asks God to bless his kingdom with justice, peace, and prosperity. The entire chapter pulses with a desire for the thriving and flourishing of the kingdom for as long as the sun and moon are in the sky. The writer's use of the phrase "from sea to sea" presumes an ancient cosmology in which a great ocean entirely encircled all dry land. Humans inhabited the solid space between the surrounding waters of ocean. Ruling "from sea to sea" essentially meant ruling the whole inhabited earth, even if the kingdom actually composed but a small portion of it. Such hyperbole was commonly used by royals in the ancient Near East to convey their profound desire for national thriving.

In his exposition on Psalm 72, the fifth-century North African church father Augustine of Hippo discerned a far grander vision.[2] Rather than reading it as a catalog of exaggerated political aspirations, he interpreted the psalm as pointing forward to the universal messianic reign of Christ.[3] The longing for a universal kingdom will be fulfilled through the church, which the Lord would spread abroad throughout the world.[4] The ancient king of Israel merely anticipated and foreshadowed Messiah's reign.

According to Augustine, "the River" (capital R) was the starting point for this global spread of the faith. Unlike most Christian commentators on Psalm 72, Augustine interpreted "the River" as the Jordan River, the place where Christ was baptized and the Holy Spirit descended upon him.[5] "From this place then His doctrine and the authority of the heavenly ministry setting out, is enlarged even unto the ends of the round world, when there is preached the Gospel of the kingdom in the whole world, for a testimony unto all nations: and then shall come the end."[6]

Augustine underscored that in its use of imagery of both the sea and the River, the psalm looked well beyond the frontiers of his own Roman Empire. "In His presence shall fall down [i.e., bow] the Ethiopians. . . . By the Ethiopians, as by a part the whole, He has signified all nations, selecting that nation to mention especially by name, which is at the ends of the earth."[7] The psalmist expresses a longing that peoples at the farthest ends of the earth would come into the church, a promise that Augustine was seeing fulfilled even in his own day and anticipated would continue until Christ's return. He proceeded to analyze the psalm's references to Tharsis (Spain), Arabia (probably Yemen/Himyar), and Saba (a kingdom of Africa):

> The kings of Tharsis and the isles shall offer gifts, the kings of the Arabians and of Saba shall lead presents. . . . But those gifts which have been foretold as to be led, seems to me to signify men, whom in the fellow of the Church of Christ the authority of kings does lead: although even persecuting kings have led gifts, knowing not what they did, in sacrificing the holy Martyrs. And there shall adore Him all kings of the earth, all nations shall serve Him.[8]

Augustine knew that this kingdom is not limited and that it stretches far beyond any specific region of the world: "The Catholic [Universal] Church has been foretold, not as to be in any particular quarter of the world, as certain schisms are, but in the whole universe."[9] His vision of the church was intrinsically global and not bound to his own political or cultural setting.

A Satellite's-Eye View of the Year 1000

In the preceding chapters, we have met Christian brothers and sisters in empires and kingdoms spread throughout "this round world" in the church's first millennium. And there were others in places not discussed in this book. Our People could also be found in India, Scandinavia, Central Asia, to name just a few examples. We have learned much from those who have gone before us as we listened to their stories, but there are many more stories that could be told.

A glimpse of the world in the year 1000 can itself continue to challenge some of our most tightly held assumptions and inclinations. When looking at either the past or the present, Christians are prone to one of two extremes: triumphalism or pessimism. On the one hand, we sometimes treat the history of Christianity as a story of progress and growth, and we demonstrate our narrative "by a selective choice of period, events, and geographical regions."[10] Our own careful selection can thus make the church appear to be always growing and expanding. On the other hand, we can dwell primarily on the losses, emphasizing the decline and even death of Christianity in certain areas. We often seem to want either a tale of triumph or one of doom and despair.

A picture of the world in the year 1000 can temper both of these extremes. As Robert Louis Wilken helpfully reminds us, "The career of Christianity is marked as much by decline and attrition as it is by growth and triumph."[11] And that holds through time. The story of the global church at any given time is never a simple tale of either-or. The exciting stories in our own day of the rise and flourishing of the Global Christian South might readily come to mind. As so often happens, the church has grown in one area while sadly declining in others. This is not to downplay or ignore the loss of Christianity in a given region. For instance, the obvious decline of the faith in western Europe in recent centuries is a true and tragic reality. Rather, it's to encourage the type of balanced assessment that history can help us develop.

In the year 1000, Christianity remained visibly strong in many of the regions to which it had spread over its first millennium. From some of these bases, it was poised to spread farther. Incidentally, that very same year two more countries—Hungary and Iceland—adopted Christianity, and large numbers of Keraites, a Mongol group, would convert to Christianity shortly thereafter. Christians still exist in many of the regions to which the faith spread in that first millennium, sometimes even still making up the majority population. In some areas that were dominated by

Islam in the year 1000, including Egypt, Syria, and Persia, Christians maintained a stalwart if diminished presence and would continue to do so for centuries.[12] In Muslim Spain, it would appear the number of Christians was even growing.

At the same time, a satellite's-eye view of the year 1000 challenges any simplistic story of triumph. All was not well in some areas. Christianity was nowhere to be found in China after several centuries of thriving there. In some parts of the Muslim world, such as Augustine's own hometown of Hippo in North Africa, the Christian faith had dwindled to essentially no witness at all. Looking ahead from the year 1000, we are faced as well with "a weighty reminder that after the end of the first millennium, the great period of Christian growth and expansion was over."[13] At least for a time. Another moment of remarkable expansion would happen, but not for several centuries. Of course, no one knew this in the year 1000.

Even unto the End(s)

How might this very mixed report fit with the glorious hope of Augustine and the words of Psalm 72? Geerhardus Vos, a Princeton theologian writing in the late nineteenth and early twentieth centuries, articulated a "kingdom theology" inspired in part by Augustine's overall vision. Vos and others famously laid out an "already but not yet" principle in which the kingdom of God is now *already* here among us but is *not yet* in its fullness.[14]

This principle can help us set the victories, successes, failures, and tragedies of Our People throughout history against the backdrop of the glorious messianic promises of Psalm 72. Augustine, for example, juxtaposed the schisms that were tearing apart the church in his own day and the glorious hope of "the Gospel of the kingdom" throughout "the whole world."[15]

Whatever enticements we might face in our own day to settle for our own nation as some sort of manifestation of God's kingdom,

257

we await that glorious future consummation. We do so amidst the joys and the sorrows, ultimately resisting both despair and triumphalism. Such has always been the call and the challenge to Our People through time and space, and it will be until time shall be no more.

Christ's kingdom has spread, is spreading, and will continue to spread throughout the round world. Right now, we are living in Christ's kingdom, even while its true fullness remains to be seen. Like Augustine in the fifth century, we in the twenty-first century look for that day.

And there shall be fulfilled with the glory of Him every land: so be it, so be it. You have commanded, O Lord, so it is coming to pass: so it is coming to pass, until that which began with the River, may attain fully even unto the ends of the round world.[16]

Notes

1. Her reference to "amber waves of grain" also calls to mind Psalm 72:16, "May there be abundance of grain in the land; on the tops of the mountains may it wave."

2. Augustine of Hippo, "Exposition on Psalm 72," from *Nicene and Post-Nicene Fathers*, First Series, vol. 8, ed. Philip Scaff, trans. J. E. Tweed (Christian Literature Publishing Co., 1886). Revised and edited for New Advent by Kevin Knight, www.newadvent.org/fathers/1801072.htm.

3. One modern commentator writes, "Though the New Testament nowhere quotes [Psalm 72] as Messianic," its "picture of the king and his realm is so close to prophecies of Isaiah 11:1–5 and Isaiah 60–62 that if those passages are Messianic, so is this." Derek Kidner, *Psalms 1–72* (IVP Academic, 1973), 254.

4. Augustine, "Exposition on Psalm 72," sec. 11.

5. Most Christian commentators through time believe this to be the Euphrates River, and several modern English Bible translations (e.g., New American Standard Bible, Contemporary English Version, New Living Translation) simply substitute "Euphrates River" for "the River." The messianic reading works with either interpretation.

6. Augustine, "Exposition on Psalm 72," sec. 11.

7. Augustine, "Exposition on Psalm 72," sec. 12. "Ethiopians" comes from the Septuagint and the Latin Vulgate. The Hebrew text simply reads "desert dweller" or something similar.

8. Augustine, "Exposition on Psalm 72," sec. 13.

9. Augustine, "Exposition on Psalm 72," sec. 12.

10. Robert Louis Wilken, *The First Thousand Years: A Global History of Christianity* (Yale University Press, 2012), 358.

11. Wilken, *First Thousand Years*, 358.

12. Some of the most harrowing stories of Christians in these areas come not from distant centuries or millennia but from recent decades.

13. Wilken, *First Thousand Years*, 359.

14. See, for example, Vos's sermon "Running the Race," in *Grace and Glory: Sermons Preached in the Chapel of Princeton Theological Seminary* (Banner of Truth Trust, 1994), 137.

15. Augustine, "Exposition on Psalm 72," sec. 11.

16. Augustine, "Exposition on Psalm 72," sec. 20.

Major Books on Early Global Christian History

I have kept the following books within arm's reach throughout this project. I would heartily recommend each of them for giving the larger picture and additional narrative and for filling in the gaps between the thirty or so key moments explored in this book.

Fairbairn, Donald. *The Global Church: The First Eight Centuries.* Zondervan Academic, 2021.

Fowden, Garth. *Empire to Commonwealth: Consequences of Monotheism in Late Antiquity.* Princeton University Press, 1993.

Jenkins, Philip. *The Lost History of Christianity: The Thousand-Year Golden Age of the Church in the Middle East, Africa, and Asia—and How It Died.* HarperOne, 2008.

Moffett, Samuel Hugh. *A History of Christianity in Asia. Vol. 1: Beginnings to 1500.* Harper San Francisco, 1992.

Wilken, Robert Louis. *The First Thousand Years: A Global History of Christianity.* Yale University Press, 2012.

Acknowledgments

Not surprisingly for a project that presumes to touch on Christian history across a good portion of the world over a thousand-year period, this one owes much to many people.

My fellow church members Doug and Mary Glenn started it all by requesting that I teach a study on episodes in Christian history. The ideas emerged week by week as "Moments in the History of Our People," and I thank Pastors Jeremy Jones and Ben Ward along with the members and many visitors at Covenant Presbyterian Church in Grove City, Pennsylvania. They all helped me more than they realize as I strove to strike a balance between being a professional historian of ancient and early medieval empires and meeting the desires of my fellow Christian brothers and sisters to learn about Our People through time. George "Van" Campbell and the Becomers Class of East Main Presbyterian Church, also in Grove City, invited me to test-drive parts of this study with them in late 2024 and early 2025. I thank this dynamic group (fifty plus years together and counting as a Sunday school class!) for their kind reception and some helpful ideas that I was able to incorporate just in time.

My friends and fellow church members, Kristi Hannon and Tiffany Ward, graciously read rough drafts of many chapters and provided excellent suggestions. Their editorial comments along the way were always right on. Rev. Daniel Howe likewise improved a number of draft chapters.

Students and alumni of Grove City College have been my co-laborers from the start, and I am grateful to those who took up the "editorial option" in a history class with me: Johnny Adkins, Zander Bedingfield, Alaina Donnell, Sam Hertzer, Oswald Hunter, Adam Nicholson, Judah-David Shay, Sawyer Wiersma, and Joseph Wolcott. Several others have helpfully commented on parts, including Jacob Feiser, Austin Zeilstra, John Hatzis, Aziz Ishler, and Ian Dolbier. Further conversations with Adam Nicholson shaped the introduction and chapter 29 in fundamental ways. Elsa Miller prepared a draft of the map. Ginger Schiffmayer and Sophie Spilak have been first-rate research assistants—crafting the timeline, tracking down illustration copyrights, and more—helping make progress possible even amidst busy teaching semesters.

Colleagues at Grove City College read portions and gave excellent feedback, including Gillis Harp, Gary Smith (emeritus), Libby Baker, Andrew Mitchell, Paul Munson, and Alden McCray. Caleb Fuller was an encouragement at every stage. I thank Paul Kemeny, Connie Nichols, and Jarrett Chapman for arranging a perfectly peaceful space for me to write each afternoon during the fall semester of 2024.

Several specialist historians received emails out of the blue and graciously agreed to look over chapters in process—among them Anthony Barrett, Stanley Burstein, Florin Curta, and Ray Van Dam. Whatever mistakes might remain here, their keen eyes saved me from more, and they each provided insightful critiques and suggestions, whether or not they resonate with the premise of this book.

Andrew Wolgemuth energetically supported this project from the start, and I am deeply grateful for his encouragement. At Baker, Eddie LaRow has been a true inspiration through both his enthusiasm for history and his skill at his craft, and Amy Nemecek opened my eyes to what an excellent copyeditor can do with a draft manuscript.

Finally, my family members dove in with their characteristic love and grace. Sarah Graham read many draft chapters, taking special interest in helping clarify introductions and conclusions. Phoebe Graham, Estelle Rampelt, Samuel Rampelt, and Zachary Rampelt (honorary family member) all shaped the project by reading sections and over dinner-table conversations. Ira Graham has been understanding of my diminished presence over the past year. Becky, my beloved wife and best friend (and proofreading queen), daily inspires the joy that can make any undertaking a delight.

Mark W. Graham is chair of the history department at Grove City College, where he has taught numerous classes on the premodern world for more than two decades. He also taught at a university in Yanji, China. As an affiliated faculty member with Centro di Conservazione Archeologica, Mark has worked on archaeological projects and sites in Sardinia, Corinth, and Rome. He also helped excavate the Byzantine emperor Justinian's church in Carthage. He earned his doctorate in history at Michigan State University. Graham has been an elder in his local Presbyterian church for over a decade and serves on several committees in his presbytery.